Black migration in America

Studies in Social and Economic Demography

General Editor

George C. Myers, *Director*, Center for Demographic Studies, Duke University

Black migration in America

A social demographic history

Daniel M. Johnson *and*
Rex R. Campbell

Duke University Press
Durham, N.C.   1981

Permission to quote has been granted by the following: Robert William Fogel and Stanley L. Engerman, *Time on the Cross*, © 1974 by Little, Brown and Company; Robert B. Grant, *The Black Man Comes to the City* © 1972, Nelson Hall Company; Daniel P. Mannix, *Black Cargoes* © 1962, The Viking Press and Harold Matson, Inc.; Ann Ratner Miller, *Net Intercensal Migration to Large Urban Areas of the United States*, © 1964, University of Pennsylvania; Reynolds Farley, *The Growth of the Black Population* © 1971, Markham Publishing Co.; "I, Too," from *Selected Poems of Langston Hughes*, © 1959, Random House, Inc., Alfred A. Knopf, Inc., & Pantheon Books; Karl E. Taeuber and Alma F. Taeuber, *Negroes in Cities*, © 1965, Aldine Publishing Company, reprinted by permission of Karl E. Taeuber and Alma F. Taeuber.

Library of Congress Cataloging in Publication Data

Johnson, Daniel Milo.
  Black migration in America.

  (Studies in social and economic demography; 4)
  Includes bibliographical references and index.
  1. Afro-Americans—Population. 2. Migration, Internal—United States. 3. United States—Population.
I. Campbell, Rex R., joint author. II. Title.
III. Series.
E185.86.J63   305.8'96073   80–16919
ISBN 0–8223–0442–2 (cloth)
ISBN 0–8223–0449–X (paper)

Contents

Preface

Historical demography is an area of study that offers the social scientist a vehicle for examining ways in which past patterns of population changes have created today's population distribution. The problems of the cities and rural areas including crime, delinquency, poverty, pollution as well as the very destinies of the communities themselves, have been strongly influenced by shifts in distribution and concentration of population. If we are to understand these problems and their relationship to contemporary demographic structures and processes, it is essential that our study and research incorporate the historical dimension.

The migrations of black people represent an important though frequently inglorious aspect of American history. Black migrations began with the slave trades in the fifteenth century, and various forms of forced migration continued to characterize black population movements well into the twentieth century. A major assumption underlying the approach of this study is that an understanding of contemporary migration patterns—particularly black migration—must include knowledge of significant historical patterns that contributed to the present population distribution, mobility networks, and attitudes toward moving. The major historical patterns of black migration are presented in this work from our perspectives as social demographers. We have attempted to determine the general character of the socioeconomic milieu within which black migration occurred historically, the volume of migration, characteristics and motivations of the migrants, and the consequences for the people and communities involved.

Not since Carter Woodson's book, *A Century of Negro Migration*, published in 1918, has there been an attempt to synthesize and integrate historical, economic, sociological, and demographic knowledge of black migration. We have made the attempt and hope that the results will provide a comprehensive but concise description of black migration in America.

This book is from a larger project on the migration of Negroes to the South, supported jointly by the Department of Health, Education and Welfare, the Public Health Service (Project Number 2-ROI-HDO 5852), and the Missouri Agricultural Experiment Station. The larger project included personal interviews with over 700 individuals and families who had moved to the South, the data from which will be put into book form by the authors.

The names that appear on the title page of this volume represent only a portion of those whose effort went into its preparation. Frank Whelan made helpful criticisms and suggestions and Mary Jokerst did an excellent job typing much of the manuscript. Our families played an important role by providing moral support in their patience with all the hours that were taken from weekends and evenings to work on the manuscript. Particular thanks must go to Mary Campbell, who spent hundreds of hours editing, checking references, and performing many other services.

The responsibility for any errors or omissions rests entirely with the authors, Daniel M. Johnson and Rex R. Campbell.

Black migration in America

1. Introduction

The study of migration

We are a nation of movers, of migrants. This is not a new phenomenon. Man, by his very nature, appears to be a migratory animal. The United States was formed by migrants—first from Asia, then from Europe, Africa, and again Asia. It is the migration of the Africans and their descendants that is considered here, that is, the migration history of black people to and within the United States.

Before we start the examination of black migration, a basic understanding of the process of migration is necessary. The movement of individuals and families from one place to another produces a wide variety of changes in the individuals and families involved, in the sending and receiving communities, and in the larger areas of which the sending and receiving communities are a part. The most obvious of these changes is a decrease in size of the place of origin and an increase in the population in the destination community.[1]

Of course, not everyone migrates. Some persons migrate more often than others, over longer distances, and in different directions. Some societies and distinctive groups within societies are characterized by greater population movement than others; and the volume, direction, and distance of the moves fluctuate at various points in the economic, political, and social histories of societies.[2]

One of the few generalizations that may be made about migration from the hundreds of studies that have been conducted, and one that is applicable to all population movements, is that all migration is selective. Some people migrate while others do not, and those who migrate are different in character from those who remain sedentary. This fact suggests that migration has patterned demographic, economic, and social determinants and consequences. It is the nature of these patterns that constitutes the area of inquiry for students of migration. Their studies have shown enormous variation in the patterns of selectivity. But this is only one starting point. It is also important to know how and why migration is selective, which groups are more inclined to move and why, and the implication of migration for society.[3]

Migration selectivity does not function similarly for all types of migration. One of the more useful typologies for the various classes of migration is that developed by Petersen, wherein five broad classes are designated: "primitive," "forced," "impelled," "free," and "mass." For our purpose these words require a fairly precise definition. Primitive migration is viewed as the result of an "ecological push," or man's inability to cope with natural forces. Forced and impelled migrations are activated not by these ecological pressures, but by social institutions. When the persons involved retain some power to decide whether or not to leave, a migration is referred to as "impelled." When no such decision-making capacity is left to the persons, it is referred to as "forced."[4]

An important form of impelled migration has been flight, such as when a stronger people move into a new territory and drive out the weaker occupants. Other classes of those who have fled their homeland include émigrés, i.e., those who regard their exile as temporary and live for the day when they may return, and refugees, i.e., those who flee and settle in a new country.

Likewise, there are several different subtypes of forced migrations. For example, displacement refers to a forced movement intended merely to remove a dissident population, such as the relocation of many native American tribes to reservations. Forced migrations also have served to furnish a labor force, as in the case of the Atlantic and domestic slave trade in the United States.

In the types of migration discussed thus far, the will of the migrants has been a relatively unimportant factor. A primitive migration results from the lack of means to satisfy basic physiological needs; in the forced or impelled type the persons involved also are subject to the purposes of social institutions. The type in which the will of the migrants is the decisive element, "free" migration, is illustrated by the overseas movement from Europe during the nineteenth century. The final type, according to Petersen, is mass migration, a form of collective behavior wherein migration becomes the style, an established pattern for a group or subgroup.

It is frequently difficult to differentiate between migration types. Many of the individuals who left Europe to come to the United States may have felt impelled or even forced to migrate. Thus, the terms are used in the most general sense to designate the primary forces behind streams of migrants.

This framework of migratory types provides a particularly useful and systematic way to view the migration processes of blacks in the United States. Viewing the patterns as they have occurred during the last four hundred years, one finds that each of Petersen's types is clearly represented. The tragic part of the history of black migration is that the predominant form has been forced or impelled.

While it is almost taken for granted that selective migration is a feature of all free mobility, at least where individual choice is operative, forced relocation of subcommunities or ethnic groups at first glance may appear to be predicated on the notion of nonselectivity. It is clear that selectivity is present for both free and forced migrations, but differs in the form it takes. Forced migration of the groups held in slavery is inherent in slavery. Slaves are displaced or forcefully removed on the basis of race, ethnicity, religion, occupation, social class, etc., and hence differ significantly from the total society in these characteristics.[5]

Black migration: an overview

This study is not solely a history of black migration, but rather an attempt to describe and answer some of the basic demographic questions about the major, as well as some of the minor, migrations that black people in the United States have made since their uprooting from Central and West Africa in the fifteenth century. While the presentation is in historical sequence, and the sources from which a large amount of information has been obtained are historical, our objective was not only to present a history but to develop a systematic presentation of the migratory patterns and processes of black Americans, using the perspectives, tools, and concepts of demography.

Black migration in the United States, like that of any social group, must be viewed as an ongoing, continuing phenomenon. Failure to take account of the migration patterns that antedate the one in question may preclude an understanding of the propensity to migrate, and the consequences for the communities and the migrants involved. Questions about when the black migration began and when it ended are based on the mistaken assumption that there was a black migration that was time specific. Since the arrival of the first black people in the United States there always has been black mobility, despite the constraints imposed by the institutions of slavery and racial discrimination. Whether by force or by choice, mobility and migration have characterized a sizable proportion of the black population. Without question the movement of slaves was restricted. Nevertheless, slave trading produced some involuntary mobility, and continued efforts by slaves to gain their freedom produced some migration.

For black Americans, the Civil War, World War I, and World War II were significant periods that brought numerous changes, including migrations. Because of the significance of these historical events, as well as for their heuristic value, black migration is presented for periods bounded by these major wars. Chapters 2, 3, and 4 exemplify the forced or impelled character of the transatlantic migration that resulted in relocation of Africans to America and their distribution along the Atlantic seaboard and across the South.

The inclusion of chapters on the Atlantic and domestic slave trade and antebellum migration is not based on any desire to uncover new facts about slaving practices, but to place the information that has been gathered on the subject into the context of forced migration. It will also provide a basis for examinations of later migration patterns.

The affected Africans of the slave trade were the most numerous Old

World immigrants to the Western Hemisphere before the late eighteenth century and were a major factor in the settlement of much of what are now the Atlantic and southern states.[6]

In chapter 5, "The turn of the century," a noticeable shift is shown to have occurred in the character of the migratory patterns of the former slaves from a forced or impelled migration to a form of mobility more closely resembling free migration. Blacks began exercising, many for the first time, some limited power over whether or not to leave their places of abode in search of different environs. Also, during this period of a little more than a half century, the first moves from the rural areas toward the cities of the South could be observed. Streams of black migrants crossed the Mississippi River into Texas, Colorado, and California.

Between the two world wars, the largest mass migration in the history of the United States brought more then a half-million black Americans out of the rural South into the industrial, urban North. Chapter 6, "The Great Migration and the post–World War I era," focuses on the subsequent years of the 1920s, and chapter 7 on the Depression years of the 1930s. In chapter 8, "World War II," the effects of the war and the demobilization are seen in the migratory patterns of blacks. Chapter 9 highlights the extent, patterns, and consequences of black migration in the postwar years.

The mass movement of black Americans to the metropolitan North during the 1950s is discussed in chapter 10. The decade of the 1960s, which shows the beginning of what may be a dramatic shift in black migration patterns, is discussed in chapter 11.

2. The Atlantic slave trade: a forced migration

Background

Until late in the nineteenth century black migration was characterized by force. Among the earliest European records of Africans is evidence of their forced removal from their homelands to the oases of the deserts and the coasts of the Mediterranean.[1] These early records show that the first black slaves were brought to Egypt. Later, whole armies of slaves were imported by the Cyrenians and Carthaginians, and again by the Egyptians, some for home use and the remainder for trade in other markets.[2] From North Africa and the Mediterranean coast to Asia Minor and from all of East Africa, blacks were brought to fill labor needs in the Orient. They were regularly imported into China, over a prolonged period. A Chinese document which has been dated 1178 refers to male and female slaves being brought from Africa and Madagascar.[3]

The traffic in African slaves to Europe began with the Portuguese, shortly after 1400, under Prince Henry the Navigator.[4] In the latter half of the fifteenth century, there was a period of slave importation to Europe, particularly Sicily, Portugal, Spain, and Italy. Estimates vary as to the size of this stream of slave traffic, from a low of 25,000 to a high of 100,000.[5]

Forced migration to the new world

The introduction of black Africans to the New World occurred simultaneously with the coming of the white Europeans. Arriving as servants or slaves to the original explorers, black Africans were present at the opening of the continent. It has become customary to date the beginning of traffic in Africans to the year 1502. In that year the first references to blacks appear in the documents of Spanish colonial administrators.[6] Later, with the failure of the first colonists to make productive use of Indians in developing plantations and working the mines, Bartolomé de Las Casas and others in 1517 sought to persuade Charles V to import black Africans as slaves. Charles V granted a patent that resulted in four thousand Africans being captured and shipped to the West Indian colonies. With this act the Atlantic slave trade was underway.[7]

It is believed that the first African slaves to arrive on what is now the United States mainland were brought by Lucan Vasquez de Ayllon in 1526. He attempted to establish a colony at what may have later been the site of Jamestown, Virginia. He brought with him five hundred colonists, eighty-nine horses, and one hundred slaves.[8] Other North American settlements of the sixteenth century also brought Africans as slaves. They were present in St. Augustine, Florida, from its founding in 1565. For a period of three centuries, from 1565 to 1865, black Africans and their children provided the town with slave labor. Further north, the slave trade began in 1619. Sailing under the written auspices of the Prince of Orange, a Dutch man-of-war arrived at the newly established colony of Jamestown with twenty Africans.[9]

By the turn of the eighteenth century, the common European belief was that African slavery was the cornerstone of overseas expansion. Not only did the sale of slaves promise great profit, but there also was the profit that could be gained through the use of their labor in the New World colonies. Without the slaves' labor, no southern colony was prepared to survive.[10]

African slaves were not the only source of cheap labor. Both Indians and indentured servants were used at various times and places throughout all of the Americas. Neither proved as practical as the black man. Indians easily eluded their white masters by drifting back to their tribes in the wilderness.[11] Use of white European indentured servants, on the other hand, generally proved more practical than attempts to enslave Indians, but the availability of these white servants depended on economic conditions in Europe. Even at best they would work only a specified number of years. Despite these limitations, the use of indentured servants was widespread throughout the colonies in the early eighteenth century. The African slaves, however, possessed distinct advantages in that they could be

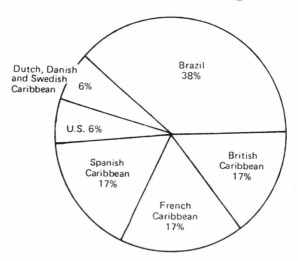

Figure 2-1. *The distribution of slave imports in the New World, 1500–1870.*
SOURCE: Robert W. Fogel and Stanley L. Engerman, *Time on the Cross* (Boston: Little, Brown & Co., 1974), p. 14.

obtained relatively cheaply, they were separated from their homeland by a
vast ocean, their skin color identified their status and discouraged their
running way, and, most important, they provided their own replacements
through their children.[12]

Volume of the Atlantic slave migration

The question of how many Africans were subject to the forced migration
of the Atlantic slave trade beginning in the fifteenth century and ending
nearly four hundred years later has long been a matter of inquiry among
historians. The most accurate answer is that nobody knows, and many of
the records needed to make even a reasonably accurate answer have been
destroyed or lost. The best that can be done is a rather crude estimate
based on incomplete data.[13]

The literature on the slave trade frequently fosters an impression of
accuracy by providing tables of the number of imported slaves during a
given period. Estimates of the number of black Africans imported to all
parts of the Americas commonly range between 15 and 20 million. However, Curtin maintains that upon close examination of these estimates, consensus turns out to be nothing but a "vast inertia, as historians have copied
over and over again the flimsy results of unsubstantial guesswork. The
passage of time brought little or no change. Instead, the hesitant guesses
of the last century have been passed off as hard data."[14]

The most commonly reported estimate of slaves brought to the Americas
is 15 million.[15] Other estimates have been offered that present widely varied views of the volume, from a low of 3.5 million to a high of 50 million.[16]

United States

Historians in the United States have an advantage over students of slavery in many other countries, since the federal census began in 1790 when
the slave trade was at its height, and regularly published population data
that identified the number of slaves. With these statistics, together with
assumed fertility rates, the rates of slave importation could be deduced
with some degree of accuracy. However, recent evidence has shown that
most early censuses underenumerated slaves, and therefore the basis for
the reliability of the estimates has been called into question.[17]

The United States, surprisingly, received only a small number of the
slaves shipped from Africa. Though the United States had about one-third
of the black population of the Western Hemisphere in 1950, it actually
imported directly only 5 to 6 percent of the slaves shipped to the Americas
during the trading era. The center of the trade was tropical America, with
almost 90 percent of it going to the Atlantic fringe from Brazil through

the Guianas to the Caribbean coast and islands. The highest ratio of slave immigration to a geographical area was found in the Lesser Antilles.[18]

It has been estimated that the total number of Africans imported during the period of legal slave trade was 333,500; 263,500 by 1790, and 70,000 from 1791 to 1807. Some estimates were even higher.[19]

While most historians agree that some slaves were imported into the United States after 1808, there is disagreement about the actual number. From the formal abolition of the trade to the beginning of the Civil War, W. E. B. DuBois estimated that 250,000 more slaves were imported. Some estimates went to the impossibly high figure of one million. Curtin believes that the evidence seems strong enough to reduce these estimates considerably. Admitting that it is "only a shot in the dark," he places the number imported at 1,000 a year, including the slave trade to Texas before it joined the Union. This gives a total estimate of 54,000 for the period 1808 to 1861. Accordingly, this places the total number of slaves imported into the United States before and after Abolition in a range between 387,500 and 399,000.[20] If, however, we accept the estimate that 9.5 million slaves were brought to the New World and 5 to 6 percent were received by the United States, we may conclude that the number of slaves transported to the United States was between 475,000 and 570,000.[21]

Northern colonies

The wholesale importation of African slaves into the English colonies in America did not begin until the latter part of the seventeenth century. There were several reasons for the long delay. The plantation system had not yet developed, and consequently, there were not yet the huge demands for labor that eventually would be needed to cultivate the sugar cane, tobacco, and rice that were mainstays of plantation society. The English had no slaving fleet in the Atlantic and no forts in Africa. Political developments such as the English Civil War between 1641 and 1649 detracted from English development of the colonies. The most significant reason was the relatively widespread use of indentured servants. Possibly as many as half of the early white immigrants were indentured servants.[22] Even allowing for their questionable accuracy,[23] the many censuses taken in the northern colonies during the eighteenth century show two noticeable trends. First, there is indication that the black population grew more rapidly than the white during the period 1700 to 1750. In 1700, when the total inhabitants of New England were estimated at 90,000, the black population probably was not more than a thousand. However, when the first general census by race of New England's population was made in 1715, there were approximately 158,000 whites and 4,150 blacks.[24] Generally, blacks were concentrated in a few cities, some of which had an even greater proportion of blacks in 1750 than in 1960. For example, in 1746, New York City's population was more than one-fifth black.[25] Similar patterns were found in other cities and regions in the northern colonies. There is little question that the size of the black population in the early eighteenth century was due, in large part, to forced immigration rather than natural increase.

The second trend was the growth of the black population in the northern colonies, which peaked around 1750 and thereafter grew very slowly, if at all. In two colonies, Connecticut and Rhode Island, a noticeable decrease was observed during the period between 1750 and 1790.[26]

Low growth rates may have been due to several factors. First, there was a general preference for white workers because it was believed that they could learn skilled trades more easily and would work more diligently. Second, there was a widespread fear that if the black population grew too rapidly it would be difficult to control. Slave uprisings and race riots had occurred earlier in the colonies. In 1712 a slave revolt in New York City resulted in the deaths of 9 whites and 27 blacks. Also, in 1714 a suspected conspiracy among slaves led to the execution of 23 people.[27] Reluctance to import slaves may also have been the result of the growing strength of antislavery organizations. The Revolutionary War took its toll of slaves, both those who served in the armies and those who were lost as a result of British raids through slaveholding areas.[28] Consequently, the slave trade failed to develop in the northern colonies during the latter part of the eighteenth century, and the slave traders had to turn elsewhere for a market.

Southern colonies

The forced migration of black Africans was received with much greater favor in the southern colonies than it was in the northern ones. Crops peculiar to the South that demanded large amounts of labor to cultivate and harvest encouraged the importation of slaves. Demand gave rise to supply, and by the late 1600s, the tobacco and rice plantations were bringing Africans for the needed labor.[29]

The total slave population of the British colonies in North America in 1714 was about 59,000. Forty years later, the number of slaves had risen to 298,000. No doubt a small part of this growth was due to natural increase, i.e., the excess of births over deaths, but considering the imbalance in the sex ratio favoring the males and high mortality, it is unlikely that a large proportion of the growth was the result of natural increase. Most of it was due to the importation of slaves directly from Africa and, indirectly, via the West Indies. By 1790 the slave population was about 700,000, almost all south of the Mason-Dixon line. By the end of the eighteenth century slavery had become the economic foundation of the South.[30]

Places of origin

It is difficult to determine accurately the exact origins of the African slaves. Evidence is scarce because documents have been destroyed by the companies and governments involved in a number of the rare instances that slavers kept such records. Most of the slaves apparently were from western Africa. They were taken from a score of principal markets, and from many smaller ones, on a 3,000-mile coastline between what is now Senegal in the north and Angola in the south. A few were taken from East Africa even in the sixteenth century.[31] It is estimated that two-thirds of the slaves came from the Gold Coast and Angola in tropical central Africa, but several other areas had periods of heavy losses. For example, during the seventeenth and nineteenth centuries, the Congo was the source of a large proportion of the slaves. During the eighteenth century the Slave Coast was the hardest hit. The Niger Delta also increased as a source for slaves during the nineteenth century. Other areas had slaves taken either sporadically or in a steady trickle.[32]

The coastal people seldom supplied slaves from their own ranks. The general practice was to purchase or otherwise obtain slaves from the tribes inland, and these in turn looked for their main supply to other peoples still farther into the interior. The best evidence suggests that this shunting process was relatively shallow. While the depth of the interior from which slaves were brought varied from century to century, it seems clear that the bulk of them were taken from a belt that reached inland from the coast (but seldom included the coast itself) for only several hundred miles.

An exception to this pattern was observed by James Bardot, a seventeenth-century trader, who noted that peoples in Angola extended their trade as far eastward as the frontiers of the kingdoms of Mombasa, Kilwa, and Sofala, all of which are on the East African coast.[33]

Characteristics of the migrants

Tribal characteristics

A large variation existed among the African tribes in physical and behavioral characteristics. The principal importing colonies frequently made careful, comparative studies of the qualities of the various tribes with certain specific tasks in mind. For example, the Senegalese, who had a strong Arabic influence in their ancestry, were considered the most intelligent of Africans and therefore particularly suited for domestic service, handicrafts, and responsible positions. The Mandingos were thought to be unusually gentle but peculiarly prone to theft. They were perceived as being easily fatigued but were well suited for less arduous work. Among the most highly prized were the Coromantees of the Gold Coast. In the folklore of slave owners the Coromantees were strong in mind and body, and some considered them to be the best and most faithful of slaves. Others viewed them as haughty, ferocious, stubborn, and frequent instigators of slave conspiracy and insurrection.

The most highly esteemed of all were the Whydahs, Nagoes, and Pawpaws of the Slave Coast. Described as lusty, industrious, cheerful, and submissive, they brought higher prices on the block. Among the less desirable were the Eboes or Mocoes. They were described as "having a sickly yellow tinge in their complexion, jaundiced eyes, and prognathous faces." While the women were reportedly good workers, the men were believed to be lazy, despondent, and prone to suicide.[34] The least desirable of all were those from the Kingdom of Gaboon. Their reputation was based, apparently, on their morbidity and mortality rates. Few survived the passage, and those who did died soon after arrival.[35]

These perceived characteristics and the variations in preferences by the slave owners and traders had a marked influence on the price offered in various markets and on the distribution of a given tribe throughout the New World and within the colonies, and later, in the United States.

Demographic characteristics

Systematic data on demographic characteristics of African slaves are not available. However, scattered plantation documents, shipping manifests, and other documents do provide some evidence on sex and approximate age, and occasionally list occupational skills or aptitude. Data on fertility, morbidity, and mortality also are widely scattered and unsystematic, if available at all.

Slaves most desired were between 15 and 25 years of age. If these were not available, older children were preferred to middle-aged adults, since they were less apt to die in the "seasoning." It was found that they would learn English easily and their service would increase instead of decrease after the first few years of slavery.[36] Likewise, it is no surprise that the ratio of males to females was high among the African slaves, since the bulk of the work was hard labor. One large plantation with 528 slaves reported 284 males and 244 females.[37] Almost all of the slaves were unmarried. Very little effort was made to import complete family units, and those that were taken by the slavers were frequently broken up during the passage.

The Middle Passage

Conditions of the migration

The journey from the West African coast to the New World is frequently referred to as the Middle Passage, by reason of its being the second leg of the triangular trading voyage between the continents of Europe and Africa, Africa and America, and America and Europe.

The slavers had two methods of obtaining their human cargoes. The first, called "boating," consisted chiefly of anchoring at the mouth of some river and sending out smaller boats to buy slaves from local traders along the coast and up the rivers. This often took weeks and was quite dangerous. The second method, likely to be even slower, was simply to drop anchor and wait for the slaves to be brought to the ship by the local traders. This took so long, at times, that the slaves purchased first, died in the heat and squalor of the ship's hold before a full cargo was obtained.[38]

After the captured Africans were taken aboard the slave ship, the men were usually shackled by attaching the right wrist and ankle of one to the left wrist and ankle of another. The women and children were often allowed to wander about the vessel during the daylight hours, though the nights were spent between decks in rooms usually barred to the male slaves but not necessarily to the sailors. The captives slept without covering on bare wooden floors, which were often constructed of unplaned boards. In rough seas, skin over the elbows would wear away to the bare bones.[39]

There were two schools of thought among the slave-ship captains as to the most profitable way to transport their human cargo. One maintained that by providing the slaves adequate room, decent food, and exercise, they would reduce the mortality rate and increase the value of each slave upon arrival. Those using this approach were referred to as the "loose packers." The others known as "tight packers," crowded their holds with bodies, permitted little or no exercise, and economized on food. They operated on the theory that, although the loss of life might be greater on each of their trips, the net receipts would be larger. The weak and emaciated could be detained upon arrival until they had regained their health and weight, and thereby increased the price they would bring at auction. While the debate between the two schools of thought continued for many years, it was evident that the "tight packers" were by far in the majority by the mid-eighteenth century. The potential profit was so great on each slave that most captains used every possible space for the storage of human cargo.[40]

The discomfort of the densely packed quarters of the slave ships has been described as wretched by even the most apologetic authors.[41] Structurally, the hold of a slaving vessel was usually about five feet high, but when rigged for "tight packing" another shelf or platform was built in the middle of it extending six feet from each side of the vessel. When the bottom of the hold was completely filled, another row of slaves was packed on the platform. If there was as much as six feet of vertical space in the hold, a second platform was usually installed to accommodate more slaves. Such arrangement left only about two feet of headroom. Slaves on such a ship, during the entire voyage, were unable to sit upright.

Disease, death, and suicide plagued nearly all voyages. Smallpox, scurvy, various forms of ophthalmia, and flux were the diseases most feared by slavers. Numerous accounts of slaving vessels losing half their "cargo" are scattered through the literature on the slave trade. The average mortality during the Middle Passage is difficult if not impossible to determine accurately from existing records. However, the "cost of the slave trade in human life was many times the number of slaves landed in the Americas." For every slave who landed alive, there were many others who died in warfare along the treks leading to the West African coast, awaiting shipment, or in the crowded and contaminated holds of the slaving vessels.[42] Historians of the slave trade estimate that loss of life during the Middle Passage leg of the journey ranged from 12 to 33 percent.[43]

Suicide was common on most voyages; on some it was epidemic.[44] In 1737, for example, more than a hundred men slaves reportedly jumped overboard from the *Prince of Orange* while the ship was anchored at St. Kitts. The cause, as it was reported, was a hoax circulated among the captives that upon arrival they first would have their eyes put out and then would be eaten.

Usually, the last leg of the Middle Passage, which frequently took about five weeks, was less restrictive. All but a few slaves were released from their irons and brought to the deck for relief. Such practices were not motivated by humanitarian purposes, but rather to prepare the slaves for the market. If the remaining stock of provisions was sufficient, the slaves were given bigger meals and as much water as they could drink. If the ship was commanded by an amiable captain, the last day was set aside for limited frolicking in the form of a costume party on deck, with the women slaves dancing in the sailors' discarded clothing. The journey completed, the captain was rowed ashore to arrange for the sale of his involuntary passengers.[45]

Destinations of the migrants

Port of entry is not demographically useful for determining destination since there were frequent additional moves before arrival at the final destination. The point of the original disembarkment was often an island in the West Indies that served as a temporary layover until a sale or a wholesale movement of slaves to another island or to the mainland could be arranged.

On the North American mainland, the majority of slaves were landed south of the Mason-Dixon line. The chief ports of disembarkment were in Virginia, the Carolinas, and to a lesser degree, Georgia. There is evidence that during the period 1710 to 1769 a total of 52,500 slaves were imported to Virginia (see Table 2-1).[46]

Nearly 86 percent of the slaves were brought to Virginia directly from

Table 2–1. Origin of Virginia slaves, 1710–69

Origin given merely as "Africa"	20,564
The Gambia and Senegal	3,652
"Guinea" (apparently the Windward Coast, the Gold Coast, and the Slave Coast)	6,777
Calabar (mostly Ibo, Ibibio, and Efik from the Bight of Biafra)	9,224
Angola (including the Congo)	3,860
Madagascar	1,011
Slaves brought direct from Africa	45,088
Slaves reimported from the West Indies	7,046
Slaves from other North American colonies	370

SOURCE: Daniel P. Mannix, *Black Cargoes* (New York: The Viking Press, 1962), p. 167

Africa, whereas 13 percent were imported from the West Indies. The remaining 1 percent were brought from other North American colonies to Virginia.[47]

South Carolina's busy port of Charleston was visited by many of the big Liverpool Guineamen. Charleston's prices were usually high, and the captains came to regard it as another West Indian island for the sale of slaves. Many of the imported slaves—about 36 percent—came from Angola or the Congo. As "connoisseurs" of Africans, the slave owners of South Carolina preferred Gold Coast slaves, chose next those from the Windward Coast, followed by Mandingos, who were used primarily as house servants.[48]

For seventeen years after its founding in 1733, Georgia was the only American colony that prohibited the importation or ownership of slaves.[49] However, the antislavery stance of the colony proved so unpopular that white settlers frequently moved to the Carolinas to be able to make use of slaves. But once in the slave trade, Georgians showed a preference for slaves from the Gold Coast or the Windward Coast. Since it was one of the less important markets, it was often necessary to import slaves into Georgia

Table 2–2. Origin of South Carolina slaves

Origin given merely as "Africa"	4,146
From the Gambia to Sierra Leone	12,441
Windward Coast (including Sierra Leone, the Grain Coast, and the Ivory Coast	7,757
"Guinea Coast" (here apparently the Gold Coast, the Slave Coast, and Calabar)	18,240
The Congo and Angola	22,409
East Africa	473
Slaves imported from Africa	65,466
Slaves reimported from the West Indies	2,303

SOURCE: Ibid., p. 168.

in small groups from the West Indies, making it somewhat more difficult
to determine their place of origin.

Consequences of the slave trade

Results in Africa

Historians and other scholars have only recently begun to examine the
impact of the 500 years of slave trade on African societies. Many of these
studies portray contrasting findings, ranging from the position that the
slave trade was responsible for virtually every unfavorable development in
Africa during these centuries to the opposite point of view that even the
slave trade was better than no trade at all.[50]

Inevitably, demographic consequences follow in the wake of any migration. One consequence of slaving was the apparent reduction in the population of Africa, though the exact extent of this reduction is difficult if not
impossible to determine. At certain times and in certain places these population losses undoubtedly crippled many tribal societies. It is estimated that
in slave migration to all destinations Africa lost at least 50 million inhabitants.[51] Much of this loss was calculated from the potential population had
the slaves remained and reproduced. Since a large portion of the slaves
died before reaching their final destination, the gain in other places was
much less.[52] Variation in the intensity of slaving in the African continent
may have caused long-term differences in population density. However,
change in the African continental population was the least important long-
term consequence of the slave trade. For example, although large numbers
of captives were shipped from the forest lands of Nigeria, this area is still
among the most densely populated regions in all of Africa.[53] This small
impact resulted from two factors: a high rate of natural increase to replace
the migrants and the long time span over which the slave trade occurred.

Perhaps more important than the demographic consequences were the
far-reaching structural consequences of the societies affected. Curtin's
analysis of the Atlantic slave trade poses the problem of the impact of the
slave trade on African social and political change. He presents two extreme
models of this relationships, the first of which depicts the transformation
of a previously peaceful peasant community into a militarized slave-catching society. In the transformed society, slave-raiding became an economic
activity consciously pursued for the European trade that could be obtained
with slaves, and only with slaves. If the European demand for slaves did
indeed force this kind of economic value system on African societies, the
slave trade can be shown to have had disastrous consequences for the hunters as well as for the hunted. In addition to the death and destruction
caused by the raids themselves, the resources and creative impulses of the

African hunters must have been diverted from the pursuit of innovation and progress in other fields.

The second model viewed African societies like those common throughout most of the European world, where disputes were settled frequently by military means. Warfare produced prisoners of war, who could be killed, exchanged, or enslaved. Slaves were a by-product of war, not its original cause. The African adaptation to the demand for slaves might have been to adapt warfare to increase the number of prisoners, without actually increasing the destruction of lives and property. If so, the slave trade might have done little to alter the African society.[54]

The question is, of course, which model has the most currency. Historically, variations of both of these models have existed. The available data can only suggest which model was dominant. According to Curtin's argument, if the dominant African model at the height of the slave trade was the militarized, slave-catching society—the second one—the export projections should show a relatively large and continuous supply of slaves from the hunter societies, the slaves being from the defeated warring neighbors.

The African export data of the eighteenth century do not support that notion. Some ports, however, did produce a continuous supply that may imply slave-catching as an economic activity. In other areas, the rapid shift in sources of supply from one region to another suggests that by-product enslavement was the dominant feature, or that if systematic slave-hunting had been tried, it could not be maintained.

The economic consequences of the slave trade for Africa are complex and difficult to ascertain with any degree of certainty. However, a number of observations can be made. One clear consequence was the diminution of human capital and resources. In exporting slaves, African communities exported their own human resource without any possible return in monetary interest or in the improvement of their economic system.[55] Unlike the more or less forced emigration of the impoverished peoples of nineteenth-century Europe, the exported African slaves were unable to enter the mainstream of capitalist expansion and thereby to benefit their mother country indirectly or by returning with their gains. They enhanced only the wealth of their owners, a wealth that never returned to Africa. While the payment received in exchange for the slaves could have benefited Africa had it been in the form of capital goods, the slave trade failed because the payments were nonproductive.

The conditions of the exchange prevented the kind of capital accumulation that could have led to advancing the economy of the African tribes.[56] The overall economic effect was a serious and continuing retardation of Africa's productive capacity, from areas like the Congo, where production practically ceased, to some parts of Guinea, where production was only slightly affected. Yet even in the area where economic retardation was not severe, the social troubles resulting from even the limited trade exacted a high cost.

The political consequences of the slave trade in Africa were likewise significant. Just as the balance of power among Europeans shifted from century to century as a result of nations pursuing slave monopolies, so African political entities were thrust into a quest for preeminence as middlemen. They developed alliances with European nations to supply slaves at a price. As international conditions changed, these alliances were altered or broken. Such a change came with the British and French abolition of the slave trade. The trade alliance that these nations had developed with African bargaining units took on the form of European domination. The old trade agreements succumbed to the subsequent economic and political triumph of industrial Europe over nonindustrial Africa.

Social consequences were far-reaching. Family disruption, tribal disorganization, and wars were immediate effects. However, they have not been systematically studied or described.

Results in the United States

The economic, political, and social consequences for the United States are also difficult to measure. Without the labor provided by the African slaves and their descendants, the economic development of the South in the particular form it took would have been severely retarded, if not impossible. While the argument of whether slavery was profitable continues, little doubt exists that the captive laborers had a major economic impact on the development of the South and the nation.[57]

The political consequences of the slave trade were among the most traumatic the United States has ever experienced. The controversy over slavery divided the nation and, in large part, brought on the Civil War with its lingering aftermath.[58]

Socially, the introduction of African slaves marked the beginning of a racially heterogeneous United States, with the Africans as a significant minority race. A social structure developed that separated the races and promoted white people to superior roles and black people to subordinate ones. It engendered a social climate characterized by fear, suspicion, hate, and sporadic conflict that continues in parts of the United States. E. Franklin Frazier has described the social significance of the introduction of blacks into American society:

That nameless Dutch vessel which arrived a year before the Mayflower, was hardly less important in American history. She carried not only twenty Negroes but, for the future, everything those Negroes and their successors would contribute to American wealth and culture, including Carolina rice, Louisiana cane, and the Cotton Kingdom. She carried, or announced, the maritime trade of New England and the training of the first sailors in the United States Navy; then the plantation system, the Abolition Society, the Missouri Compromise, and the Civil War; then Reconstruction, the Solid South, Jim Crow, and the struggle for integration. She carried the spirituals, jazz, the researches of such Negro scientists as George Washington Carver, the contributions to American culture of younger Negro musicians, statesmen, scholars, and writers; and she also carried, for this age of international struggles, the first link between the United States and Africa.[59]

Upon arrival in the United States, slaves from Africa had to be "resocialized" to fill their new roles and to meet their owners' expectations. It is also likely that the new slaves with their African ways and memories had to endure the disdain, if not the hostility, of the Africans imported earlier, who had already adjusted to the slave regimen and had acquired a new conception of themselves.

The acculturation of the slaves to the new environment varied, depending on the degree of isolation from the new culture. Where slaves were assigned to household responsibilities, the acculturation proceeded more rapidly than for those working in the fields, removed from contact with whites and resocialized slaves. The notion that resocialization of the slaves obliterated any and all African culture traits has been held by many and challenged by others.[60] Part of the African culture, however, survived, including traces of language and elements of religion. For example, Lorenzo D. Turner identified approximately four thousand words of West African origin in the Gullah vocabulary of blacks on the coast of South Carolina and Georgia.[61] In his study, he also discovered numerous African given names and African phrases that had been translated into English.

W. E. B. Du Bois argued that careful research would reveal traces "of the African family in America," giving the example of the Zulu practice of bride-chasing that was reported as having occurred in Lowndes County, Alabama, in 1892.[62] On the other hand, Frazier's study of the destruction of the African family as slaves in America indicated that there was scarcely any evidence that recognizable elements of the African social organization survived, that such survivals associated with the African family are "rare and isolated."[63]

Survivals of African religious behavior in the United States have been noted by some scholars. During slavery there were reports of the dancing and singing of slaves that supposedly indicate that African religious ceremonies had been carried over, but except for a few instances occurring among isolated groups of blacks, it has been difficult to identify religious traits that could correctly be called African survivals.[64]

Thus, the experiences of the African slaves following their forced migration to the United States resulted in a virtually complete resocialization.

While traces of African language, family structure, and religion have been noted, their influence on the social organization of black American has been quite limited. African patterns of thought and behavior could survive only where the black newcomers were isolated, and where there was sufficient common understanding among them to give significance to surviving African ways.[65] With few exceptions, isolated black enclaves were nonexistent because the majority of the slaves were scattered over broad areas on small farms and plantations. Internal slave trade further precluded the possibility of maintaining black cultural enclaves in the United States.

According to Frazier, the most important factor prohibiting retention of African culture was

> the fact that the African family system, the chief means of cultural transmission, was destroyed. Under such circumstances African languages were lost and the African social organization could not be reconstituted in the new environment. Consequently, Negroes acquired new habits and modes of thought, and whatever elements of African culture were retained, lost their original meaning in becoming fused with their experiences in the New World.[66]

3. The domestic slave trade

Structure of the trade

The domestic slave trade in the United States represents the largest systematic, forced redistribution of people in American history. While there have been other forced migrations in the United States, e.g., the relocation of the native Indian population to reservations and the encampment of the Japanese-Americans during World War II, the domestic slave trade was unique in that the migrants were viewed as chattel. The temporal span of the migration era was nearly two hundred years, and it was carried out by private parties and business interests and not by the government directly, although it certainly had official sanction.

The domestic slave traffic, a form of forced migration, was the means by which the black population was first redistributed in the United States. With the legal abolition by the British of the Atlantic slave trade after January 1, 1808, and the opening of the Midwest and Southwest during the nineteenth century, there was an increased demand for slave labor. The result was illegal traffic in African slaves, slave breeding, and domestic slave trade.[1] The domestic slave trade provided the basic labor for the developing agricultural economy of the South.[2]

Though given impetus by the abolition of the Atlantic trade, the domestic trade actually began earlier. Trade from North to South, although small in scale compared to what was to follow, existed in colonial times.[3] The internal trade was more noticeable near the end of the eighteenth century in various parts of the South. With the official closing of the African trade, the domestic trade became profitable and began to assume the character of a regular business. By 1815 it had become a major economic activity in the country. The structure for handling the traffic quickly developed, and an institution emerged that served as a substitute, or a supplement, for the African trade.[4]

While the form varied from time to time, the domestic trade was often handled by farm-supply business firms that frequently took on a "line" of slaves. Auctioneers who dealt in real estate and personal property sold slaves along with other commodities. Organizations frequently sold slaves by lottery. Planters who were leaving their farms or cutting back their operations would advertise or pass the word around that they had slaves for sale.[5]

The domestic slave trade first developed in Maryland and Virginia and later was extended to the Carolinas, Kentucky, and Missouri, the latter four becoming major states of origin. At first the movement of slaves was into the upper South and border states. As it progressed, continued agricultural and economic expansion resulted in the movement of slaves into Florida, Alabama, and Mississippi; then later into Arkansas, Louisiana, and Texas. Trading centers developed in the major cities of both the destination and origin states. The principal trading centers in the destination states were Baltimore, Washington, Richmond, Norfolk, and Charleston. In the origin states, Montgomery, Memphis, and New Orleans became the principal marts.[6]

At various times during the nineteenth century, most southern states attempted to prevent slave traders from marketing their merchandise within their borders. Many of the state constitutions contained clauses authorizing their legislatures to "prohibit the introduction of any slave for the purpose of speculation, or as an article of trade or merchandise."[7] The only states never to pass such laws were Missouri, Arkansas, Texas, and Florida. Until 1849, Kentucky even prohibited residents from importing slaves for their own use, unless they were acquired by inheritance. With few exceptions, the law against the introduction of slaves by professional traders remained in force for only short periods of time. Some states—for example, Mississippi—adopted legislative prohibition of slave trading, but made no serious effort to enforce the provision, and speculators continued to sell slaves in violation of it.[8]

Few good words have been written about the slave traders. They have been called, variously, "southern Shylocks," "slavemongers," "nigger traders," and "traders in human misery." Few were liked, some were tolerated, but most were hated. Traders were condemned morally at the same time they provided a service that most slave owners wanted, if not needed. The slave trader was portrayed as

a brutal, keen speculator, a ruthless sharper. He watched for bargains at the public and private jails; he started the bidding at the auctions, but dropped out if there was ambitious competition, for he would purchase only at the lowest prices and sell at the highest. He often had, and always pretended to have, ample cash, but seemed meanly sparing of it. He was conspicuous and inquisitive in public places and on public occasions—on sale-days and during the session of the county court, at the musterings, the barbecues, the joint debates and even the Fourth of July celebrations where "liberty," "freedom," and "state sovereignity" were on every tongue—collecting scraps of news or gossip about fortunes and misfortunes of farmers, planters, professional men and merchants that might be induced to buy or compelled to sell slaves. He was intrusive and impertinent privately, eager to argue that a certain sum of money would be much more useful than the services of some boy or girl, cook or hostler, or that a "breeder," a carpenter, a blacksmith, a drayman, a barber or a hairdresser would surely be a good investment. He bubbled over with assurances and recent instances designed to relieve all doubts and to encourage all expectations, whether he wished to buy or to sell, although his largest profits often came from children separated from their mothers, or *vice versa*, and the palming off of unsound or vicious slaves as "prime" and "of good character." To planters able to buy, he was obsequious; before slave owners needing cash, or plain farmers, mechanics or tradesmen that had saved it so as to join the slaveholding class, he posed as benevolently willing to furnish what was desired. He negotiated as secretly as any hypocritical master wished, and hastened away at night, so as to prevent sad partings and escape public notice, but treated his purchase like so many sheep or refractory cattle. Imagine a compound of an unscrupulous horsetrader, a familiar old-time tavern-keeper, a superficially complaisant and artful, hard-drinking gambler and an ignorant, garrulous low-politician and you will get a concoction that resembles the Southern antebellum notion of the "nigger trader."[9]

Although this conception was not an accurate composite of all slave traders, few regular traders were without some of these traits.[10]

The domestic slave trade consisted essentially of two forms. On the one hand, a large amount of the trade was in local transactions. A rural owner who wanted to sell a slave often would pass the word around among his neighbors or publish a notice in the county newspaper. Frequently, in such cases, there would be appended to the notice a statement that the slave was not to be sent out of the state or that no dealers need apply.[11] The other form of the trade was conducted on an interstate basis. The long-distance trade, though open to anyone who wanted to engage in it, appears to have been conducted primarily by business firms engaged in slave trading. Many of these trading firms had assembling headquarters with field agents to collect slaves and selling agencies at the centers of slave demand.

While the domestic slave trade began in the early 1700s and lasted to 1860, the heaviest trading took place during the period 1815 to 1860. The greatest activity was just prior to the Panic of 1837, and thereafter the flow was held somewhat in check, first by the hard times in the cotton belt and then by an agricultural renaissance in Virginia.[12] The trade ended with the Civil War.

Size of black population in the United States

When the first federal census was taken in 1790, there were 757,000 blacks in the United States, of whom almost 700,000 were slaves. Slaves and freemen constituted 19 percent of the total population. Moreover, the significant feature of the black population was that more than nine-tenths were concentrated in the South, where the plantation system of agriculture had created the need for cheap labor. More than 40 percent of the black population (305,000) was in Virginia. Maryland, North Carolina, and South Carolina each had a black population exceeding 100,000, Georgia had nearly 30,000, and Kentucky and Tennessee had 12,500 and 3,770, respectively.[13]

From 1790 to 1860 the slave population of the United States grew from about 700,000 to nearly four million. This growth was a result of the switch from tobacco to cotton production and the resulting plantation economy[14] was effected by the legal and illegal entry of African slaves into the United States as well as by their natural increase.[15]

The domestic slave trade brought about a significant redistribution in the slave population in response to the demands of the expanding plantation system that moved toward the Gulf states and the Mississippi Valley. Three quarters of a million slaves were removed from the old slave states of Delaware, Maryland, Virginia, North Carolina, and the District of Columbia to states in the Deep South and the Southwest. Another 835,000 slaves were imported into the origin states from 1790 to 1860, with the largest movement occurring between 1830 and 1840. It is estimated that nearly a quarter of a million slaves were transported over state lines during that decade. In the last decade for domestic slave trading, 1850–1860, migration accelerated, with 193,000 slaves transported over state lines.[16] The percentage of slaves in the total population showed a decrease in the border states from 1820 to 1860, and a corresponding increase in the states of the lower South.[17] During the last half of the period from 1790 to 1860, slave traffic was three times as large as during the first half.[18]

The slave states of the South can be viewed as three types, depending on the particular period in question. There were states that were primarily exporters of slaves, such as Virginia, Maryland, and, to a lesser extent, South Carolina. There were states that were originally importers but gradually became exporters as the demand for slaves became more intense in other areas, generally to the West and South. Among those states that engaged in both importing and exporting were Kentucky, Tennessee, Georgia, and later, and to a lesser extent, Mississippi. States that engaged primarily in importing slaves were most often the frontier states, such as Arkansas, Louisiana, and Texas, the inhabitants of which were converting virgin land into cotton.

It was estimated by a committee of the South Carolina House of Representatives that during the period between 1840 and 1850, 234,000 slaves were removed from Maryland, Virginia, North Carolina, South Carolina, and Kentucky.[19] This figure is considered by some to be excessive by 50,000. Fogel and Engerman show that by 1860 the exporting states had only 60 percent of the slave population they would have had if they had grown at the national average.[20]

The extent of importation by states in the Southwest, including Alabama, Arkansas, Florida, Georgia, Mississippi, Louisiana, and Texas, has been estimated to be more than 263,000 for the decade 1850 to 1860. This estimate is considered to be excessive in the amount of 32,000.[21] There were, of course, significant variations by states and for different years during the decade. But on the whole, migration swelled the slave population of the origin states to 3.6 times the level it would have attained if these states had grown at the national average.[22]

States midway between the Atlantic seaboard and the Southwest were often major importers during the early decades of the century, but several gradually gave way to the profits that could be obtained by exporting as well. Mississippi's market role in the domestic slave trade reflects such a pattern, as does that of Kentucky.

Each state's slave-trade structure was unique in some respects, and each state developed a reputation that was reflected in the desirability and prices of the slaves. Slaves from Virginia and South Carolina, for example, were in greater demand in the markets of the Southwest than those from North Carolina. Few traders boasted of obtaining slaves from North Carolina unless they could say they came from "up near the Virginia line" or "down near the border of South Carolina."[23] Quite apart from the quality of the slaves, the reasons for this poor reputation were said to be the lack of social attractions for the traders and the lack of first-class slave markets in the North Carolina cities.

Impetus to the developing economies of midwestern cities was provided by the domestic slave trade. Of the cities in the central South, Memphis had by far the largest trade. The city's location was considered very favorable—on the Mississippi River midway between St. Louis and Natchez and in the midst of a fertile region where cotton planting was increasing rapidly. Slaves were brought by water from Virginia, Kentucky, and Missouri. After completion of the railroad in 1857, they were brought from the Carolinas, Georgia, and Tennessee. Memphis was also the most convenient market place for the planters of Arkansas, northeastern Louisiana, and western Mississippi.[24]

Volume of slave migration

Assessing the redistribution of any population requires an ongoing system of residence reporting. Obviously, such reporting systems were not available during the eighteenth and nineteenth centuries; they are not available even at the present time. The most reliable and extensive bases for determining the extent of the domestic slave trade are the United States decennial census reports of the population between 1790 and 1860. But, at best, they provide little more than approximations.[25]

Few systematic studies of the volume of the domestic slave trade have been conducted. Bancroft's 1931 study however, attempted to estimate the volume of the interstate domestic slave trade in an average year during the mid-1800s using the residual method. Simply stated, growth or decline of a population is viewed as the result of natural increase and migration. If the natural increase component of the population growth can be determined, the residual component is due to migration. The precise natural increase of the black population in any state during the antebellum period is not known, but a reasonable estimate for the whole South during the period 1830 to 1860 was between 23 and 27 percent. Of course, the percentage of natural increase was not the same in any two states, but the variations were presumed to be small.

In estimating the volume of slaves removed from a wholly exporting state or taken into a wholly importing state, the slave population at the beginning of a decade as determined by the census is added to the estimated natural increase for the decade. If the sum is less than the actual slave population at the end of the decade, it is obvious that there were exportations; if more, there were importations. Bancroft shows for example that Virginia's slave population in 1830 was 469,757, and with a natural increase of 24.2 percent or 113,681, it should have risen, without exportation, to 583,438 by 1840. But it was only 448,987—showing apparent exportations and their natural increase amounting to 134,451.[26] Runaways and emancipations were taken into account. However, without an adequate basis for providing an accurate determination of the extent of these occurrences, they were merely estimated to be 2,000. By applying this procedure to each state, Bancroft was able to estimate the volume of interstate slave trade in a systematic way.

To the extent that the domestic slave trade constituted interstate commerce, the volume of slaves relocated was subject to control by the federal government. Repeated efforts by antislavery groups to persuade Congress to exercise its constitutional prerogatives to limit, if not abolish, the slave traffic, met with little success. State regulation was sporadic and generally ineffective.[27] Such limited restraining legislation as was adopted was motivated primarily by the desire to protect the interests of the purchasers and to maintain the security of the white communities. Only a few states sought to control the flow of slaves for humanitarian reasons.[28]

Characteristics of the migrants

Scattered historical evidence on the characteristics of slaves that made up the interstate trade would indicate that in terms of demographic characteristics, i.e., age and sex, the slaves were relatively similar to a "normal" population, with some notable exceptions that were no doubt due to the demands of the market. From the available data, it would appear that the relative proportions of male and female were similar. Although, when age is controlled, it also appears that the sex ratios reflect a greater proportion of young women than young men. This was perhaps due to the fact that young mothers with several small children were extremely valuable, and buxom girls of ages 14 to 18 were usually at a great premium because of good looks or proven or expected fecundity.[29]

Age characteristics were frequently noted on shipping manifests. From four manifests of shipments to New Orleans dated 1834 and 1835 the following age characteristics of slaves are indicated:

> Of the four cargoes making a total of 646 slaves, 396 were owned by Franklin and Armfield. Among these 396 there were only two full families; the fathers were 21 and 22 years of age, the mothers 19 and 20 and the children 1 and 1½. There were 20 husbandless mothers with 33 children, of whom one was 2 weeks old, 4 others were less than 1 year old, 19 were from 1 to 4 years old, and 9 were from 5 to 12 years of age. The remaining 337 were single and may be grouped thus:
>
> > 5 were from 6 to 9 years old, both inclusive
> > 68 were from 10 to 15 years old
> > 145 were from 16 to 21 years old
> > 101 were from 22 to 30 years old
> > 9 were from 31 to 39 years old
> > 8 were from 40 to 50 years old
> > 1 above 50, a man of 60.
>
> Of these 337, 93 percent were from 10 to 30 years of age.[30] Additional support for the generality of these findings is that the slaves whom the dealers preferred to buy for distant sales were "likely" Negroes from ten to thirty years old.[31]

Characteristics other than the most basic, age and sex, are even more difficult to come by. Some records carry limited occupational background information, but the fact that slaves were frequently shifted from one type of work to another as ownership changed or as the seasonal needs of the plantations changed makes this information difficult to interpret meaningfully. Behavioral characteristics are known to have played a role in the selection of those slaves that were marketed. The owners were most eager to be rid of the slaves that were indolent, unruly, or under suspicion.[32] Buyers, on the other hand, were careful to avoid those slaves thought to be planners or participants in plots or revolts. Some of the slaves were actually convicted felons sold by the states in which their crimes had been committed. The purchasers of these were generally required to give bond to transport them beyond the limits of the United States; some of the traders, however, broke their pledges on the chance that their breaches would not be discovered.[33]

Migration conditions

There were three methods of moving slaves to distant market: by ships down the coast or the Ohio and Mississippi Rivers and their tributaries, by overland march, and by railroad. The largest of the cargoes shipped via the coastal route went from Alexandria, Baltimore, Norfolk, Richmond, and Charleston to places farther south or on the Gulf or the Mississippi. Many of the ships were built expressly for the slave trade and the others were remodeled to suit it.[34] One such ship, the *Tribune*, was described as follows:

> The hold was appropriated to the slaves and divided into two apartments; the afterhold would carry about 80 women, and the other about 100 men. On either side were two platforms running the whole length; one raised a few inches, and the other half-way up the deck. They were about five or six feet deep. On these the slaves lie, as close as they can stow away.[35]

From shipping manifests, which were required by law after 1808, it appears that the volume of the coastal slave trade between 1815 and 1860 varied from two to five thousand slaves per year.[36] A greater portion of the interstate trade from Maryland, Virginia, and the Carolinas is reported to have occurred during the 1830s than during the later decades.[37] One firm alone, the Franklin and Armfield operation, at the peak of their business shipped cargoes of as many as a hundred slaves every two weeks.[38]

The slave voyages down the coast and through the Gulf frequently were subject to actual or attempted slave mutinies by land or sea. The *Nile's Register* alone reported at least three attempts in a five-month period in 1829 and 1830.[39] Storms and the danger of grounding increased the risks of the voyages. However, the sufferings and fatalities of the marine domestic slave trade were not as severe as the African slave trade. Reviews of shipping manifests that provide for the recording of any or all births and deaths in transit indicate that morbidity and mortality were not sufficiently high to cause concern among the insurance brokers.[40] Yet, conditions on the ships engaged in the domestic slave trade were rarely sanitary or commodious.

The greatest inland channel of the trade was the Mississippi River. Descriptive assessments of the river trade indicate that conditions of slave travel on the rivers, including the Ohio, the Missouri, and others, were harsh. Men commonly were chained to prevent their escape, and it was frequently necessary to do the same to the women. The men and women occasionally were handcuffed together and closely watched in the event the shackles should be slipped and an escape attempted.

The most common form of moving slaves was in coffles, which varied in size from less than a half-dozen slaves to more than one hundred. Women were often tied together with a rope about their necks, like a halter, while the men were handcuffed and wore iron collars, fastened to a chain. The men were placed in double file in front, with the women following in similar fashion. The drivers rode where they could best watch and direct their coffle. At the end of the day the slaves were placed in secure quarters or were left shackled and handcuffed while they slept on the ground without shelter.[41]

Overland traders reported that they were accustomed to covering 25 miles per day, depending upon the number of slaves making up the coffles, the nature of the terrain, and the weather. The children were often placed in wagons. It was believed that 25 miles per day was not excessive for sturdy slaves, and there were generally facilities so that the sick could ride with the children in wagons.[42] Thus, the trip from Virginia to Louisiana usually required from six to eight weeks.[43]

The building of railroads speeded the transport of slaves and correspondingly reduced the costs.[44] By the middle of the century, it became customary to use the train for overland transport. Most railroads instituted separate cars for slaves, most of which were simply freight cars. By 1858, the Central of Georgia Railroad improved its service by instituting a sleeping car for slaves.[45]

In the late 1850s, the number of slaves taken through or from Virginia caused a great deal of comment. For example, in 1859 the Portsmouth, Virginia, *Transcript* reported that "Heavy shipments of Negroes for the far South are made almost every day by the Seaboard and Roanoke railroad. Yesterday about a hundred arrived here from the eastern shore of Maryland and passed through, and this morning another carload from Delaware was sent on."[46] In Montgomery and Mobile it was noted that the shipments of slaves by rail had averaged not less than 200 slaves daily during a two-month period in 1859.[47]

Consequences of the migration

The intent of the domestic slave trade was simply to provide cheap labor in the developing South and Southwest and to provide an economic base in those mid–South Atlantic states where soil depletion required a new source of income. It carried with it, however, demographic and sociological consequences.

The chief demographic consequences of the trade were to reduce the black population, absolutely and proportionately, in the mid–South Atlantic states, and to increase the same in the East South Central and Southwestern states. Had the trade not existed, states such as Maryland, Virginia, and South Carolina would probably have a much higher proportion of black people today. States such as Arkansas, Louisiana, Mississippi, and Texas would have had a significantly lower black population during their period of agricultural and economic development prior to the Civil War as well as at the present time. There is little question that agricultural development would have been greatly retarded or at least of a different character in the East South Central and Southwestern states had the labor supply been limited to the whites who migrated there in the early 1800s.

The significance of the slave trade for the nation's westward movement is frequently overlooked. It has been argued that without slavery and the slave trade, the westward movement on the southern frontier would have been unsuccessful. According to U. B. Phillips,

> It was the slaves, brought in either by the settlers or the traders, who transformed the Southern frontier from a wilderness to flourishing cotton and sugar plantations. It was the slaves, moreover, who represented one of the most substantial forms of capital to be found in the cotton kingdom. Frederick Jackson Turner, an historian of the frontier, always described the trader as having preceded the farmer. He was, of course, referring to the person who carried on barter with the Indians. In this instance, however, the trader followed the farmer. He was the person who brought the labor supply to the farmer. Although the order is, in this case, reversed, it would not be too much to say that the slave trader, with his black workers, had a more profound effect on the history of the Southern frontier than did the Indian trader, with his trinkets and fire water.[48]

Not only did the domestic slave trade produce marked consequences for the areas of origin and destination, but it also produced a lasting effect on the people who took part in the system. One of the most significant aspects of the slave trade was its effect on the structure and stability of the black family. There has been considerable agreement that the domestic slave trade was highly destructive of slave families, that trading was essentially an economic activity motivated by profit and there was little or no reluctance to divide families when market conditions justified such actions.[49] Some recent studies, however, indicate that the notion that slave practices destroyed the black family is largely myth.[50] These studies maintain that the family was the basic unit of social organization under slavery, and that it was in the economic interest of planters to foster the stability of slave families. Fogell and Engerman argue that most sales were either of "whole families or of individuals who were at an age when it would have been normal for them to have left the family."[51]

However, the fact was that the everyday practices in selling slaves to pay debts and settle estates divided families. The interstate traders were suspected of intending to divide families even when they advertised for them. The fact that all but a small percentage of the slaves for sale were "single" or young mothers with small children is strongly indicative of family separations.

Some families were advertised frequently as being for sale together, but they were not always sold that way. The principal reason for dividing families was that they frequently brought higher prices when sold separately.[52] The practice was made easier by the fact that neither marriages nor parenthood among slaves was legally recognized and there were no laws prohibiting the separation of "husband" and "wife" when put on the market.[53] The separation of children from their mothers was legally permissible throughout the southern states with the exception of Louisiana, which prohibited the separation of slave children under ten years of age from their mothers.[54] But this law was disregarded almost totally and was, therefore, entirely without effectiveness.[55]

The separation of families, while not looked upon as a desirable practice, was justified on the grounds that family ties among slaves were either extremely loose or nonexistent and that slaves were indifferent to separation.[56] Slave owners, however, frequently admitted that a fugitive perhaps had returned to a plantation where there was a wife, a husband, or children. Moreover, the fact that a slave might be returning to his family suggests that dividing families was not rare.[57]

Antebellum migration: slaves

In all of human history, flight has been an important form of migration[58] and, in the case of slaves in the American southland, it was particularly important because of the volume of runaways and for its political significance. Therefore, it has been argued that "the Underground Railroad was one of the greatest forces which brought on the Civil War, and thus destroyed slavery."[59]

There is little doubt that slaves began escaping the moment slavery started. In the early decades of slave expansion in the colonies, there was little pattern to the direction runaways took. There is some indication that fugitives would often band together in remote areas of the swampland in the Deep South. Others were reported to have gone to live with Indians on the frontiers. By the end of the eighteenth century, however, a new pattern emerged, resulting from the efforts of hundreds of abolitionists in the North and scores of sympathetic southerners, thereby linking nearly all parts of the South to Canada and the free states of the North. The underground system is believed to have extended from Kentucky and Virginia across Ohio, and from Maryland through Pennsylvania, New York, and New England to Canada. The system also extended westward to embrace the middle states east of the Mississippi. Iowa and Kansas likewise provided escape routes for slaves in the Southwest.[60] The extent and organization of what has been called popularly the "Underground Railroad" is disputed by some historians. Certainly there was a movement of fleeing slaves northward that was supported by people white and black.[61]

Motivations

The motivations to escape were inherent in the system of slavery. As one author stated, "liberty was the subject of dreams . . . and the object of . . . prayers."[62] While the desire for freedom was nearly universal among the slaves, usually it was not sufficiently strong to motivate escape without some precipitating factor. One such factor was the fear of being sold from one of the northern slave states to the far South—"down the river."[63]

During the decade 1830 to 1840, increased activity along the Underground Railroad was matched by the expansion of cotton in the Gulf states. The opening of vast new lands there meant higher prices for slaves that, in turn, meant increased numbers of slaves would be sold to southern owners.

Personal grievances were precipitating factors as well. Perhaps the most common grievance was being separated arbitrarily from family and friends. It was not uncommon for slaves, upon separation, to take flight mainly to visit relatives on other plantations. For many, this act represented little more than truancy. Since many slave owners were kept informed of their slaves' friends and relatives, they usually recaptured these runaways without much difficulty.[64]

Flight also was a means by which slaves resisted attempts to work them too severely. The heavier labor burdens as well as the more favorable climatic conditions accounted for the higher incidence of runaways in the summer. A few slaves also ran away to avoid punishment for misdeeds or to get revenge for punishments already received. Only a few runaways had whip marks, healed or fresh; it seems slaves who resisted slavery by running away were not likely to get themselves into situations where they could be beaten.[65] In other cases escape was simply the result of a longing for relief from the restraints, discipline, and hardships of slavery.[66]

Origins and destinations

While the state origins of the slaves who embarked upon flight via the Underground Railroad are not well documented, it is believed that most states were represented proportionally to the number of slaves in each. The destinations included both Canada and the northern states. The rural areas and farm lands of Canada West and Upper Canada become the new homes for many self-emancipated slaves, while others went to towns and cities like St. Catherines, Hamilton, Toronto, and London.

In the northern states, many were content simply to cross the Mason-

Dixon line, whereupon they made their residence. Others scattered across the North, taking up residence in both the rural areas and cities. Some were drawn by the affinities of race or the forces of racial prejudice to seek permanent homes in all-black communities. Many fugitives are known to have settled among their Quaker protectors in New Jersey on the edge of a slave state. Columbus and Akron, Ohio, Elmira and Buffalo, New York, and Detroit, Michigan, also were major centers of attraction for fugitives in search of a new home.[67]

Volume

The volume of slaves taking flight to the North has been the subject of considerable controversy. A wide divergence among the various estimates was, and continues to be, the result of difficulty in getting reliable information regarding the number of runaway slaves. A number of very general estimates were made by participants of the underground. These estimates ranged from about 20,000 fugitive slaves in 1850 to about 50,000 in the various free states in 1852.[68]

The United States Census of Population for 1850 and for 1860 also provide some statistics on fugitive slaves. These official reports appear to show that the number escaping from their masters was small and inconsequential, and that it rapidly decreased during that period. According to the census, approximately 1,000 slaves escaped from their masters in 1850 and 800 in 1860. But scattered diaries and records of blacks passing through the Underground Railroad indicate that the census figures on fugitive slaves fall short of the most modest estimates.

For the period 1830 to 1860 in Ohio alone, no less than 40,000 fugitives were aided, according to one estimate. Moreover, the number increased during the 1850s rather than decreased (as was indicated by the census). A record kept by the Vigilance Committee showed an average of one fugitive a day assisted through Philadelphia during the 30-year period, 1830 to 1860, or more than 9,000 runaways.

Some evidence of the volume of runaways is offered by statements of certain southerners. Governor Quitman of Mississippi declared that between 1810 and 1850 the South lost 100,000 slaves.[69] Kenneth Stampp's assessment of southern newspaper advertisements of runaways led him to conclude that fugitive slaves numbered in the thousands every year.[70] Frederick Douglass wrote in his *Narrative* that thousands more would have escaped but for the strong cords of affection that bound them to their friends. Describing his own feelings as the time approached for him to make his second attempt for freedom, Douglass wrote: "The thought of leaving my friends was decidedly the most painful thought with which I had to contend. The love of them was my tender point, and shook my decision more than all things else."[71]

Method of travel

It is known that a variety of methods were used to convey fugitives from station to station. Runaways usually went singly or in small groups of two or three. Some, however, escaped in groups of a dozen or more, and in a few instances in groups of more than fifty. Most travelers were on foot, but a few went on horseback. It was also common for fugitives to be carried by covered wagons, closed carriages, and deep-bedded farm wagons. On occasion, conductors (persons who helped fleeing slaves and conservatively estimated to have numbered 3,200) had special wagons built with hidden compartments that permitted them to carry fugitives undetected. Nearly all escape operations took place under the darkness of night. The use of disguises was common, and supplies for the journey generally were taken from the master. Light-skinned slaves sometimes attempted to pose as whites, and at times posed as master while the dark ones posed as servants. Every conceivable disguise was used.[72]

On the eastern coast, runaways often were carried by ship from New England into Canada, and, after the railroads were completed around 1850, many fugitives traveled in freight cars or, disguised, in passenger cars to their northern destinations.

Migrant characteristics

There is disagreement about the characteristics of fugitives, but some of the myths surrounding them can now be dispelled. Stampp, for example, describes the runaways in the following terms:

They were generally young slaves, most of them under thirty. . . . The majority of them were males, though female runaways were by no means uncommon. It is not true that most of them were mulattoes or of predominantly white ancestry. While this group was well represented among the fugitives, they were outnumbered by slaves who were described as "black" or of seemingly "pure" African ancestry. Domestics and skilled artisans—the ones who supposedly had the most intimate ties with the master class—ran away as well as common field hands.[73]

The fugitives who reached Canada seem to have been nearly representative of slaves in general. While it is true that in the early days of the Underground Railroad the fugitives were most often men, women and children became a common sight once the system began working with regularity.[74]

Behaviorally, it was difficult, if not impossible, to identify those with the greatest propensity to escape. An observer on a southern plantation could hardly have selected would-be fugitives as being different from their fellow slaves in any way. The average slave was shrewd enough to tell what he thought least likely to arouse suspicion. If questioned about their desire for freedom, most agreed with their fellows that they were content with their present lot. However, such discretion did not necessarily indicate a lack of desire for liberty, as is shown by the numerous escapes.[75]

Consequences

Despite the action by Congress in 1792 prohibiting slave escapes, and an even more severe action in 1850 against such slave behavior, flight from the plantations and the South was an ongoing phenomenon.[76] In appraising the consequences of running away, and of the Underground Railroad, a number of significant effects are worth noting. Demographically, the flight of slaves resulted in a degree of population decline of blacks in the South and an increase in their numbers in the North. The significance of the flight for the white South, however, lay in its economic effects. The continuous exodus from the South of its slave "property" caused constant irritation to slave owners and slave traders. Several Congressmen attempted to calculate the economic loss to their states. Pratt, of Maryland, stated that the loss to his state through runaways was not less than $80,000 per year. Mason, of Virginia, declared an excess of $100,000 per year. Butler, of South Carolina, reckoned the annual loss of the southern section at $200,000. Other southern states provided similar estimates. Governor John A. Quitman of Mississippi estimated no less than $30 million was lost by the flight of 100,000 slaves from the South in the course of forty years, from 1810 to 1850.[77] These economic losses engendered a regional identification characterized by wrath, suspicion, and hostility in the minds of southerners for northerners who were defying the laws of Congress and the decisions of the highest courts.

Others have argued that the Underground Railroad was perhaps beneficial in that it served as a "safety valve to the institution of slavery." It furnished a means of escape for persons well qualified for leadership among slaves who were, conceivably, candidates for insurrection. As leaders arose among the slaves who refused to subject themselves to slavery, they would nearly always strike out for the North. Had they remained, it is likely that many would have worked to increase the number of uprisings and insurrections. While the flight of these slaves represented an economic loss, their retention would have, in all likelihood, resulted in even greater losses.

The demographic consequences for the North were significant in that the introduction of an additional 40,000 to 100,000 blacks provided the necessary population base for a more racially heterogeneous society. Blacks were found in many northern cities from New England across the Midwest. As noted earlier, several all-black communities sprang up in Ohio and western Pennsylvania. Politically and socially, the consequences were stress-producing for most northern communities. Many communities and states enacted restrictive legislation to prevent blacks from full participation as citizens. The exclusion and colonization movements were evidence of the hostility of the white population towards blacks. At the individual level, the migration meant an opportunity to flee slavery, a chance to enter a society as a normal individual, and for families, the possibility of remaining together as a unit.

Antebellum migration: free blacks

Several northern states had prohibited slavery and others had developed programs of gradual emancipation before the end of the eighteenth century. Consequently, the number of free blacks became a substantial element in the population by the early nineteenth century. Free blacks were found not only in the North but in the South as well, despite the fact that their presence tended to undermine the very foundation on which slavery was built.[78] In the North most blacks were freeborn. In the South, freedom was obtained by enterprising slaves who were able to save enough money to purchase their freedom. Thousands of others in the North and South obtained their freedom by running away.

In 1790, the year of the first decennial census, there were 59,000 free blacks in the United States—32,000 in the South and 27,000 in the North. By 1830 there were 319,000 free blacks in the United States and 30 years later the number had increased to 488,000, of which 44 percent lived in the South Atlantic states and 46 percent in the North. The remainder were located in the South Central States and the West. The largest state population of free blacks was found in Maryland, 83,900 in 1860. Virginia was next with 58,000, followed by Pennsylvania with 56,000, the state's entire black population.[79]

Free blacks were primarily urban residents, especially in the latter years of the antebellum period. The greater economic and social opportunities accounted for the tendency of free blacks to concentrate in cities.[80]

It would be misleading to think of free blacks as being significantly better off economically than their slave counterparts. The economic panic and depression of the 1830s, the mass immigrations from Europe, and the resulting competition for jobs prevented all but a very small group of free blacks from achieving significant social and economic upward mobility throughout the antebellum period. A fortunate few overcame the obstacles of racism and overt discrimination to become financially independent, while others made contributions to their professions and communities in dentistry, pharmacy, law, teaching, and the ministry.[81]

Volume

Despite their status as "free" persons and the fact that certain individuals were financially able to relocate, free blacks often had more difficulty moving than slaves did. In no southern state could free blacks move about as they wished, and in some northern communities it was dangerous to try because of the risk of being mistaken for a fugitive slave. In certain places in the South, free blacks were prohibited from going beyond the county adjoining the one in which they resided. Likewise, most of the seaboard states prohibited black sailors from leaving their ships while in port. Virginians, as early as 1793, prevented free blacks from entering their state, and by 1835 most of the southern states and many of the northern ones restricted or prohibited free black immigration.[82] Free blacks in the South never enjoyed the rights of full citizenship. Laws required that the free black carry on his person a certificate of freedom, and without this document he might be claimed as a slave. Some local laws required that he be registered with the police.[83]

Early in the nineteenth century a small but important migration from the South to the North began, largely as a consequence of North Carolinian Quakers freeing their slaves and assisting them in their efforts to reach free soil. First, the manumitted slaves were sent to Pennsylvania. But as early as 1812, a report recommended that these freedmen be settled in Ohio, Indiana, and Illinois. Settlements were also established in western New York, west Pennsylvania, and the states of the former Northwest Territory.[84]

After 1830, increasing numbers of blacks were migrating north and west from the South. Not only were slaves running away in increasing numbers, but free blacks were looking toward the North Star in the hope of finding greater opportunities and better treatment. Their destinations centered largely in the cities of the Northeast, while others migrated to free states in Ohio, Indiana, and Illinois along with white immigrants from Europe. Some indication of the volume of black migration in the last years before the Civil War is evidenced by the sizable population increases in the popular destinations. For example, between 1850 and 1860, Michigan's black population increased from 2,500 to 6,700, Iowa's more than tripled, and California's increased from 962 to 4,086.[85]

The North of the antebellum period was not yet the "promised land" it was destined to become in another half-century. In fact, conditions in the North were not greatly dissimilar to conditions in the South. An overwhelming majority of white Americans in both the North and the South had a firmly held belief in the superiority of the white race.[86] The South claimed no monopoly on the belief that America was a white man's country, and, consequently blacks could not have a political voice and only a prescribed social and economic role.

The reception of the free blacks by the North was not pleasant. Fearing that the immigration of the former slaves would increase to the point of making them an important force in the community, some of the northern and northwestern states attempted to discourage black settlers by requiring them to register their certificates of freedom at a county clerk's office and to present bonds ranging from $500 to $1,000, guaranteeing that they would not disturb the peace or become public charges. Accordingly,

> toward the end of the antebellum period, Illinois, Indiana and Oregon excluded Negro migrants entirely. Only Ohio, after a long battle, repealed its restrictive immigration legislation in 1849. Though such anti-immigration statutes were only erratically enforced, nevertheless they intimidated Negroes. In 1829 an attempt to enforce an 1807 law requiring a $500 bond precipitated a race riot at Cincinnati and a mass Negro exodus to Canada.[87]

Other efforts, designed, in part, to discourage immigration or at least to control its effects, included disenfranchisement. In New Jersey, disenfranchisement came in 1807, in Connecticut in 1814, in Pennsylvania in 1828, and restrictions were added in New York in 1811, 1823, and 1824.[88]

In addition to antiimmigration statutes and disenfranchisement, opposition to black migrants also consisted of prohibiting the children of migrants from attending public schools. The irony of this prohibition was the fact that quality education was one of the foremost aspirations of the northern black. It was through education that blacks hoped to improve their economic status, produce their own literary and scientific figures, and break down the racial barriers of discrimination. This quest for educational advancement prompted strong and often violent protests in various areas of the North. The "possibility that Negro children would be mixed with white children in the same classroom aroused even greater fears and prejudices than those which consigned the Negro to an inferior place in the church, the theater and the railroad car."[89] Various proposals to educate blacks were highly controversial. Opponents often warned that increasing educational opportunities for blacks would only encourage their increased in-migration and antagonize southern-born residents.[90]

The problems of finding and keeping a job in the face of increasing white resistance to the increased number of blacks competing in the labor force were problems for blacks in the North as well. The black labor force, increasingly augmented by emancipated and fugitive slaves, aroused the concern of several white citizens' groups and several northern legislatures and constitutional conventions. In 1834, a group of petitioners in Connecticut declared that "the white man cannot labor upon equal terms with the Negro," and unless the legislature adopted appropriate entry restrictions the sons of Connecticut would be driven from the state by the great influx of "black porters, black truckmen, black sawyers, black mechanics, and black laborers of every description." In nearly every antebellum northern legislature and constitutional convention, similar fears were expressed over blacks entering occupations formerly dominated by whites.[91]

The problems of obtaining employment were compounded by the Panic of 1837 and the ensuing depression. Only the most menial of jobs were filled by blacks, and many expressed the concern that as economic conditions worsened and whites began stooping to accept these lowly jobs, blacks would face certain destruction.

The nation's economic conditions began improving, but black workers were faced soon with a new and serious challenge to their already deprived economic condition—the Irish immigrant.[92]

Immigrants from most of the northwestern European countries began pouring into the United States during the 1820s and ensuing decades. Between 1830 and 1860 alone, there were nearly five million immigrants that entered the United States, most of whom were from Germany, Norway, Sweden, and Ireland. Most of the Germans and Scandinavians settled in the farmlands of the Midwest, but the Irish usually remained in the cities, seeking any kind of employment, regardless of conditions or wages.[93]

Although the Irish immigrant did not immediately replace the black worker, it was only a short time before blacks and Irish were to be pitted against one another for the bottom rung of the occupational ladder. Increasing antipathy and economic competition soon gave rise to violence between black and Irish workers. In 1842, competition for jobs in the coal mines of Pennsylvania erupted into conflict. Again in 1853, conflict erupted over jobs on the Erie Railroad. Two years later, the scene was the New York docks, and once again in 1863, blacks and Irish clashed in the New York Draft Riots.[94]

Many black migrants found more congenial destinations beyond the border of the United States in Canada. Some of the migrants moved directly from the South to Canada, but the majority moved first to the free states and then, if they chose, on to Canada. The stream to Canada from the free states was contemporary with that from the South to the free states. That migrations occurred from both the South and the free states to Canada is evident from the fact that of the 60,000 blacks in Canada in 1860, 15,000 were born free.[95]

Migrant characteristics

Very little is known of the social and economic characteristics of black migrants during the antebellum period. Most of what can be said about characteristics must be inferred from what is known about migrant selectivity in general and the social, economic, and political climate of the times.

Migrants are rarely, if ever, socially or economically similar to the population from which they are drawn. Frequently, they tend to be somewhat superior occupationally, educationally, and in other ways—particularly those migrating over long distances. But with the restrictive legislation and social customs impeding the mobility of free blacks, the selectivity of migrants is intensified considerably. Thus, only the most enterprising migrants are likely to be successful in relocating across county and state boundaries. Although the necessary data to test this hypothesis are not available, there is some evidence which tends to support it. It has been argued that migrants were drawn disproportionately from the more enlightened southern blacks because in 1840 there were more intelligent blacks in the South than in the North, but that by 1850 the situation had changed as a result of migrant selectivity.

Consequences

The consequences of the increased migration were not always pleasant even for free blacks. The adjustment of the migrants to urban life styles in the North was a difficult process for both the migrants and the recipients. Northern whites had shown no unusual hostility to blacks who were already living in their midst, but they did not welcome black newcomers from the South, most of whom were considered rough and crude. In fact, many people living in the West had hoped to keep their region free not only of slavery but of blacks as well.[96]

Prior to 1800, the living conditions of blacks in the North were generally inferior to those of their white counterparts but, in turn, were superior to those of most blacks still living in the South. In fact, until the turn of the nineteenth century, abolitionists, mostly Quakers, believed that whites and blacks would eventually reach a stage of living together on the basis of absolute equality. At that time, blacks had not exceeded the number that could be assimilated by the sympathizing communities in the North. Later, however, the ideal of racial equality was quickly discarded as the migration to the northern cities from the rural South reached such proportions that adjustment of migrants was significantly retarded. It was not only the migration of blacks to the northern cities that created housing and job shortages, but also the increasing flow of Europeans, particularly during and after the 1840s. The migrants, black and European, were arriving faster than they could be assimilated. In Pennsylvania alone, the number of free blacks increased from 22,492 in 1810 to 37,930 in 1830. By 1860 this number had increased to 56,949.[97]

Conditions continued to deteriorate for blacks in the North during the antebellum period. Physical and social conditions in the 1830s were so harsh that many believed blacks would eventually be annihilated.[98] The increasing numbers and deteriorating social and economic lives of the migrants were met by rising hostility and prejudice on the part of the whites. DeTocqueville observed that blacks were more detested in the free states than in those where they were held as slaves.[99]

As the migration of blacks—both free and slave—increased, racial animosity grew in both the North and West and in many places became violent. Stonings occurred in Philadelphia, and interracial fights broke out in the mining camps of California. At times the violence reached the proportion of riots. In New York state, Ohio, and Pennsylvania, racial riots were frequent during the 1830s and 1840s.[100]

4. The Civil War and Reconstruction

The continuity of life in the South was seriously interrupted in the latter half of the nineteenth century. The experiences of the Civil War—invasion, defeat, emancipation, occupation, and reconstruction—were traumatic. A basic social institution, slavery, was dismantled, affecting not only the economy, but the entire social structure.

The movement and migration of blacks during the Civil War consisted chiefly of two kinds of flight: from the advancing Union troops and from the masters to join or seek the protection of the Union forces. In addition to the effects of the war, an active domestic slave trade continued and resulted in the relocation of thousands of slaves until the war ended.

In the first year of the war, Union forces penetrated only a small portion of northern Virginia and the seacoast areas of the Carolinas. Life for blacks in the South outside the immediate areas of invasion went on in much the same manner as before.[1] Even after the invasion of western Tennessee, northern Mississippi, and other peripheral portions of the South, the pattern of slave life in the interior was not appreciably changed.[2]

In the invaded areas, however, there were pronounced and radical changes in the lives of the slaves. If time permitted, some planters moved their slaves into the interior. In other cases, masters and slaves who postponed their departures too long or who were unaware of the Union advances were forced to "disordered flight."[3] When planters, threatened by Union forces, were reluctant to relocate their slaves, Confederate military authorities would force them to relocate the stronger males out of reach of the Union army. In such instances transportation was provided by the military.

Migration under these circumstances usually involved some selection of who was to go and who was to remain. Limited time and shortages of transportation facilities meant that those slaves of limited utility either to the masters or to the invaders were likely to be left behind. The planter usually selected his more valuable domestic slaves and field hands and left the old and very young behind for the "Yankees."[4]

As the war intensified and the Union forces began their extensive campaigns of 1862 it became necessary to remove larger numbers of slaves from the war zones. The practice of moving thousands of slaves along the highways became common and was called "running the Negroes."[5] When time prevented an organized journey to more protected or isolated areas of the "up country," planters took temporary cover in woods, swamps, or canebrakes.[6]

Throughout much of the war, large numbers of blacks, together with planters and sometimes their families, became refugees. The hardships were often severe. Lack of adequate food and shelter was common for those in flight. Families were divided, some temporarily, others permanently. The disappointment of not being freed by the Union troops and the hardships of becoming refugees were difficult to endure. Often, these were sufficient to motivate many blacks to flee toward the Union lines.[7]

No sooner did the Union troops march into a town than the problem of the black refugees had to be solved. Each day, as the war pushed farther into the Confederency, the number of escaping slaves seeking the protection and freedom of federally controlled areas seemed to increase. How to handle the fugitives quickly became an insistent problem of the Lincoln administration.[8] Large numbers of the refugees offered their services to the Union forces but were rejected, and no policy was formulated by the federal government to deal with them.

Many of the escaped slaves, in fact, were forced by the Union armies to return to their masters. During the early summer of 1861, several Union military officers spoke out in favor of returning all fugitives.[9] It was not until the Confiscation Act of August 1861 that a relatively uniform policy was adopted by Congress. In general, the act provided that property used in aiding and abetting insurrection against the United States with the owner's consent was the lawful subject of prize and capture wherever found. When the property consisted of slaves, they were to be freed.[10]

The price of freedom came high in the camps of the Union army. For most slaves it meant suffering, even death. In 1864 a Union official stated that mortality in the refugee camps was "frightful" and "most competent judges place it at not less than twenty-five percent in the last two years."[11] Freedom, however, also had its compensations. Schools were established for the refugees both in the North and the South. By 1863 schools were established in most areas occupied by Union troops. Most of the teachers and other resources were provided by northern whites; "the people responsible for establishing these schools . . . made a most significant contribution to the adjustment of Negroes coming out of slavery."[12] The former slaves were also active participants.

In the South, trading in slaves continued, even though 200,000 blacks, most of whom had left the slave system, provided their services to the Union armies during the war.[13] Slave trading resulted in forced migration and relocation for a large proportion of the slaves that were sold. Although there is no way of determining the number of slaves relocated under these conditions, it was on such a scale that the market for the sale of slaves plunged into depression not only in those areas from which they were being evacuated, but also in their destination communities. In October 1862, for example, the condition in Richmond was described as one in which "bidders are few and the market is stocked—owing to the large number of slaves brought from the upper counties of Virginia. Parties having slaves in such localities and wishing to obtain high prices for them would do better to take them farther South, for the present, at least."[14]

Despite declines in prices and sales in late 1862, the slave market in the South made a significant comeback in the first months of 1863. Newspapers frequently commented on the good prices and large sales, although it is certain that the prices were as much a product of speculation and patriotism as utility.[15] By June of the same year prices for slaves were into another slump, resulting from the steady advance of the Union forces. For example, in Louisiana many owners, driven from their homes by invasion, sold their slaves at greatly reduced prices. Cotton planters in Texas, as yet untouched by the war, took advantage of the depressed prices and imported large numbers of blacks.[16]

After a prolonged period of vacillation, indecision, trial balloons, and preliminary proclamations, President Lincoln issued the Emancipation Proclamation, declaring that after January 1, 1863, all slaves held within the states that were in rebellion would be "thenceforward and forever free."[17] It was then clear that, as much as to preserve the Union, the purpose of the war was to free the slaves.

The sale of slaves continued throughout the South, although in 1863 slave sales were slow in most places. As late as 1864 there was a brisk upturn in sales in several of the larger markets, including Savannah, Mobile, Atlanta, Columbia, and Charleston. In some localities, the sale of slaves continued until the end of the war, and there is some evidence to suggest that some slaves may have been sold even after the war.[18]

The Reconstruction period

The immediate problem after the war was the disposition of the landless, moneyless freedmen. Many white southerners were concerned that a massive migration of former slaves to the North would reduce the needed labor supply for agriculture, as well as the labor supply of servants and tradesmen for urban areas. This fear was based on the century-old practice of slaves escaping and striking out for the North and the freedom the region represented. It was reasonable to suppose that the ultimate exercise of their newly acquired freedom would be to move, unrestricted, to the North.

There was little apprehension by northerners that they would be overrun by blacks. The census figures prior to the Civil War did not indicate such a movement by blacks already free in the South. For example, in all the northern states in 1860, there were 225,000 free blacks compared to 258,000 in the South.[19] That there were more free blacks in the South than in the North suggested that a mass exodus was not imminent.

Following the war there was extensive relocation of freedmen in the South that took on more of the character of a confused, random, or purposeless movement than that of a migration.

The first thing the Negro did after realizing that he was free was to roam over the country to put his freedom to a test. To do this . . . he frequently changed his name, residence, employment and wife. . . . Their emancipation . . . was interpreted not only as freedom from slavery but from responsibility. Where they were going, they did not know. . . .[20]

Despite its appearance, the movement of freedmen was not completely confused or entirely random. Many—perhaps most—of the former slaves sought the cities and the towns of the South, probably as a refuge from the grueling work of the fields. Others crowded into the cities thinking the government would care for them there.[21] The military also played a role in the urbanward trek of the blacks by bringing wagonloads in from the country and simply leaving them there to shift for themselves.[22] In some cities the migrants were so numerous that, even with government assistance, the resources were inadequate to meet the needs. The exodus of slaves from the plantations of Louisiana into the city of New Orleans alone has been estimated at 10,000.[23]

Unfortunately, many publications describing the conditions of blacks in the early postwar years are based on the testimony of whites who have, wittingly or not, exaggerated the vagrancy of the blacks in order to justify the methods in dealing with it.[24] It is true that there were large numbers of blacks without homes, jobs, or money all through the South. But it is also true that large numbers of whites, many of whom had had their homes and farms destroyed by the war or were generally shiftless, were roaming the highways and city streets, and in some cases became marauding bands.[25]

Volume. The migration of blacks from the South to the North during the Reconstruction was small compared to the streams that would develop early in the next century. The principal movements were from the border states, mainly Virginia, and were a continuation and enlargement of streams that were active during the war. Much of the migration from Virginia was to the metropolitan areas of New York and Boston. The motivation and means to migrate came largely from labor agents and contractors from businesses in the northern cities seeking cooks and maids for hotels and laborers for construction.[26] This early postwar migration is reported to have reached its peak about 1870.[27]

For blacks in the Deep South, there was little northward migration during this period. The North seemed too far away, and the former slave showed little disposition to seek his fortune in the strange and distant lands.[28] He lacked the means to undertake such a long journey without some assurance of employment when he arrived, and there was little initiative for such a venture at a time of possible change in the South. What the ex-slaves wanted most of all was land of their own to cultivate and the opportunity to obtain an education.[29]

Following the war a small stream of blacks migrated back to the South from the North for a short period of time. Many who had run away during and prior to the war returned home to be with friends and families.[30] Others, who had acquired an education and political contacts in the North, went to the South to take a role in the Reconstruction.[31] It was common practice to refer to these workers as "carpetbaggers," but in reality many of them were natives of the South returning home. Other motives also impelled blacks to go South following the war. Some had found unexpected hostility in the North. Competition for housing and jobs with arriving immigrants, particularly the Irish, in the northeastern seaboard cities created hardships reminiscent of the South. Still others were motivated to return by a sense of adventure and expected opportunities of the Reconstruction. The extent of the postwar migration to the South was not large, but this movement, together with the migration to large urban communities in the North, resulted in the decline of several black communities in the North after 1865.[32]

Prior to and during the Civil War numerous slave owners removed their human chattel closer to the frontier in the Southwest where agricultural and economic development was less affected by the invasion and destruction of the Union forces. After the war this small, forced migratory stream developed into a migration of considerable size. The areas of out-migration were chiefly plantations located in the states of South Carolina, Georgia, Alabama, and Mississippi, while the destinations were largely in the states of Louisiana, Arkansas, and Texas.[33]

The principal causes of the southwestern migration were the pioneering spirit of the migrants, economic opportunities, land speculators who were inducing whites and blacks to go west and southwest, and a developing railroad system linking the ever-expanding frontier with the Deep South. In the main, the out-migrants were leaving territories that were densely populated, by the standards of the time, and in economic decline, resulting in rising levels of poverty.[34] While these conditions were increasing in the southeastern United States, the demand for common labor in the Southwest was rising.

Some of the social factors that added impetus to the propensity to migrate were reenactment of the Black Codes, the forming of numerous white protective societies, and the emergence of a kind of guerrilla warfare against blacks, particularly against those who represented the Washington government.[35] The Congressional Committee on Reconstruction collected substantial evidence indicating that landholders were using the Black Codes to take advantage of blacks by suppressing agricultural wages, binding them to unfair labor contracts, and often refusing to pay them wages at all. Blacks were found to have considerable difficulty receiving fair trials in state and local courts and were often threatened and sometimes assaulted by bands of "regulators."[36]

Political motivation as a factor fostering the migration to the Southwest was minimal, as demonstrated by the fact that the leaders of the blacks did not migrate. A politically motivated migration certainly would have included the leaders.[37]

Despite the fact that it was not a mass movement, but a migration of individuals rather than whole communities, it is reported that one agent boasted that he personally had induced 35,000 blacks to leave South Carolina and Georgia for Arkansas and Texas. While it is likely that the agent's claim was exaggerated, little doubt exists as to the considerable black migration to the Southwest in the decade following the Civil War.[38]

One measure of the volume and direction of the migration is the decennial change in the "center of population." Theoretically, the center of population is a point which responds to each change in residence on the part of individuals making up the population, and which responds to the growth or decline of population. The center's movements in any direction from census to census is the result of growth or decline, or the net drift of population during the intervening decade. The average decennial movement of the center of the black population for the nine decades from 1790 to 1880 was 49.2 miles. By 1880 the center was located 10.4 miles east of Lafayette, Georgia.

Consequences. The consequences of the migration for the migrants were varied depending upon the migrants' characteristics, the timing of the move, the places from which they migrated, and their destination. For many blacks the result was often disappointment. The expectations of the freedmen for full civil rights were soon smashed in most parts of the nation—North or South, urban or rural. Moving from the Deep South to the developing Southwest or the cities of the North often provided some relief from the harsh postwar civil and social repression by whites. The postwar period has been described as "a dream betrayed," a period which experienced few changes in white sentiment. Blacks still had to battle every step of the way for the recognition of basic citizenship rights.[39]

Beyond the commonly known unfavorable treatment that all blacks received, it is difficult to determine the consequences of migration for those blacks who sought their fortunes on the frontier or in the cities of the North. It is known that the press published reports of the destitution and dissatisfaction of migrants who had gone to the Southwest. Stories were circulated that epidemics of "consumption" were widespread and that ill fortune followed most who ventured to leave. These reports also were known to be nothing more than propaganda designed to keep blacks from leaving those areas where out-migration had already severely reduced the labor supply.[40]

The effects of the propaganda efforts to retain the black labor force are not known, except that black out-migration from many areas of the Piedmont was sufficient to reduce the supply of black labor. The net result was an improvement in the bargaining power and economic opportunities for those blacks who chose to remain.[41]

Segregation soon became the modus operandi for relations between whites and blacks in most northern cities. Though segregation in the churches was largely voluntary, the separations in other institutions were largely involuntary.[42] Opposition to black suffrage emerged, often led by Irish laborers. Using the Democratic party as a weapon, the Irish campaigned in a Chicago parade for "NO NIGGER VOTING," and "WHITE SUPREMACY."[43]

Black migrants to Philadelphia found the social and economic environment inadequate to meet their needs. The more than 15,000 blacks who migrated to that city between 1870 and 1896 were faced with crucial housing shortages and intense competition for jobs. These newcomers to the "City of Brotherly Love" were not warmly received by the older residents, white or black. The earlier black migrants viewed the later migrants as a threat and as competition for housing and jobs, as did the other vulnerable social segments of the city.[44]

The consequences of black out-migration from the mid-Atlantic states were quite severe for the agricultural economy in certain locales. In some areas the out-migration was so heavy that the resulting labor shortages made the cultivation of large acreages impossible, thereby depressing the land values. For many planters the idle land meant smaller returns on their investments. Those forced to sell their land found that land that sold for ten dollars or more an acre before the war brought from one to three dollars an acre at court-ordered sales.[45]

The Kansas Exodus

Emancipation made freedmen of slaves, but Reconstruction failed to bring about any significant changes in their basic civil, social, or economic status. The majority of blacks still were found on farms and plantations that whites owned. The only commodity blacks owned was their labor. No more than 1 percent of the black farmers in 33 of Georgia's largely black counties owned land; the same proportion was reported from 17 predominantly black Mississippi counties. Throughout the entire state of Tennessee, only a very small proportion of the blacks owned land or even the houses in which they lived. Conditions were generally similar throughout most of the other southern states.[46] The black farmer worked the white man's land, and he worked it with a white man's plow drawn by a white man's mule.[47]

While the landless blacks worked either for wages or for shares—under a variety of different arrangements—a large proportion of landlords used the wage system. According to the 1880 census, monthly wages for a man's work "from sun to sun" ranged from $5 to $15 throughout the southern states. Wages for women were generally less. The census made no distinction between the wages of whites and blacks, but it is unlikely that the difference was very large. In general, annual wages in the central cotton belt of Georgia ranged from $60 to $100 a year but might reach $125 a year in a few of the other cotton states.[48]

Housing conditions, diets, and clothing of blacks reflected their low wage scale: typical houses consisted of crudely constructed one- or two-room cabins without windowpanes or ceilings. Diets were generally coarse and consisted largely of hominy, corn bread, bacon fat, and some vegetables. Clothing was tattered, filled with holes or a variety of patches. Morbidity and mortality, in turn, reflected the inadequacy in meeting basic physical needs. The death rate for blacks in Charleston, for example, increased from 26.4 per thousand before the war to 43.3 afterward. Major diseases, except for yellow fever and alcoholism, took a greater toll among blacks than whites.[49]

In the years following the Compromise of 1877, blacks throughout the country, and particularly the South, found themselves victims of prejudice, discrimination, and violence. Once the federal military support for the "radical" governments was withdrawn and Washington accepted the white Democratic hegemony in the South, blacks were left without any effective defense. Henry Adams, a former Georgia slave and Union war veteran living in Louisiana, who later played an important part in the Kansas Exodus, described blacks living in the South as being almost hopeless: "the whole South—every state in the South—had got into the hands of the very men that held us as slaves . . . and they were holding the reins of government over our heads in every respect . . . even the constable up to the governor."[50] Thus, a new system of white social control of blacks was developed to replace the old institution of slavery, and black political participation was forcefully curbed through violence and the threat of violence.[51]

The streams of black migration that had set in during the Civil War and Reconstruction continued to move in the same general direction for some years after "redemption," the restoration of white political domination. These migrations were largely of three kinds: from the rural areas to the towns and cities; from the poorer, exhausted lands to the fertile bottoms and delta land of the Mississippi; and from the older states to the newer states of the Southwest. However, socially and economically, it did not matter where they moved. Denial of civil rights, educational and occupational discrimination, landlessness, inadequate health provisions, and domination by whites continued to be the lot of blacks. They continued to dream of freedom, a piece of land of their own, and the right to full and equal citizenship. Voluntary migration to a new community or state, perhaps even to the far-off African homeland of their ancestors where life could be better, was a common consideration and aspiration of blacks in many areas of the South and in some northern communities. Hopes of the whites were often as visionary; many clung to the belief that farm life with the blacks as freedmen was an impossibility. More than a few planned migration to Mexico or Brazil; others hoped the blacks would migrate and be replaced either by European immigrants or northern purchasers of plantations.[52]

The problem became one of the major issues in the numerous postwar conventions held by blacks throughout the country. Studies of the problems were conducted by the conventions, and proposals for federal assistance followed, but to no avail. One proposal requested the president and the Senate "to help us out of our distress, or protect us in our rights and privileges." When the plea went unheeded, money was requested for the purchase of land in the West or to finance a return to Liberia. Later, in some conventions, proposals asking foreign governments for assistance in leaving the United States also were given serious consideration, and requests were made.[53] Following their failure to obtain federal assistance, a number of black leaders began to organize what later came to be called the Exodus of 1879, or, more commonly, the Kansas Exodus.

The Kansas Exodus is the first general migration of black people after the Civil War.[54] Although free blacks and slaves had been migrating freely or by force for nearly two centuries, it was the first planned movement involving a substantial number of blacks relocating to a common distant destination under the leadership of a small group of people.

Most prominent among the leaders of the exodus were two individuals— Benjamin "Pap" Singleton and Henry Adams. Singleton, self-proclaimed "Moses of the colored Exodus," was born a slave in 1809 in Nashville, Tennessee, and worked as a carpenter and cabinetmaker. Singleton, according to one description,

> was of a restless disposition, and probably his master considered "trifling," for "Pap" asserted that although he was "sold a dozen times or more" to the Gulf states ... he always ran away and came back to Tennessee. Finally he decided to strike for Canada and freedom, and after failing in three attempts he made his way over the "Underground Railroad" to Ontario. . . . Soon after he came back to Detroit where he worked, he says, until 1865 as a "scavenger," and also kept a "secret boardinghouse for fugitive slaves."[55]

Singleton returned in 1865 to Tennessee and his trade of making cabinets. Upon his return to the South he became anxious about the lack of progress by blacks and launched his "mission" to encourage blacks to save their earnings and establish themselves by buying property. To aid in his program of racial betterment through property ownership, Singleton, with the help of others, founded the Tennessee Real Estate and Homestead

Association at Nashville in 1869. Because of high prices demanded for good land and the limited monetary resources of blacks, the association failed. Singleton concluded that the only hope for blacks was to leave the South and separate themselves into all-black colonies in a new territory where competition with whites would be minimal. Rejecting Tennessee as unsuitable for black colonization, and after considerable investigation, Singleton decided upon Kansas, the state of "Old John Brown," as the ideal location to carry out his vision.

Henry Adams, like Singleton, was illiterate, but a man of "energy, courage, and ability." Following his discharge from the Union army in 1869, he returned to his native Louisiana where he was confronted with the poor treatment of blacks. Outraged by what he witnessed, Adams traveled through the lower Mississippi Valley organizing a committee—at one time numbering 500—to survey social conditions in the South. A convention held in New Orleans to deliberate over the findings of his survey adopted a resolution recommending "organized and systematic emigration."[56]

The Kansas migration plan did not receive support from all black leaders. Frederick Douglas, among others, objected to any scheme of moving masses of blacks to the North.[57] Douglass maintained that blacks had been too impatient, that they had not given democracy enough time to assert itself in the South, and that they should stand by to assist in the progress. Douglass's position was sharply criticized in the black press. For example, the Chicago publication *Inter-Ocean* asked, "Why had Mr. Douglass not remained in the South as an example for his persecuted race?"[58]

The idea of migrating to Kansas fired the imaginations of even the most illiterate peasants of the Deep South, for the song "John Brown's Body" and the abolitionist's martyrdom at Harper's Ferry were known to all.[59]

Beginning in the spring of 1879, the Kansas Exodus quickly grew to a black migration of unprecedented size in a short period of time. While the majority of the migrants came from the lower Mississippi Valley states of Louisiana and Mississippi, others were reported from states further east including Alabama, Georgia, and South Carolina.

Volume

The actual size of the migration is widely disputed. In a survey by Henry Adams and his workers, it was reported that 98,000 southern blacks were willing to move to Kansas.[60] However, estimates of the actual number who moved vary from 6,000 to 82,000. The census provides some evidence of the scope of the migration by the population growth. In 1860 there were only 627 blacks in Kansas; two decades later, migration and natural increase brought the population up to 43,100.[61] Even before the migration was completed, there was a claim that 60,000 blacks had moved to Kansas, two-thirds of whom arrived destitute. Approximately 30,000 settled on farms, 25,000 went to the towns and cities, and the remainder became laborers and moved about wherever their work took them. However, a significant but unknown number returned to the South after a short period of time.[62]

Singleton's estimates of the number of migrants were not always consistent and there were those who observed that his estimates seemed to grow with his age.[63] Late in life, "Pap" Singleton boasted that he had led 82,000 blacks out of the South.[64] Few doubt that this figure is greatly exaggerated. Though the statistical dimensions of the movement have never been accurately determined, the general opinion is that less than 10,000 is more realistic.[65]

Causes

The causes of the migration to Kansas have been variously labeled as economic, social, and political. "Pap" Singleton viewed the migration as the necessary first step toward economic independence for poor blacks. While he recognized the social and political forces that gave rise to the disadvantaged economic position of blacks, he argued that the situation could be remedied only after blacks gained control of their economic system. Moreover, this type of economic control could be achieved only in a frontier setting unfettered by a white power structure.[66]

Henry Adams viewed the causes of the migration more in social and political terms. In his testimony before a United States Senate committee investigating the movement, Adams stated:

> "Well, the cause is, in my judgement, and from what information I have received, and what I have seen with my own eyes—it is because the largest majority of the people, of the white people, that held us as slaves treats our people so bad in many respects that it is impossible for them to stand it. Now, in a great many parts of that country there our people must as well be slaves as to be free; because, in the first place, I will state this: that in some times, in times of politics, if they have any idea that the Republicans will carry a parish or ward, or something of that kind, why they would do anything on God's earth. There ain't nothing too mean to do to prevent it; nothing I can make mention of is too mean for them to do. . . ."[67]

Historians and other students of the migration, however, have come to view the causes of the Kansas Exodus as more complex. Several interacting factors that contributed to the migration were identified: low prices of cotton and widespread crop failure; a credit system that permitted mortgaging crops before they were invested or in some places before they were planted; the denial of civil and political rights; and rumors of free land, mules, and money in Kansas supplied by the federal government.[68] Added impetus was provided by the railroads and steamship companies offering special rates for migrants to Kansas.[69] Extensive advertising and other forms of promotion also helped to spread the propaganda of Singleton and his cohorts about Kansas. Singleton used $600 of his personal finances to advertise the migration. One poster read:

> All Colored People
> that want to
> GO TO KANSAS
> On September 5th, 1877
> Can Do So for $5.00[70]

The migration quickly took on the character of a religious social movement. Singleton claimed that he was the "whole cause of the Kansas immigration" and that his idea for the exodus was a "divine revelation." Singleton's self-styled title "Moses of the Colored Exodus" added to the religious tone of the movement. Songs were "composed" and sung in black churches describing "The Land That Gives Birth to Freedom." Poetry and verse equating the Kansas migration with the Hebrew Exodus from Egypt became popular and were quoted widely in sermons and classrooms. While political, economic, and social conditions played an important part in motivating blacks to leave, the argument has been made that the worst epidemic of yellow fever in the history of central and southwestern Mississippi was at its peak and played a major role as well, resulting in the economic disaster that precipitated the migration to Kansas.[71]

Though self-styled black leaders claimed credit for the movement, the causes were in the structure of race relations as they emerged during Reconstruction. The exodus can best be viewed as a combination of protest against the tightening post-Reconstruction conditions in the South, the efforts of a loose organization of blacks supporting the migration, and the collective results of a social movement that succeeded—perhaps too well.

Consequences

The consequences of the Kansas Exodus were far-reaching and felt not only by the migrants themselves, but also by native Kansans, by blacks who remained in the South, and by southern whites. For the migrants, those who arrived early and had the resources to make a crop fared well. The major problem, however, was the attraction of Kansas to the have-nots who arrived too late with too little to produce the resources to carry them through the cold Kansas winter. But there was no holding them back. Once they made it to Kansas, they reasoned, their troubles would be over.[72] The inclination to go to Kansas—with or without resources—was reinforced by Singleton and other black leaders, including Richard T. Greener, one of the nationally prominent blacks of the period.

The number of blacks coming to Kansas without adequate means for earning a living or surviving was so great that some organized relief had to be offered. Many arrived in the winter months with no shoes or winter clothing. Some had never seen snow and were not prepared for the cold.[73] Among several relief efforts, the Kansas Freedmen's Relief Association was formed by a Quaker group to raise funds and secure food and clothing for the newcomers. With the support of Kansas Governor J. P. Saint John, the Relief Association raised $40,000 and acquired 500,000 pounds of clothing and bedding for distribution and migrant assistance.[74] Private sympathizers in England contributed $8,000 and 50,000 pounds of goods. The Relief Association also supplied the new farmers with teams, seed, and cabins.

As the migrants continued to arrive it was soon apparent that the resources for establishing impoverished families were not available. Reluctantly, Singleton was forced to use his influence to check the migration. In mid-year, 1879, and later in the spring of 1880, he advised prospective "exodusters" to stay in the South or to scatter into other northern states.[75] Messengers also were sent throughout the South urging blacks to come to Kansas only if they had the necessary resources to sustain themselves, including tools, seed, and clothing.

While most native Kansans were not openly hostile to the migrants and many were involved in relief organizations to assist the newcomers, there were others who openly opposed the migration and resisted efforts by blacks to settle. The City Council of Atchison passed an ordinance prohibiting the "importation of paupers." Civil authorities in Leavenworth halted a steamboat loaded with migrants in midstream and prevented it from docking, forcing the newcomers to disembark at another destination. In Topeka, a group of citizens descended upon the barracks being built to house the destitute migrants and, after razing the building, threw the building materials into the river.[76]

Several Kansas and other midwestern towns passed "sundowner" ordinances that remained in effect for almost a century and that prohibited blacks from remaining overnight within the corporate limits. This had the net effect of preventing any black immigration.

The majority of the migrants homesteaded or bought farms, while others settled in towns and cities of the state. There were others, however, who sought to build their own black communities. In addition to several crossroads settlements that eventually disappeared, the towns of Baxter Springs, Nicodemus, Morton City, and Singleton developed into thriving all-black communities for a time.[77]

The result of the migration often brought about somewhat better conditions for those who remained in the South. This was particularly true in areas of the heaviest out-migration. The reduced labor supply resulting from the migration enabled those who remained to obtain rent decreases and promises of higher wages and favorable treatment for staying.[78] For the first time since the Civil War, planters along the Mississippi River and in other parts of the South were impressed with the dependency of the South's agricultural economy on the black man's labor.[79]

In the areas hardest hit by the black out-migration, white planters took steps to halt it. Black leaders of the movement were publicly denounced as troublemakers and local agents for the exodus were often driven out of town or otherwise threatened. When these efforts failed to diminish the out-migration, white Mississippians closed the river and threatened to sink all boats carrying black migrants. A letter from General Thomas Conway to President Hayes reported: "Every landing is blockaded by white enemies of the colored exodus; some of whom are mounted and armed, as if we are at war."[80] One migrant who had returned from Kansas to get his family was seized by whites, who cut off both his hands and threw them in his wife's lap, saying, "Now go to Kansas and work!"[81]

Return migration from Kansas

The movement to Kansas was not all one way. The harsh conditions of the Kansas frontier, the hostility of some Kansas communities to the migrants, homesickness, and the somewhat better wages being paid in certain areas for farm labor influenced some blacks to return. The best evidence seems to indicate that the exodus was a fairly "efficient" migration, i.e., the size of the counterstream was small compared to the major stream.[82] Elizabeth L. Comstock, a Quaker missionary working for the Freedmen's Relief Association, reported that in her talks with the exodusters, she found that many "preferred death on the cold Kansas prairies to retreat to the balmy Southland."[83]

5. The turn of the century

Though the Kansas Exodus was, by far, the most dramatic black migration stream of the late nineteenth century, it was by no means the only migration of the period. Depression in 1873, civil and political disorder accompanying the return to power of southern Democrats, and the expansion of the economy and railroads created pressures and opportunities for movement throughout the North, South, and West.

Post-Reconstruction period

Quality of the data

Much of the data upon which the remainder of this chapter and the following chapters are based are derived from the U.S. Census. The accuracy of the census information about blacks has long been questioned because of known irregularities in the procedures used to define a person as a Negro, or black, and in the completeness with which the enumerations were carried out. In fact, until 1880, the Census Office had no control over enumerators or enumeration districts and little control over enumeration procedures.[1]

The Census of 1870 was believed to be particularly inaccurate in its enumeration of the South. United States marshals and their appointees had the responsibility for gathering the census information and many of these men lacked the necessary skills, knowledge of the locale, and dedication to carry out an accurate count of the population. Francis Walker, superintendent of his census, described the count as "inadequate, partial and inaccurate, often in shameful degree."[2]

Later census enumerations also were believed to have undercounted the black population. The Census of 1890 appeared to underenumerate blacks when compared to the returns of 1880 and 1900. The validity of the Census of 1920 also has been questioned because the enumeration was moved to January 1 and inclement weather is believed to have impeded census workers, particularly in the rural areas. Later studies have shown that the black population was underenumerated by about 10 percent in 1960 and by a slightly larger amount in 1940 and 1950.[3] Moreover, it is likely that a mobile population such as migrants would stand a greater chance of not being included in the census. Thus, it is difficult to draw firm conclusions about the extent and nature of black migration from the census, yet it remains our one best source of information of a continuous nature for the last century. We should also note that the type of presentation will change from this point onward in the book, because for the first time-period we do have some rather detailed primary source data.

Volume

Crude estimates of the volume of interregional black migration during the 1870s are provided by place-of-birth census data. The data in Table 5-1 suggest very little interregional black migration prior to the turn of the century. By 1870, fewer than 150,000 blacks born in the South lived outside their region of birth. By 1880, the number was still less than 200,000. In that same year, of those born in the North and West, fewer than 23,000 were living outside the region of their birth. Indicative of the relative stability of the southern black population prior to the turn of the twentieth century is the fact that the proportion of northern- and western-born blacks who moved to the South was larger than the proportion of southern-born blacks who moved to the North and West. Whereas 5 percent of the northern- and western-born blacks lived in the South in 1880, only 3.2 percent of the southern-born blacks lived in the North and East.

Despite the fact that a larger proportion of northern blacks were moving South than southern blacks moving North, the absolute size of migration streams resulted in a larger migration from the South to other regions. From 1880 to 1890, an additional 36,300 southern blacks moved North while 7,500 moved West. But taken on the whole, the decade of the 1880s had less interregional black migration than either of the decades before or after. From Table 5-2, it may be seen that the migration from the South to the North and West during the 1880s was down more than 10 percent compared with that of the previous decade. Migration from the North and West to the South experienced a drastic decline of nearly 80 percent, according to these place-of-birth census data.

Table 5–1. Annual growth rates of the black population by region, 1790–1900 (percentage)

Period	Total population (% growth)	Northeast (% growth)	North Central (% growth)	South (% growth)
1790–1800	2.8	2.1	–	2.9
1800–1810	3.2	2.1	–	3.2
1810–1820	2.5	0.8	–	2.6
1820–1830	2.7	1.2	–	2.8
1830–1840	2.1	1.3	7.7	2.0
1840–1850	2.4	0.5	4.2	2.4
1850–1860	2.0	0.4	3.1	2.0
1860–1870	0.9	1.4	3.9	0.8
1870–1880	3.0	2.4	3.5	3.0
1880–1890	1.3	1.6	1.1	1.3
1890–1900	1.8	3.6	1.4	1.6

SOURCE: Reynolds Farley, *The Growth of the Black Population* (Chicago: Markham Publishing Co., 1971), p. 42.

Table 5-2. *Migration of Negroes out of and into the South, by states, 1870-80*

| Section, division, and state | Negro population born in the South | | |
	1870	1880	Increase 1870-80
North and west	149,100	198,029	48,929
North	146,490	194,630	48,140
New England	8,269	10,824	2,555
Maine	366	227	-139
New Hampshire	173	162	-11
Vermont	199	142	-57
Massachusetts	4,347	5,851	1,504
Rhode Island	1,385	2,013	628
Connecticut	1,799	2,429	630
Middle Atlantic	33,754	48,332	14,578
New York	8,147	14,373	6,225
New Jersey	5,166	7,401	2,235
Pennsylvania	20,441	26,558	6,117
East North Central	63,856	75,217	11,361
Ohio	31,378	31,880	502
Indiana	13,459	20,355	6,896
Illinois	14,408	19,150	4,742
Michigan	3,752	3,282	-470
Wisconsin	859	550	-309
West North Central	40,611	60,257	19,646
Minnesota	391	558	167
Iowa	2,258	2,919	661
Missouri	30,754	30,785	31
North Dakota	. . . .	. . . .	. . . .
South Dakota	. . . .	. . . .	. . . .
Nebraska	353	1,035	682
Kansas	6,793	24,810	18,047
West	2,610	3,399	789
Mountain	754	1,606	852
Montana	71	80	9
Idaho	26	22	-4
Wyoming	96	108	12
Colorado	248	942	694
New Mexico	80	187	107
Arizona	18	65	47
Utah	38	60	22
Nevada	177	142	-35
Pacific	1,856	1,793	-63
Washington	33	99	66
Oregon	102	63	-39
California	1,721	1,631	-90

| | Negro Population born in the North and West | | |
	1870	1880	Increase 1870-80
South	15,583	22,039	6,456
South Atlantic	2,425	5,207	2,782
Delaware	429	772	343
Maryland	677	999	322
District of Columbia	279	960	681
Virginia	207	530	323
West Virginia	224	477	253
North Carolina	122	438	316

Table 5–2. (cont.)

South Carolina	127	231	104
Georgia	211	390	179
Florida	149	410	261
East South Central	4,564	7,017	2,453
Kentucky	977	1,622	645
Tennessee	1,231	1,653	422
Alabama	358	1,455	1,097
Mississippi	1,998	2,287	289
West South Central	8,594	9,815	1,221
Arkansas	2,032	2,806	774
Louisiana	2,497	2,686	189
Oklahoma	*		
Texas	4,065	4,323	258

SOURCE: U.S., Bureau of the Census, *Thirteenth Census of the U.S.: 1910* (Washington, D.C.: Government Printing Office).
NOTE: *No enumeration for Oklahoma and Indian Territory in 1870 and 1880.

Destination selectivity also was quite pronounced in the migrations of the 1870s and 1880s. The most popular state for migrants from the South during the 1870s was Kansas. The decade witnessed an increase there of more than 18,000 blacks from the South. Indiana, New York, and Pennsylvania each attracted more than 6,000 migrants during the decade. Illinois, New Jersey, and Massachusetts were the only other states to attract more than a thousand southern migrants over the same period.

Quite different patterns of destination selectivity emerged for the black migrant in the 1880s. The state of Kansas, the most attractive state for southern blacks during the previous decade, experienced an out-migration. Undoubtedly, some returned to the South because of the intense hardships migrants encountered. The rather significant increase in the number of southern blacks in Nebraska, Colorado, and California suggests that some of the Kansas Exodus migrants moved farther North and West rather than return to the South.

The principal destinations for blacks leaving the South during the 1880s were the industrial states of Pennsylvania, New York, and New Jersey. More than 30,000 blacks moved to these three states. More than 15,000 moved to Pennsylvania alone. Illinois continued to attract migrants, but only half as many as in the previous decade. The Oklahoma territory also began emerging as a potentially attractive area for blacks late in the 1880s, but it would take another decade before Oklahoma realized any significant in-migration.

Considerable interstate migration also occurred within the South during the post-Reconstruction decades. Among the more pronounced patterns were those linking the South Atlantic states of Virginia, North and South

Carolina to the Gulf states of Louisiana, Mississippi, and Texas. These streams were, in large part, continuations of those formed in the latter years of the antebellum period. Thirty-five thousand blacks from South Carolina and Georgia moved to Arkansas and Texas in the decade following the Civil War.[4] Substantial out-migrations from Georgia, Alabama, South Carolina, and Mississippi to the Southwest also were evident in the period 1865–1875.[5] These movements were stimulated by labor agents from the destination states.

While the pull to the Gulf states and the Southwest was the promise of jobs, the push was political and social oppression. In one incident in South Carolina, migrants complained that they had been driven away from their homes by political persecution and that when they returned for their friends, some of the migrants were shot at by white farmers who accused them of enticing away the laborers.[6]

The largest single out-migration from South Carolina during the post-Reconstruction period came from "bloody Edgefield," near the western border of the state, in the last week of 1881: an estimated 5,000 blacks left their homes for Arkansas.[7] Political oppression was reportedly more severe in and around Edgefield than in other parts of the state; blacks complained that they could not vote in elections, or if they did, their ballots were not counted.[8]

Some argue against the political oppression theory, claiming that the migration was economically motivated. One study of South Carolina blacks states that "in most cases the economic push was stronger than the fear of personal danger and political persecution."[9] Narcisco Gonzales, a young reporter for the *Charleston News and Courier*, wrote:

> For ten years we have tried to make money and have not been able to do so. We are poorer now than when we began, we have less, in fact we have nothing. We have not lived extravagantly, we have exercised all the economy we knew how to use and we are going further downhill every day. There is not help for us here, there's no use in trying to get along under the old conditions any longer, and so we have just determined to go somewhere else and take a new start.[10]

Migration from the South Atlantic states was given further impetus by the numerous emigration societies that sprang up in the late 1870s and early 1880s. Membership dues in one such society were one dollar, and meetings were held regularly, often twice a week. With the money received from dues, scouts or "spies" often were sent west to bring back reports of what the country was really like. Earlier migrants had frequently been duped by labor agents spreading stories about the "tropical country of Arkansas, where coconuts, oranges, lemons and bananas grow and soft balmy breezes blow." Scouts brought back more realistic but still slightly exaggerated stories of wages of $12 to $20 a month and government lands that could be bought for twelve and a half cents per acre.[11]

When a majority of the members of a society decided to migrate, another assessment was levied by the emigration organization and a representative was selected to make travel arrangements. Migrants commonly traveled in groups of 10 to 50. Some groups could afford to travel by train at special rates provided to emigrant societies; others walked or borrowed horses and wagons. At their destination, the migrants were sometimes met by land agents who took charge and provided accommodations near the area where small plots of ground could be purchased. Those without means sometimes were helped until they obtained work.

Families and groups passing through Greenville, Chattanooga, Atlanta, and other southern towns and cities on their way to Arkansas, Mississippi, Louisiana, and Texas were frequently cited in local newspapers or were subjects of magazine and journal articles. Their migratory behavior was called "Arkansas fever." They were made the objects of scorn and stigma in the communities they left, but were sought by communities throughout the Gulf states and the Southwest to meet the labor demands of an expanding economy.

Black migration toward the end of the century

For 15 years following the Civil War, much of the South remained economically stagnant. With the exception of Atlanta, Richmond, and Nashville, the major cities of the South failed to recover from the ravages of the war and the disorders of the Reconstruction.[12] Poverty and dilapidation pervaded the countryside and small towns as well. Highways and railroads were in disrepair, stores lacked customers, and the beautiful antebellum homes of the planters were often abandoned and falling in ruins. Blacks lived in shacks or "wretched huts," and "everywhere the people show by their dress and manner of living that they are poor."[13]

The South's poverty stood in marked contrast to the relative wealth found in the North. In 1880 the per capita wealth in the South was 27 percent of that in the northeastern states of New York, New Jersey, and Pennsylvania. In the Northeast per capita income was $1,353 as compared with $376 in the South.[14]

The southern economy seemed to reach a turning point in 1880. Depression had ended the year before and northern and English capital began trickling into the South as a modest but renewed commercial life appeared. The editor of the *New Orleans Times-Democrat* called it "a commercial evolution unparalleled in the annals of American progress."[15] Construction began to get underway, railroads were built, seaports bustled, tobacco and cotton were in demand, and the iron industry in the South was transformed from a potentiality to a reality.

The principal migration patterns in the two decades following the Civil War were from one agricultural region to another within the South, gradually shifting the nation's black population in a southwestward direction.[16] With the exception of the period between 1878 and 1881 (the Kansas Exodus) most of the migration occurred in steady, continuous, but undramatic streams.

By the end of the 1880s a period of increased migration appeared about to reoccur. The upswing in the southern economy, together with industrial expansion in the North, brought about a renewed incentive to relocate in order to take advantage of the improving economy and to escape exploitation, intimidation, and injustice. Black migration toward the end of the century clearly revealed, however, that improving one's economic position was easier than escaping social injuries. The curses of second-class citizenship were to follow blacks regardless of their choice of destination.

Volume

The volume of black migration in the 1890s was substantially larger than in previous decades. The number of blacks born in the South and living in the North increased by 36,300 from 1880 to 1890; from Table 5-2 it may be observed that the number increased by more than 105,000 from 1890 to 1900. There was a substantial decrease in the number of southern blacks moving to the West. During the 1880s there had been an increase of more than 7,500 compared with an increase of only 2,600 during the 1890s. The number of blacks moving from the North and West to the South increased from 1,200 to over 7,000.

By far the majority of the interregional migrants were moving from the South to four states in the North: Pennsylvania, New York, Illinois, and New Jersey. More than 35,000 southern blacks moved to Pennsylvania, 21,000 went to New York, and about 15,000 went to New Jersey and Illinois. Indiana and Massachusetts each attracted more than 5,000 southern blacks during the decade. During the 1880s, Missouri experienced a significant out-migration, but this trend reversed during the 1890s and the state attracted nearly 4,000 southern blacks.

Migrants from the North and West traveling to the South were fairly evenly divided between the South Atlantic and West South Central divisions; slightly less than 3,000 moved to each area. About half of that number migrated to the East South Central division. The single most attractive southern state for migrants from outside the South in the 1890s was Oklahoma, which received over half of the southbound migrants. The result was a continuing shift in the distribution. By 1900, several states in the West South Central, especially Texas and Louisiana, had more than 10 per-

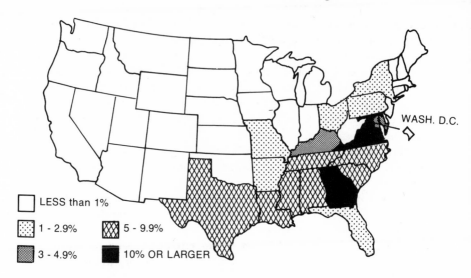

Figure 5-1. *Distribution of black population, 1870 (percent by state).*
SOURCE: U.S., Department of Commerce, Bureau of the Census, *Statistical Abstract of the Un~
States, 1947* (Washington, D.C.: Government Printing Office, 1947), Table 19, p. 20.

cent black population. The increase in most states was a combination of natural increase and migration. However, in the states outside the Old South migrants made up a disproportionate amount.

Causes

The level of migrations is influenced greatly by economic recessions and depressions as well as economic expansion. Both of these trends were found in the last decades of the nineteenth century, and the patterns of black migration reflected the vicissitudes of the economy. In the late 1880s and early 1890s, rural blacks and whites flocked to the developing mine districts of central Alabama and eastern Tennessee to take jobs as miners or mill workers.[17] Earlier, foreign immigration met the demand for labor, but when this supply became inadequate labor agents were sent into the surrounding countryside to hire black workers to compensate for the shortage.[18] The developing mines in West Virginia and southern Ohio attracted blacks from Virginia and the Carolinas. Indicative of the growth there, the black population of West Virginia in 1870 was 17,900; by 1900 it had grown to 43,500.[19]

About 1890, the "great black march westward" into Oklahoma began. In the preceding discussion on volume it was noted that Oklahoma was the single most attractive southern state for black migrants from outside the South during the 1890s. As part of the "westward expansion" large numbers of blacks moved to Oklahoma, in a fashion reminiscent of the Kansas Exodus a decade earlier, forming approximately 25 all-black communities.[20] These all-black communities were, in part, "Utopian" communities, established by various religious and sociopolitical sects, though others were established as a result of spontaneous rushes for gold, land, oil, and other natural wealth offered by the virgin territory. Promotional enterprises and businesses also established communities in order to sell land.[21]

Clearly, the largest movement of the 1890s was into the industrializing towns and cities of the mid-Atlantic states and Illinois. Black migration was only one of many streams of migrants contributing to the rapid industrial, commercial, and demographic expansion of the urban areas. Immigration from Europe was contributing ever-increasing numbers of persons to the United States, and more important, immigration was undergoing a transition from northwestern Europeans settling in the Ohio and Mississippi valleys to southeastern Europeans settling in the major cities. An overview of the census shows clearly that the immigration and migration patterns at the turn of the century closely mirrored the availability of economic opportunity and the related processes of urbanization and industrialization.

Following the Civil War, Chicago had developed something of a "mecca" image among southern blacks. Whites living in southern Illinois frequently characterized Chicago as a "nigger-loving town."[22] Between 1870 and 1890, Chicago's black community grew from less than 4,000 to almost 15,000, and in the process developed a well-delineated class structure and numerous secular and religious organizations.[23] Prior to the great fire in 1871, blacks lived throughout most of the city; however, after the fire they became more concentrated geographically. Between 1890 and 1915, the black population of Chicago grew from slightly less than 15,000 to more than 50,000. Most of the city's black population growth was the result of migration from outside the state of Illinois: in 1900 over 80 percent of Chicago's blacks were born in other states. The majority of the migrants— 43 percent—came from the Upper South and border states, the largest number coming from Kentucky. Migrants from Tennessee and Missouri were also well represented in the city's black population. Alabama, Mississippi, and Georgia were areas of origin for over 3,000 black Chicagoans. Nearly 3,000 blacks from Ohio and Indiana also moved to Chicago.[24]

It would be exceedingly difficult—probably impossible—to identify a single cause explaining the migration of blacks during this or any other period. The fact that there were many different migrations of different sizes and directions suggests that any realistic explanation of the movement would involve numerous factors. Moreover, migration for a single person or family is seldom motivated by a single cause. More often, the factors causing migration are complex and interactive, involving conditions in both the areas of origin and destination, as well as reflecting migrant characteristics. And, as students of migration are learning all too well, the reasons migrants give, their true motivations, and the real causes are seldom one and the same.

Efforts to identify the major causes of black migration during this period have been attempted. A pioneering black sociologist, Charles S. Johnson, attributed the chief cause of black migration in Georgia before 1910 to discontent with the land-tenure system. His findings indicated that blacks tended to go where they could rise from being farm laborers to either sharecroppers, cash renters, or landowners. One of the more important and controversial aspects of his survey was the finding that there was no correlation between racial persecution and migration. In some cases, the black population increased significantly in the very counties where there were large numbers of lynchings. Johnson concluded that "persecution plays its part—a considerable one. But when the whole of the migration of Southern Negroes is considered, this part seems to be limited. It is indeed more likely that Negroes, like all others with a spark of ambition and self-interest, have been deserting soil which cannot yield returns in proportion to their population increase."[25]

There were other observers of black migration in the late nineteenth century who, while not discounting the economic interpretation completely, viewed the movements more in social-psychological terms. Some argued that it was racial discrimination that motivated blacks to search out new alternatives by migrating.[26]

There was also ample incentive on the part of northern industry to encourage black in-migration during this period. Employers believed that the real or threatened presence of black workers was an effective instrument for keeping wages low, preventing strikes, and breaking them when they did occur. As early as 1855, black workers were used as strikebreakers in New York City. In the 1870s and the 1880s the practice of bringing blacks as iron, steel, and coal workers from the South to help break strikes in the North occurred with greater frequency.[27] It is important to note that the newly formed United Mine Workers of America was careful to avoid interjecting the racial issue with strikebreaking. Though union members fought and often killed blacks imported as strikebreakers, the violence was occasioned by their interference in the strike, not by racism.[28] A strike by Chicago's stockyard workers in 1894 and again in 1904 precipitated the use of black workers as strikebreakers, and when the Teamsters' Union struck the next year, the city's leading merchants sent agents south to hire blacks for the same purpose.[29] Though it would be impossible to determine the number of blacks who moved north either permanently or temporarily as strikebreakers, it was clearly a common mechanism for migrating with an assurance of work upon arrival from the late 1800s through the early 1900s.

Migrant types

Very little is known about the type of people that made up the migration streams, and the problem is compounded by conflicting reports. On the one hand, it is argued that the economically prosperous blacks with land and businesses in the South, as well as political leaders dependent on black vote support, were largely opposed to the migrations. These eminent southern blacks did not appear to have migrated themselves, even where they agreed that others should do so. "The principal, if not the entire, impetus for migration came from among the lower classes."[30] On the other hand, some have argued that the migrants were the elite blacks, the "talented tenth." The migrants to Chicago at the turn of the century were described as " . . . prominent preachers and politicians who, for a brief spell after the Civil War, sat in Southern state legislatures and in Congress; less distinguished individuals who occupied minor political posts in county and town; and all the restless educated and half-educated, who were not content to live life on Southern terms."[31]

Though concrete evidence is lacking to support or reject either of the interpretations, it is likely that both were partially right. The great majority of southern blacks were poor not only by national norms but also by those of the South. It is possible that the "talented tenth" were represented in a larger proportion than other migrants, but considering the volume of migration, it would have been extremely unlikely that they dominated the movement in terms of absolute numbers. The number of migrants far exceeded the number of economically advantaged and socially prominent blacks. Moreover, the extensive relief programs that were founded to provide assistance to the "exodusters" and the developing social welfare organizations in New York, Chicago, and other major metropolitan destinations strongly suggest that for a sizable number of migrants personal resources were inadequate for their adjustment.

Consequences

There were several important demographic consequences resulting from the end-of-the-century migration streams. Although there was little or no significant regional redistribution of the black population until after 1910, there were sizable increases in the proportions of blacks living in urban areas, particularly in the North and West. The states of Kansas, Oklahoma, Nebraska, and Colorado, which had few blacks prior to the 1880s, became the destinations for several thousand black migrants. Several metropolitan areas, including New York City, Chicago, Philadelphia, Newark, and Boston, experienced major population increases in their black communities at a time when southeastern Europeans also were arriving.

Table 5–3. Percentages of blacks living in urban and rural areas, 1890–1920

Year	United States		South		North and West	
	Urban	Rural	Urban	Rural	Urban	Rural
1890	20	80	15	85	62	38
1900	23	77	17	83	70	30
1910	27	73	21	79	77	23
1920	34	66	25	75	84	16

SOURCE: Reynolds Farley, *The Growth of the Black Population* (Chicago: Markham Publishing Co., 1971), p. 50.

For the migrants, the consequences varied depending largely on their characteristics and destinations. In some communities, black workers were welcomed to help break striking unions. In other communities, they were less welcome. It is impossible to determine with certainty the amount of economic improvement blacks derived from moving West or to northern cities. There is little doubt that many of the social evils which oppressed blacks in the rural areas and small towns of the South were not automatically removed simply by moving to a different city, state, or region.

Even though the migration streams were relatively small when compared to later periods, they may have served a very important function, i.e., they developed pathways and linkages that served as mechanisms for facilitating and even encouraging later movements.

Black migration in the new century

The first decade of the twentieth century was an anomaly from the standpoint of black migration. European immigration to America was at its peak; between 1870 and 1920, total immigration amounted to more than 26 million—more than three times as much as during the whole of the previous two and one-half centuries. The sizes of the total immigration for the decades 1870 to 1920 were as follows:[32]

1871–1880	2,812,191
1881–1890	5,246,613
1891–1900	3,687,564
1901–1910	8,795,386
1911–1921	5,735,811

From these figures, it may be observed that European immigration rose slowly during the 1870s, reaching a peak the following decade. The depression era of the 1890s resulted in a significant decline, but immigration rose again in the early twentieth century, until it was checked by the outbreak of World War I and increasingly restrictive legislation. Until 1890, most of the immigrants came from north and western Europe and usually settled on farms after reaching the United States. The "new immi-gration," on the other hand, coming largely from southern and east-ern Europe, brought settlers chiefly to the cities in the Northeast and the Middle West.

Heavy immigration from Europe to industrialized northern cities from 1900 to 1910 had a significant effect on the volume and direction of black migration from the South. While blacks continued to move northward, there was a noticeable decline in the net increase over what it had been the previous decade. For example, the net gain in numbers of southern-born blacks living in Pennsylvania increased by nearly 36,000 from 1890 to 1900, but the increase amounted to slightly over 19,000 from 1900 to 1910. Increases in the southern-born population also were less in New York, New Jersey, Illinois, and Indiana, as well as in most other northern states. One notable exception was Ohio, where southern-born blacks increased in number by 2,500 during the 1890s, then by more than 9,500 from 1900 to 1910. Although the propensity for southern blacks to migrate north had been dampened somewhat, the westward movement was more vital than ever. The principal destination for westbound blacks was California. Southern-born blacks living in the West had increased by only 2,600 in the 1890s—a major decrease from the previous decade. From 1900 to 1910 southern-born blacks increased by more than 11,400. More than half of the increase occurred in California, with Washington and Colorado expe-riencing large increases as well. Little or no increase occurred in such states as New Mexico, Montana, Utah, Idaho, Arizona, and Oregon.

Perhaps the most interesting black migration streams were those from the North and West to the South. It has already been noted that northern- and western-born blacks had migrated to the South during the last decades of the nineteenth century, largely to Oklahoma, and particularly to Ken-tucky in the 1890s. From 1900 to 1910, however, the most significant in-crease of northern- and western-born blacks living in the South occurred in the South Atlantic states, chiefly Virginia, West Virginia, and the District of Columbia. Blacks continued migrating to Oklahoma as well, but at a slower pace. From 1900 to 1910, the number of northern- and western-born blacks living in the South increased from 30,400 to 41,450. Of that increase, 6,350 were in the South Atlantic states. The smallest increases were in the East South Central states of Mississippi, Alabama, Tennessee, and Kentucky. In the West South Central states, the increase was slightly more than 3,000.

One investigation of black migration during this period revealed sub-stantial intraregional movement; not only were blacks moving from the South to the North and West, but they were moving about freely within the South, usually in a westwardly direction. Though the urbanization of the black population has been shown, even within the South, one student of Georgia's migratory patterns has documented that the principal shift in the black population in that state before 1915 was from one district to another. Such rural-to-rural migrations were common throughout the southern states.[33] After the turn of the century and during the continuing rural relocation of a sizable number of blacks, an increasing proportion became permanently detached from the land to take up residence in one of the nation's growing cities.[34]

Black migrants at the turn of the century were largely young adults. Among the male migrants the majority were moving mainly from one agricultural section to another. Female migrants tended to select cities and towns as destinations due to the great employment opportunities there for them.[35] While blacks were generally migratory, the extent of their interstate mobility was less than that of whites during the first decade of the twentieth century. In 1910, 16.6 percent of the black population had moved to some other state than that in which they were born, while the percentage for whites was 22.4.[36]

The causes of the migrations remained largely unchanged from previous decades. The push factors included the continuation of the land-tenure arrangements that kept the great majority of blacks landless and dependent on white landlords, and the continuation and intensification of the doctrine of white supremacy that manifested itself in every aspect of community life. There were also major changes in the pull factors, owing to the marked increase in European immigrants flooding the major cities of the North and Midwest. The increased competition for jobs and housing gave impetus to the westward stream, and the increased black migration to the South was probably the result of the European influx. But one argument was that the reason for increased migration to the South was the greater opportunity there for a black person to pursue a career in teaching, medicine, or business.[37]

A considerable amount of migration within the South, as well as out of the South, was due to the advance of the boll weevil. The entrance of the boll weevil into Georgia uprooted many farming and plantation families, although the states north of Georgia were not affected and hence did not suffer nearly the same loss in black population. However, states west of Georgia had been previously affected. The slight population increase in Texas and the decrease in Louisiana was due, in part, to the effect of the boll weevil after 1910.[38] Other factors contributing to migration during this period included floods in Oklahoma and problems in Louisiana's sugar industry. Superior farming opportunities in the Upper Piedmont and Wiregrass regions of Georgia between 1900 and 1910 also attracted migrants from the Old Black Belt counties of southern Georgia.[39]

6. The Great Migration and the post–World War I era

The decade 1910 to 1920 was a period of international crisis and domestic social change in the United States. Although this country had been increasingly concerned with international power politics for a generation prior to 1914, most Americans believed that they could remain aloof from European conflicts. But more than two years after the outbreak of World War I, America's precarious neutrality gave way, and the nation was drawn into the conflict as a fully embattled participant.

In addition to the international political effects of the war, important demographic changes resulted in the United States, one of which was the redistribution of the nation's black population. Domestic social changes—industrialization and urbanization—gave added impetus to the spatial mobility of blacks. The concentration of the black population in the South began to dissolve as the small stream of out-migration swelled to sizable proportions.

It was a revolutionary period for the black migrants, for the areas from which they departed and for the cities to which they moved. Major economic, social, and political consequences were felt by blacks and whites alike in both the cities of the North and the communities of the South.

Despite the earlier migrations of blacks, the sudden and large-scale exodus from the South to the North, which has since been referred to as the Great Migration, was not expected. Migrations from the South had occurred in the antebellum period via the Underground Railroad, during the Civil War and the Reconstruction, in the late 1870s to Kansas, in the late 1880s to Oklahoma, and during the years at the turn of the century to the North. In fact, the Great Migration bears such a significant resemblance to the earlier migrations that it may be regarded as a continuation of the same movement with intervals of a number of years. However revolutionary its effects may have been, viewed in the context of the preceding century, the migration of 1915 cannot be separated from the ongoing exodus from the South.

The exact point in time when this Great Migration began, if there was a start to it, is uncertain. Many students argue that it began about 1916. It is known that the migration was underway a considerable time before any notice was taken of it. Conditions for the mass migration to the North were set by the outbreak of World War I, which resulted in the virtual cessation of European immigration to the United States. This reduction in immigration cut sharply into the supply of foreign immigrant labor needed by northern industries. In the first 14 years of the century, more than 12 million immigrants had arrived in the United States. In 1914 alone, more than one million immigrants arrived. But the following year, the number of immigrants declined to about one-third that number, in 1916 to about one-fourth, and by 1918, there were only 110,000 new arrivals to the United States. At the same time, almost 100,000 emigrated from the United States to return to their European homeland.

To meet the labor demands created by the dwindling European migration, northern industries sent recruiting agents to the South in the spring of 1915 to help fill the labor vacuum. The initial response of southern blacks to the appeals of the agents apparently was not noteworthy. Relatively few responded. In the following year, 1916, however, there was a sudden increase in the number of migrants from the South. This escalation was due, in part, to the efforts of national philanthropic organizations to assist black students in obtaining summer employment.[1] One organization arranged with a few northern tobacco growers to bring a number of black students from southern schools to work in the tobacco. In May 1916, two trainloads of students were brought from Georgia for such work. Railroads and industries in the North, seeing the public relations value of the incident, sent agents of their own to the South to spread the word about the workers going North. Pictures of high wages and better social conditions were portrayed to the southern blacks, most of whom were more than ready to move.

Also contributing to the effort of the pull factors drawing southern blacks to the North were black newspapers, which exalted the economic promises in the North, and letters written home by migrants, who generally reported optimism about their newfound prosperity. Complementing these factors were strong push factors motivating migrants to get out of the South: unemployment was high and social conditions poor. A combination of these push and pull factors set a stage of prior conditions, so that relatively few triggering events or activities set off the migration.

Sources and quality of migration data

Basically, there are two major sources of information about the Great Migration. One is found in simple estimates by public and private individuals and organizations who used a variety of methods such as counting arrivals and departures at train stations, school enrollments, and military draft figures. The validity and reliability of such measures are open to question. Nevertheless, they do provide crude approximations of the size of various components of the migration stream.

A second source of information is the 1920 census. The data compiled by the Bureau of the Census clearly documents the net northward migration of large numbers of southern blacks between 1910 and 1920. However, there are two fundamental problems associated with the use of census data for analyzing the Great Migration. As noted previously, data are often unreliable for the South and especially for the black population. The 1920 census, in particular, has been criticized for errors in this respect. An additional problem is created by the ten-year time period, 1910 to 1920, which the census covers. Apparently the distribution of the black population that prevailed in 1910 changed very little until about 1916, or until the effects of World War I upon immigration, industry, and other aspects of national life began to be felt.[2] However, the use of census data prohibits any delineation of yearly movements and includes any migration that may have occurred prior to the period that is the focus of this discussion. We must generally accept, without quantitative evidence, the consensus that the bulk of the migration during this decade occurred between 1916 and 1919.[3] We also must remember that the census figures do not include persons who may have moved North and back again before 1920.

Distribution of black population

The black population remained highly concentrated in the plantation sections of the South prior to the Great Migration, despite the migrations prior to and after the Civil War. In 1910, the proportion of the total United States black population in the South was only slightly less than in 1870.

Major changes in the distribution of the black population prior to 1910 were between rural and urban areas in the South. In the urban areas, the proportion of blacks more than doubled in the four decades from 1870 to 1910, changing from slightly over 9 percent to nearly 19 percent. The percentage in rural areas of the region declined from 81 to 70 during the same period.[4] This was a time of urbanization for blacks and whites in both the North and South.

The black population, except in the Secessionist South, was more urban than the white population in every region in every decade from 1870 to 1940. In the Secessionist South, blacks were only slightly less urban than

Table 6–1. *Percent distribution of the black population by regions of the coterminous United States, 1900–1940*

Year	United States	North-east	North Central	South	West
1900	100.0	4.4	5.6	89.7	0.3
1910	100.0	4.9	5.5	89.0	0.5
1920	100.0	6.5	7.6	85.2	0.8
1930	100.0	9.6	10.6	78.7	1.0
1940	100.0	10.6	11.0	77.0	1.3

SOURCE: Daniel O. Price, *Changing Characteristics of the Negro Population*, U.S., Bureau of the Census, 1960 Census Monograph (Washington, D.C.: Government Printing Office, 1969), p. 9.

the white population, and the urbanization of the black population increased similarly to that of the white population. In other regions, blacks were more urban than whites in 1870 and have continued to become concentrated in urban areas at much higher rates than whites.[5]

From 1870 to 1910 the total population and the white population exhibited larger increases in the urban percentage than did the black population. Beginning in 1910, however, blacks showed greater urban increases than did the white population. It is likely that this increase among blacks was fostered by the problems of southern tenant farmers during the economic depressions in the late 1890s and early 1900s and the somewhat greater availability of various types of "relief" in urban areas.[6]

During the first decade of the new century, the nation's black population increased by nearly one million, or about 11 percent. Although the population in the North and West increased more than in the South, the differences were not great. In the decade beginning in 1910, however, the growth rate of the nation's black population declined by almost half, to an average annual growth rate for the interdecennial period of 6.3 percent.[7] But more important than the overall decline in the nation's growth rate were the pronounced differences in the regional growth rates. The black population increased 43 percent for the decade in the North, 55 percent in the West, but only about 2 percent in the South. Unquestionably there had been major changes in the demographic behavior of America's black population.

Volume and direction of migration

In June 1916 the Department of Labor had been appraised of "a disturbing labor condition in the South. A great migratory stream of Negro wage earners was reported as flowing out of southern and into northern states. . . ."[8] Estimates of the size of the migration varied, depending on the time period in question. The range was from 200,000 from June 1916 to September 1917[9] to 350,000 from 1916 to 1917[10] to an estimate "hardly less" than 750,000 in the period 1915–1918.[11] Estimates of out-migration for the various states ranged from 75,000 to 90,000 leaving Alabama; 35,000 to 50,000 from Georgia; and 75,000 to 100,000 moving north from Mississippi.[12]

A crude estimate of the amount of interregional black migration that had occurred by 1920 was reported by the census (see Table 6-2). In that year 343,000 eastern-born black Americans were living west of the Mississippi River and southern-born blacks living in the North numbered almost 740,000. But counterstreams also were evident, as indicated by the fact that there were approximately 96,000 blacks who were born in the West living east of the Mississippi River and about 44,500 northern-born blacks living in the South. Despite the counterstreams, the net gains were ap-

Table 6–2. Summary of results of migration of the black population east and west, and north and south, 1920

Section & net gain	Number
Born east and living west of Miss. River	342,931
Born west and living east of Miss. River	96,110
Net gain of the West	246,821
Net gain of the East	. . . .
Born in North and living in the South	44,536
Born in South and living in the North	737,423
Net gain of the South	. . . .
Net gain of the North	692,887

SOURCE: U.S., Bureau of the Census, *Population*, vol. II, General Report, *Statistics by Subject, 1930* (Washington, D.C.: U.S. Government Printing Office, 1933), p. 140.

NOTE: The cumulative effects of interdivisional black migration may be determined from state of birth as well.

proximately 695,000 in the North and 245,000 in the West. For example, in 1910 there were about 120,000 blacks living in the East North Central division who were born outside it. By 1920, the division gained approximately 175,000 net additional blacks through migration from other divisions, bringing the cumulative in-migrant population to nearly 300,000. Other divisions that were affected particularly included the Middle Atlantic states with 110,300 more black migrants in 1920 than were there ten years earlier. The number of net migrants to the West South Central division actually declined from approximately 195,000 in 1910 to about 125,000 in 1920.

Origins of the migrants were a matter of conjecture some time before the migration abated. One of the early assessments was published in the June 1917 *Literary Digest*, which indicated that nearly half of the migrants came from Alabama, Virginia, and Georgia. Other estimates, including one by the U.S. Department of Labor, indicate that the *Literary Digest* fig-

Table 6–3. Net population change: gain (+) or loss (−) through interdivisional migration (state of birth data)

Geographic division	1910	1920
Northeast	+ 20,310	+ 21,325
Middle Atlantic	+186,384	+296,664
East North Central	+119,649	+296,111
West North Central	+ 40,497	+ 68,222
South Atlantic	− 392,827	− 455,410
East South Central	− 200,876	− 405,511
West South Central	+194,658	+127,350
Mountain	+ 13,229	+ 20,085
Pacific	+ 18,976	+ 31,164

SOURCE: Ibid., p. 142.

Table 6–4. Source of black migrants by state, October 1916–May 1917

State	Number	State	Number
Alabama	90,000	Tennessee	22,632
Virginia	49,000	Kentucky	21,855
Georgia	48,897	Louisiana	16,912
North Carolina	35,576	Florida	10,291
Mississippi	35,291	Texas	10,870
South Carolina	27,560	Oklahoma	5,836
Arkansas	23,628	Total	398,348

SOURCE: *Literary Digest*, 54 (June 23, 1917) cited in Henderson H. Donald, "The Negro Migration of 1916–1918," *Journal of Negro History* 4:404.

ures were reasonably close, with the exception of Mississippi, which probably had between 75,000 and 100,000 out-migrants.[13]

Thirteen states experienced absolute loss of black population from 1910 to 1920. The largest net loss occurred in Mississippi (nearly 75,000 fewer blacks than in 1910). Interestingly, the state with the largest proportional decrease was not in the South but in New England—Vermont, with a black population decrease of nearly 65 percent. It should be noted that this loss involved small numbers. With the exception of West Virginia, the low average annual growth rates for the interdecennial period strongly suggest that no southern state was exempt from out-migration immediately prior to and during World War I.

Twenty-six states representing all geographical census divisions experienced net black population declines from rural areas. In the South, however, the divisional losses from rural areas were greater than in other regions. While the great majority of the migrants came from the rural areas of the southern states, many southern cities also lost black population because of out-migration. Of the 50 southern cities that had black populations of 10,000 or more in 1930, five experienced absolute decreases in their black populations: Louisville, Kentucky; Nashville, Tennessee; and Jackson, Vicksburg, and Meridian, Mississippi. (Of the 23 cities outside the South with black populations of at least 10,000, none showed net losses of their black populations during the same period.)

In terms of net population increase, the single most attractive state for northbound black migrants was Pennsylvania, where the black population increased more than 90,000 from 1910 to 1920. Ohio, Illinois, and New York increased by more than 210,000, collectively, and Virginia, a border state, increased by more than 65,000. However, in terms of proportionate population increase, Michigan's ten-year growth represented a 251 percent increase, the largest for any state and far greater than the 67 percent growth in both Ohio and Illinois.

The largest proportionate increase for any city occurred in Gary, Indiana, where the black population swelled by more than 1,280 percent. Ak-

Table 6-5. Average annual
growth rates for interdecennial period, 1910–20

State	Growth rate
Delaware	-2.7
Maryland	5.3
District of Columbia	16.4
Virginia	2.8
West Virginia	34.6
North Carolina	9.4
South Carolina	3.5
Georgia	2.5
Florida	6.7
Kentucky	-9.8
Tennessee	-4.5
Alabama	-0.8
Mississippi	-7.4
Arkansas	6.6
Louisiana	-1.9
Oklahoma	8.6
Texas	7.5

SOURCE: Robert B. Grant, *The
Black Man Comes to the City* (Chicago: Nelson Hall Company,
1972), p. 25.

ron and Detroit increased by 749 and 611 percent respectively. In the
South, two cities increased by more than 300 percent—Tulsa and Miami.
In terms of absolute increase, Chicago, New York, Philadelphia, and De-
troit experienced the largest growth.

The migratory streams exhibited striking order and regularity, i.e., specific areas of origin were strongly related to specific areas of destination.
Migrants from a given region in the South did not move randomly over
the North. For a vast majority of the migrants, movement involved a destination that was nearly due north of the origin. Migrants from the South
Atlantic states of North Carolina, South Carolina, and Georgia generally
moved to New Jersey or New York. Migrants from Alabama tended to
move to Ohio, Michigan, and Indiana, and those from Mississippi and
Louisiana moved to Illinois and, to a lesser extent, Missouri.[14]

By 1920 the black population of the United States was 10.4 million—10
percent of the total population. In the next ten years the black population
increased 14 percent. Despite the wave of migration to the cities, blacks
remained predominantly rural, but during the 1920s the rural proportion
declined by 10 percent and comprised 56 percent of the black population.[15] Perhaps the most prophetic figures were revealed in the percentage
increase in population in the urban areas. For the 1920s the black urban
population increased 46 percent, compared with 24 percent for whites.[16]
This disproportionate difference was due largely to a marked slowdown in

immigration from Europe (a combination of domestic policy and antiemigration measures by the Soviet Union and fascist Italy) and the continuation of black migration from the South. According to one estimate,[17] 614,000 blacks migrated to urban areas during the 1920s. Although the total migration population was of mixed origin, most of it came from the South.[18]

The flow from the Deep South was particularly large. Georgia, for example, the state with the largest black population in the nation, lost 11 percent of its black population during the 1920s. Of course the largest population gains were in the North, especially considering previous levels of black population there. In New York between 1920 and 1930 the black population jumped more than tenfold (108 percent). The black population in Michigan grew 182 percent. In terms of numbers, New York, Illinois, New Jersey, and Pennsylvania were the biggest recipients of black migrants.

Urban areas with more than 100,000 population got the heaviest concentration of blacks. Of these, seven cities had black populations of more than 100,000 by the end of the 1920s, and four of these—all in the North: New York, Chicago, Detroit, and Philadelphia—showed the greatest population gains.[19] Blacks moved into New York City at a rate that amounted to an increase of 114 percent by the end of the decade, most of them jammed into Harlem, almost five times more densely populated in 1930 than it was when it was considered crowded ten years before.[20] Growth was similar in Chicago (113 percent), Detroit (194 percent), and Philadelphia (64 percent).[21] Westward migration flowed principally to Los Angeles, where the increase over the decade was 150 percent.[22]

At the same time the blacks were moving into the North, southern cities were showing the effects, both with black population declines and net losses. As the 1930 census clearly stated: "In almost every Southern City the proportion of Negroes to the total population has been decreasing while in the Northern cities the proportion has been increasing."[23]

Characteristics of migrants

The characteristics of the participants in the Great Migration varied somewhat from one year to the next and one locale to the other. In 1916 and 1917, for example, the majority of the newcomers appear to have been men, particularly younger, detached men without families or other responsibilities. Census figures for 1920 show the largest number of black urban residents were between the ages of 25 and 29, but by 1930 the age grouping had shifted and the largest number were between 20 and 24.[24] This drop in age can be attributed at least partially to migration. Being prone to move in search of opportunity, this younger age group, like their older brothers and sisters, saw the chance to change their lot. Another group consisted of a large number of single women, detached from their families, and attracted by the potential job opportunities in domestic service. These two groups were followed by a third type—the laboring man, unskilled or semiskilled. These men frequently brought their families or sent for them as soon as they could find employment. Some of the migrants were from broken families. Widows and divorced women with children or grandchildren were attracted by the opportunities for public school education for the children and wages from domestic jobs. In addition, the aged relatives of earlier migrants also frequently followed to join their children in the North.[25]

The areas from which the majority of the migrants came were predominantly rural, characterized by a system of tenant farming. For example, in 1920 three out of every four black farmers were either croppers, share tenants, or cash tenants. These tenant farmers usually were scattered widely over large areas, living in small cabins with little more than a lean-to kitchen and a room or two. Their income ranged from fifty cents to one dollar a day. The majority of the public schools, which were generally ungraded, were conducted from three to six months per year; the teachers were poorly paid and often poorly trained; and facilities commonly consisted of ramshackle buildings or churches with little or no teaching equipment.[26]

The experiences of migrants from small towns and cities differed little from those from the rural areas. The schools sometimes had better facilities, a longer school term, and teachers with slightly better pay and better training. A majority of the blacks in towns and cities also enjoyed somewhat better housing than those from the farms. Even a few black families were reported to have had homes that compared favorably with the better white families.[27]

The migrants were not solely from the unskilled and semiskilled occupations. An article in the Birmingham *Age-Herald* noted:

> It is not the riffraff of the race, the worthless Negroes, who are leaving in such large numbers. There are, to be sure, many poor Negroes among them who have little more than the clothes on their backs, but others have property and good positions which they are sacrificing in order to get away at the first opportunity. The entire Negro population of the South seems to be deeply affected.[28]

One observer wrote that even "Negro professional men moved North to continue to serve their clientele."[29]

Causes of migration

Few migrations are precipitated or caused by a single, isolated factor acting singularly upon the person or persons involved. The factors giving rise to the uprooting and resettling of the nearly half million southern blacks were likewise numerous and complexly interrelated. Not all students of migrations agree as to the nature of the causes, or which ones deserve the most attention. Moreover, any interpretation of the Great Migration must address itself to the question, why did the volume of black migration to the North grow so rapidly and to such proportions just at the time it did? Indeed, the sudden increase in the migration rate poses important substantive, as well as theoretical, questions, especially in view of the fact that it was not until 50 years after the Civil War when greater freedom of migration was possible that northward migration became a mass social movement. Such an explanation of the volume and suddenness with which the migration occurred involves assessing conditions that encourage or discourage out-migration from the South as well as foster or retard in-migration to the North.

Although blacks living throughout the South had ample reason to leave the region prior to World War I, relatively few did so. The ties of family and home were strong and exercised a "natural restraining influence."[30] But more important than the ties of home was the lack of opportunity for blacks to earn a living outside southern agriculture. As country after country was drawn into the war, the tide of European migration was reversed abruptly. Foreign-born men working in New York, Philadelphia, Chicago, Cleveland, Detroit, and other industrial cities returned to their homeland and left thousands of unfilled jobs.[31]

Another point of view was that before 1915 there was an "existing and widening difference in living conditions between South and North which did not express itself in a mass migration simply because the latter did not get a start and become a pattern."[32] Thus, the conditions were becoming increasingly conducive to migration. There was the push in the South and pull in the North. The absence of any major migration was due to the lack of a precipitating event. World War I was such an event.

Broadly conceived, the conditions producing the migration were economic and social. Although the debate continues as to which was the more powerful motive for migration among blacks, the migration during World War I generally is viewed as being economically motivated. It should not be assumed that, having explained the factors and conditions that produced the migration, an accurate picture has been given of the actual motivation of the individuals moved.[33] According to one argument, in nearly all migrations there are countless factors that hold people within an area or attract people to it, and there are other factors that tend to repel them. Some of these factors affect people in much the same way, while others affect people differently. It is not only the actual factors at origin and destination but also the perception of these factors that results in migration.[34]

A chief motive for migrating to the North was unquestionably the desire for economic improvement. One observer at the time of the migration stated that "the fundamental and immediate cause of this Negro exodus is economic."[35] Specific job opportunities were announced throughout the South by letters, labor agents, and newspaper advertisements. Black publications, particularly the *Chicago Defender* with its large readership outside Chicago, spread the news of job opportunities. In its news columns, help-wanted ads, and editorial pages, the *Defender* urged migration to the North:

[December 1, 1917]
Rochester, N.Y., February 10—the State Employment Bureau hopes to effect a partial amelioration of the domestic problem by cooperating with Rev. L. B. Brown, pastor of Olive Baptist Church, to bring about 75 here from the south to take places in households, which it has been found next to impossible to fill. Seventy-five women are wanted here from 18 to 30 years old. Part of their fare will be paid. Women workers are in great demand. Such places are open; shirt makers, bindery workers, laundry workers, weavers, pastry cooks, children's nurses and laundresses.

[February 10, 1917]
The Defender invites all to come north. Plenty of room for the good, sober, industrious man. Plenty of work. For those who will not work, the jails will take care of you. When you have served your 90 days at hard labor you will then have learned how to work. Anywhere in God's country is far better than the Southland. Hensen was with Perry [*sic*] white at the north pole. No pneumonia there. He still enjoys life in Brooklyn, N.Y. Don't let the crackers fool you. Come join the ranks of the free. Cast the yoke from around your neck. See the light. When you have crossed the Ohio river, breathe the fresh air and say, "Why didn't I come before?"[36]

The help-wanted advertisements found their way into the hands of thousands of willing workers, many of whom left immediately for the North. Others lacked the money for fare or needed more assurance of a job. Although a large proportion of those who went north left home precipitously, many planned carefully before setting out on such a long and important journey. Some turned to the *Defender* with letters that inquired about these prospects—and that told the story, in human terms, of the Great Migration:

Port Arthur, Texas, 5/5th/17
    Dear Sir: Permitt me to inform you that I have had the pleasure of reading the Defender for the first time in my life as I never dreamed that there was such a race paper published and I must say that its some paper.
    However, I can unhesitatingly say that it is extraordinarily interest-

ing and had I known that there was such a paper in my town or such being handled in my vicinity I would have been a subscriber years ago.

Nevertheless I read every space of the paper dated April 28th which is my first and only paper at present. Although I am greatfully anticipating the pleasure of receiving my next Defender as I now consider myself a full fledged defender fan and I have also requested the representative of said paper to deliver my Defender weekly.

In reading the Defenders want ad I notice that there is lots of work to be had and if I havent miscomprehended I think I also understand that the transportation is advanced to able bodied working men who is out of work and desire work. Am I not right? With the understanding that those who have been advanced transportation same will be deducted from their salary after they have begun work. Now then if this is their proposition I have about 10 or 15 good working men who is out of work and are dying to leave the south and I assure you that they are working men and will be too glad to come north east or west, any where but the south.

Now then if this is the proposition kindly let me know by return mail. However I assure you that it shall be my pleasure to furnish you with further or all information that you may undertake to ask or all information necessary concerning this communication.

Dapne, Ala., 4/20/17.

Sir: I am writing to let you know that there is 15 or 20 families wants to come up there at once but cant come on account of money to come with and we cant phone you here we will be killed and they dont want us to leave here & say if we dont go to war and fight for our country they are going to kill us and wants to get away if we can if you send 20 passes there is no doubt that every one of us will com at once. We are not doing any thing here we cant get a living out of what we do now some of these people are farmers and som are cooks barbers and blacksmiths but the greater are farmers & good worker & honest people & up to date the trash pile dont want to go no where These are nice people and respectable find a place like that & send passes & we will all come at once we all wants to leave here out of this hard luck place if you cant use as find some place that does need this kind of people we are called Negroes here. I am a reader of the Defender and am delighted to know how times are there & was to glad to, know if we could get some one to pass us away from here to a better land. We work but cant get scarcely any thing for it & they don't want us to go away & there is not much of anything here to do & nothing for it Please find some one that need this kind of a people & send at once for us. We dont want anything but our wareing and bed clothes & have not got no money to get away from here with & beging to get away before we are killed and hope to here from you at once. We can't talk to you over the phone here we are afraid to they dont want to hear one say that he or she wants to leave here if we do we are apt to be killed. They say if we dont go to war they are not going to let us stay here with their folks and it is not any thing that we have done to them. We are law abiding people want to treat every bordy right. These people wants to leave here but we cant we are here and have nothing to go with if you will send us some way to get away from here we will work tell we pay it all if it takes that for us to go or get away. Now get bust for the south race. The conditions are horrible here with us. They wont guve us anything to do & say that we wont need anything but something to eat & wont give us anything for what we do & wants us to stay here. Write me at once that you will do for us we want an opportunity that all we wants is to show you that we can do and will do if we can find some place. We wants to leave here for a north drive somewhere. We see starvation ahead of us here. We want to imigrate to the farmers who need our labor. We have not had no chance to have anything here thats why we plead to you for help to leave here to the North. We are humane but we are not treated such we are treated like brute by our whites here we dont have no privilige no where in the south. We must take anything they put on us. Its hard if its fair. We have got no cotegous diseases here. We are looking to here from you soon.[37]

As each wave of migrants arrived at their northern destination, they wrote the folks back home telling them of their experiences and how wonderful it was in the North. Armed with firsthand reports from trusted friends and relatives, another contingency of migrants frequently set out for the "promised land."

Just as World War I accelerated black migration to the urban North, postwar prosperity with its consequent heightened expectations further encouraged migration in the 1920s. A large influx of black people thus created a political, economic, and cultural base for development of the black bourgeois. White America had to recognize blacks as more than racial "non-persons." By the 1920s, the average black in the urban North was "working class"—semiskilled at best and unskilled at worst. Men were porters, waiters, messengers, elevator operators, and janitors.[38] Women, in the slight majority in the North, were predominantely employed as domestics. In 1925, for example, 60 percent of New York's black female population were employed as either laundresses or servants.[39] Chances for social and economic advancement were limited, since most labor unions systematically blocked black membership. Among the few that did not were the longshoremen and the International Ladies Garment Workers: in 1925 five thousand blacks were members of the longshoremen's union in New York City, compared to only 56 black apprentices in 1920 among almost 10,000 apprenticeships in the skilled trades unions.[40]

It was not until the New Deal era that the unskilled gained leverage with employers. The best example of this is A. Philip Randolph's Brotherhood of Sleeping Car Porters, which was founded in the 1920s but did not receive full recognition by the Pullman Company until 1937.[41]

Antagonism on the part of ethnic whites in the North greeted the large number of blacks moving into the cities. Prejudice and fear of mixed neighborhoods sparked a summer of riots in 1919. The most violent outbreak was in Chicago, where 13 days of violence left 15 white and 23 black fatalities and almost a thousand families homeless.[42] Gangs of young white and black toughs provoked further violence.

The dramatic nature of the urban change was drawn into focus by the sudden shift of whole neighborhoods. An article on Harlem described it vividly:

> Then the whole movement in the eyes of whites took on the aspect of an "invasion"; they became panic stricken and began fleeing as from a plague. The presence of one colored family in a block no matter how well bred and orderly was sufficient to precipitate a flight. House after house and block after block was actually deserted. It was a great demonstration of human beings running amuck. None of them stopped to reason why they were doing it or what would happen if they didn't.[43]

Before the Great Migration, blacks had to beg for rooms in Harlem, at the time a predominantly middle- to upper-middle-class district.[44] By 1925 blacks and whites regarded Harlem as the center of the "New Negro" black culture movement.[45]

The major social reasons that contributed to general dissatisfaction with the South mostly remained constant from the period before the Great Migration through the 1920s: injustice in the courts, denial of voting rights, discrimination in public conveyances, inequalities in the separated educational systems, marginal living conditions and racial violence, including lynching.[46] Justice was too often illusory after the Civil War and Reconstruction, and gross inequalities dictated the image, if not the reality, of the courts. When a white man assaulted a black person, he was seldom punished. The reverse was only rarely, if ever, true. Black witnesses counted for little or nothing in most southern courts, except when testifying against blacks. On the other hand, the testimony of a white person was conclusive against blacks in most instances.[47]

Racial violence on the part of both southern officials and the Ku Klux Klan became factors so important in out-migration that the effects on the southern labor force were evident. As one southern newspaper commented (as quoted by the Chicago Commission of Race Relations in its investigation of the social factors contributing to the mass migration of blacks to Chicago):

While our very solvency is being sucked out from underneath we go out about affairs as usual—our police officers raid poolrooms for "loafing Negroes," bring in twelve, keep them in the barracks all night, and next morning find that many of them have steady jobs, valuable assets to their white employers, suddenly left and gone to Cleveland, "where they don't arrest fifty niggers for what three of 'em done."[48]

Both blacks and whites mentioned lynching as one of the most important causes of the out-migration of blacks from the South during World War I. Migrants from Florida mentioned the lynchings that had occurred in Tennessee as their reason for moving north. The white press in Georgia maintained that lynchings were driving blacks away from the state in large numbers. The Chicago Urban League reported that many migrants from towns where lynchings had occurred registered for jobs in Chicago very shortly thereafter.[49] It is also noteworthy that a study of the northward migration of blacks from 1916 through 1918 indicated that mistreatment by police resulted in almost as many persons leaving the South as did lynchings; whereas lynchings were more or less sporadic, mistreatment by authorities was a problem that all blacks had to bear continually and from which they were anxious to escape.[50]

Denial of suffrage for blacks in many areas of the South was achieved both through legal statute and social pressure. Several state legislatures in the South passed literacy tests and "grandfather clauses," which effectively eliminated a large sector of the black vote. Those votes the legal process failed to suppress, social pressure and mob violence often did. Many black workers employed by whites were "too smart" to be seen around the polls on election day. "Jim Crow" train cars were separated; inferior waiting facilities of public transportation systems likewise were viewed as white expressions of contempt for the black communities. Segregated schools with disproportionately lower fiscal allotments for the black institutions resulted in inadequate plant facilities and frequently poor instruction. Such arrangements were viewed by many as the major factor creating and ensuring prolonged inequality in the South. The belief was widespread among most black parents that without quality education the hope of future generations was little more than illusory.

Since leaving the South had become easier than trying to change it, migration became the immediate solution to the many pressing social problems of southern blacks. Although there is little doubt that oppression played a significant role in motivating blacks to move, the fact that there were similar patterns in white migration suggests that migration was motivated more by economic considerations than by social injustice. Compared with blacks, whites had a slightly higher mobility rate going largely to the North and West. Until 1915, one of the major directions of black migration had been south and west. Thus, it is argued that if racial oppression had been a major cause of the migration, it would appear that there would have been appreciably more blacks moving than whites, and that the direction would not have been south and west, but north.

Of course such arguments overlook the fact that, despite the relatively more desirable social system in the North, the labor market was being amply supplied by European immigrants before 1915. There were simply no occupational opportunities for the blacks in the North until the European immigration was reduced. The fact that blacks did not go north does not mean that oppression was not a factor in the motivation of the migrants when they relocated within the South. The image of the North as a desirable place for blacks likewise had been tarnished by the growth of the Ku Klux Klan, restrictive covenants, racial zoning, and other manifestations of discrimination in the North. It was not until newspapers, labor agents, and blacks already living in the North began to extol the superiority of the northern cities over the caste system of the South that the North once again acquired the promised-land image it had during the slave era. Others have argued that the social factors were important but did not enter the motivational structure of the migrants until after the migration was underway. After the movement started, there was substantial discussion among blacks throughout the South centering on various social grievances.[51]

Perhaps a more realistic approach to the question of relative significance of the various motivating forces is the view that the social *and* economic factors are interrelated, manifesting the values upon which the social order of the South was based. Both the economic and the social problems of blacks in the South and elsewhere were the result of the philosophy of white superiority. The black migrant was motivated primarily by the desire to escape the caste-like social system of the South with all of its economic and social manifestations. Until the war, the problem was that there was no place for him to go that would substantially change his situation, and if there had been, there was no realistic way to get there. But this situation was changed with the sudden reversal of the supply and demand for labor in the North, which created a place to go as well as a way to get there. The demand for labor, together with the railroad companies working jointly with industry to provide transportation, offered the black southerners a way to achieve their desire of freedom and social advancement.

There were other versions of the causes of the migration. Many southerners blamed the exodus on a Republican political conspiracy; others claimed it was the work of the United States Department of Labor. W. H. Crawford, the chairman of the Committee on Naval Stores, advocated that German propaganda induced blacks to leave in order to reduce the supply of American cotton. An editorial in the *New York Times* even speculated on possible Bolshevist causes for the migration as well as the riots.[52]

In many respects, the migration took on the character of a mass movement. As such, it has been described as having "created a sort of . . . suction which drew others along."[53] A Department of Labor report characterized the migration in the following manner:

> The unusual amounts of money coming in, the glowing accounts from the North, and the excitement and stir of great crowds leaving, work upon the feelings of most Negroes. They pull up and follow almost without a reason. They are stampeded into action. This accounts in large part for the apparently unreasonable doings of many who give up good positions or sacrifice valuable property or good businesses to go North.[54]

The "milling" effect of the discussions is apparent from many of the reports describing southern communities during the period of heavy out-migration. For example:

> One of the chief stimuli was discussion. The very fact that Negroes were leaving in large numbers was a disturbing factor. The talk in the barber shops and grocery stores where men were wont to assemble soon began to take the form of reasons for leaving. There it was the custom to review all the instances of mistreatment and injustice which fell to the lot of the Negro in the South. It was here also that letters from the North were read and fresh news on the exodus was first given out. In Hattiesburg, Mississippi, it was stated that for a while there was no subject of discussion but the migration.[55]

In addition to milling, characterized by excited discussions, social contagion was enhanced by the circulation of rumors. In the absence of verifiable information needed to provide the basis in decision-making, "improvised news"—rumors—often substituted credibly:

> When a community is wrought up, it is less difficult to believe remarkable tales. To persons beyond the influence of this excitement it is somewhat difficult to conceive how the rumor that the Germans were on their way through Texas to take the southern states could have been believed. And yet it is reported that this extravagant fiction was taken seriously in some quarters. The rumor gained circulation that the Indians were coming back to retake their land lost years ago. It was further rumored that the United States Government was beginning a scheme to transport all Negroes from the South to break up the Black Belt. Passed from mouth to mouth, unrestrainedly, these reports became verities.[56]

With the transmission of each rumor, additional support for leaving the South was created.

One aspect of the migration that distinguished it from some of the earlier migration was its lack of leadership. The Great Migration did not have a leader of the stature of "Pap" Singleton or Henry Adams as did the Kansas Exodus. Rather, the migration of 1916–1918 was a leaderless mass movement.[57] From the reaction of the white South and its attitude toward the migration, it was readily apparent that anyone who openly encouraged the exodus would have been in serious personal danger. There were, however, some who did venture their support of the migration, but in most cases, they were quickly silenced. One such case was a Methodist minister who was sent to jail because he was said to have been enticing laborers to go north and work for a New York firm that would give jobs to 50 of his congregation.

Other efforts to control the out-migration took the form of laws. Various state and local governments in the South attempted to prevent the "labor raids" by enacting legislation providing for fines and imprisonment for anyone convicted of enticing, persuading, or influencing any laborer to leave his home area for employment at any other place.[58] Such activity on the part of labor agents required a license in most southern states, counties, and cities. For example, Alabama required a licensing fee of $500 for the state plus $250 for each county. Moreover, Birmingham required an additional $500 license and nearby Bessemer required a $300 license. Even with licenses costing over $1,000, Birmingham had at least four licensed labor agents and Bessemer had three between June 1916 and July 1917.[59]

The aftermath

Disillusion about the promise of the North set in shortly after the war and during the 1920s, especially among the poor. Attempts to cope with city life ended in frustration—frustration that surfaced in a black nationalist movement. Known popularly as the "Back to Africa" movement, it was headed by a young West Indian, Marcus Garvey, who attracted a large following before his conviction for mail fraud in 1925. Garvey was neglected until recently as an important figure in the history of black nationalism.[60]

A greater influence on middle-class blacks was the "New Negro" movement, although there was disagreement about what a "New Negro" was. The models were largely the result of ideals of black pride established by white and black intellectuals. Still, the movement sparked the Harlem Renaissance, an outpouring of black culture financed by wealthy whites who considered themselves patrons of the arts. It was through their help that black writers like Langston Hughes, Countee Cullen, and Claude McKay were able to publish. Although they reflected the black experience, these authors used the conventional models of the white culture around them.[61]

To most Americans it was black music that had the greatest impact. Jazz went from brothels in New Orleans to New York's Aeolian Hall and the upper class via George Gershwin and Paul Whiteman.[62] The appeal of Harlem to whites who went "slumming" were the black cabarets that flourished and folded. Most important of these night clubs was the Cotton Club where Duke Ellington got his start in 1926.

Yet the foundation of black prosperity was fragile, more so than for whites, and when the economy faltered in the late 1920s the underpinnings of black economic progress came undone. "Last hired, first fired" became a brutal economic fact of life familiar to black people as industry cut back. When the rich likewise cut their household expenses, the black servants were first to go.[63] Black businesses, marginal at best and hardly supported by the capital base typical of white businesses, were mostly service-oriented, and when faced with a shrinking economy in their communities they could not pay their mortgages.

The black cultural movement contracted as white patrons were forced to cut off their support for black writers and artists. Black cabarets closed and did not reopen. With the end of black prosperity and the black pride movements, blacks had to put aside the dreams of Langston Hughes' poem, "I Too"

> I too sing America
> I am the darker brother
> They send me to eat in the Kitchen
> When company comes
> But I laugh
> And eat well
> And grow strong
>
> Tomorrow
> I'll sit at the table
> Nobody'll dare
> Say to me
> "Eat in the kitchen"
> Then
> Besides they'll see how
> Beautifull I am
> And be ashamed—
> I too am America

Hughes' "tomorrow" was delayed thirty years.

7. The depression years

For the student of migration, the decade of the 1930s represents an anomalous period in the nation's demographic history. Many of the prevailing population movements and patterns were altered—some slightly, others radically—by the depressed economy and disrupted social structure. Profound changes in the national economy brought about equally profound changes in the national temper and life style. The nation's quest for material success that characterized the Roaring Twenties gave way to a struggle for survival in the 1930s.

Well over half the present population were born late enough to have no memories of the Great Depression. Stereotypical images of what has been called the "greatest economic calamity in the nation's history"[1] persist, and like most stereotypes, contain elements of truth. Many farmers from Kansas and Oklahoma whose soil had dried and blown across the plains by storms during the Dustbowl did strike out for California, like the Joads in John Steinbeck's *The Grapes of Wrath*. Some stockbrokers did commit suicide by jumping from the windows of Wall Street skyscrapers. Soup lines, hobos, and the unemployed were familiar sights in most of the nation's cities. It is interesting to note that few of the stereotypes of the Great Depression reflect the conditions of life among the nation's black population. Perhaps even more significant is the general paucity of research and information about blacks during this period in America's history.[2]

The central questions of this chapter attempt to address some of those stereotypical and informational gaps, particularly as they relate to the questions of population distribution and change. For example, how did the migration patterns of blacks during the 1930s differ from those of earlier periods? What were the major factors contributing to mobility and stability among blacks? How did the migratory patterns of the black population differ from the white segment during the depression? And, what were some of the more significant consequences of black migration during the thirties? Any understanding of the social and demographic processes of this period requires at least a brief overview of the nation's economy.

A profile of the depression

Prior to the Great Depression, the United States was described as "the richest nation in the world; the richest in all history."[3] The nation could boast that its 122 million people had more real wealth and real income per capita and in total than the people of any other country, despite the conspicuous poverty of the black population and other minorities. The nation's endowment of vast natural resources, its growing stock of capital

goods, its advanced technology, and the quality of its labor force contributed to the belief held by most Americans that the growth potential of the
economy was more than promising and would be achieved indefinitely
without serious interruptions.[4]

From the summer of 1929, however, economic indicators revealed a
sharp deterioration in the nation's economic health, and by October the
depression had begun, signaled by the crash of the stockmarket late in the
month. The year following the crash witnessed continued deterioration of
economic conditions. The leading economic indicators dropped even more
steeply in 1931 and 1932, but the worst was yet to come. Using the gross
national product (GNP) as a measure of real output valued at constant
prices, the extent of economic decline from 1919 to 1932 was nearly 30
percent; by 1933, the decline was even slightly larger.

The lowest point in the depression occurred between President Herbert
Hoover's defeat for reelection in November 1932 and Franklin D. Roosevelt's inauguration on March 4, 1933. It has been argued that during those
four months "capitalism almost failed."[5] To characterize capitalism as a fail-

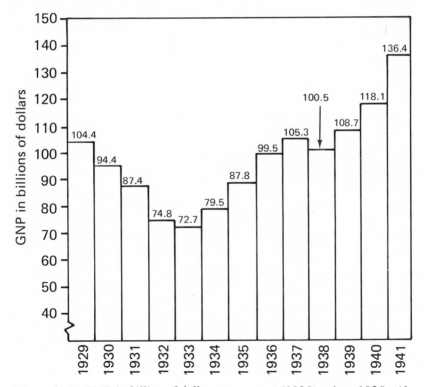

Figure 7-1. GNP in billion of dollars as constant (1929) prices, 1929–41.
SOURCE: Lester V. Chandler, *America's Greatest Depression, 1929–1941* (New York:
Harper & Row, Publishers, 1970), p. 3.

ure only during those four months, however, overlooks the almost total exclusion of black Americans from the capital system since the founding of the Republic. Insofar as the black population is concerned, it would be misleading to argue that American capitalism was a "success" or "failure."

Perhaps the best index of national economic privation is unemployment.[6] Estimates of the average levels of unemployment during the depression years are presented in Table 7-1. In 1929, there were 1.5 million employed workers in the United States, or 3.2 percent of the labor force. The following year the number of unemployed increased to 4.3 million, or 8.7 percent of the nation's labor force. During the two worst years, 1932 and 1933, the number of totally unemployed was more than 12 million each year with an average unemployment rate in excess of 24 percent.[7]

Estimates of unemployment differed, however, reflecting the varied interests of the economy. For example, the National Industrial Conference Board, which represented the business community, places unemployment in 1933 at 11.8 million. The American Federation of Labor (AFL) reported it as 13.2 million. The left-wing Labor Research Association placed the figure at 16.1 million. It will never be known which, if any, of these statistics was correct.[8]

Economic recovery, as reflected in unemployment rates, was slow in coming. In four years following the bottom of the depression (1933), unemployment rates declined from nearly 25 percent to 14.3 percent in 1937. In the spring of 1937 the economy lapsed into a sharp recession that lasted into 1938 and that again brought a return to excessively high rates of unemployment. It was not until 1941 that the number of unemployed fell

Table 7–1. Labor force—employed and unemployed in the United States, 1929–41 (number in millions)

Year	Labor force	Employed	Unemployed	
			Number	Percent of labor force
1929	49.180	47.630	1.550	3.2
1930	49.820	45.480	4.340	8.7
1931	50.420	42.400	8.020	15.9
1932	51.000	38.940	12.060	23.6
1933	51.590	38.760	12.830	24.9
1934	52.230	40.890	11.340	21.7
1935	52.870	42.260	10.610	20.1
1936	53.440	44.410	9.030	16.9
1937	54.000	46.300	7.700	14.3
1938	54.610	44.220	10,390	19.0
1939	55.230	45.750	9.480	17.2
1940	55.640	47.520	8.120	14.6
1941	55.910	50.350	5.560	9.9

SOURCE: U.S., Department of Commerce, *Historical Statistics of the United States* (Washington, D.C.: Government Printing Office, 1960), p. 70.

below 7.7 million, or in which the average unemployment rate declined below 14.3 percent.Even with the expanding economy prompted by the rearmament program, the average number of unemployed in 1941 was still over 5.5 million, with an unemployment rate of 9.9 percent.[9]

Despite the geographical, occupational, and social pervasiveness of unemployment during the depression, it was also highly uneven in its impact. Particularly hard hit were the young, elderly, and black people. Those who have studied the depression are generally agreed that the economic effects on the black population were more severe than they were on any other group.[10]

Surveys in several cities in early 1931 found that the incidence of unemployment of negroes was far above that for whites. . . . Another survey relating to the same period revealed appallingly high unemployment rates among negro women in cities with generally high unemployment rates. Some of the reported rates are highly credible . . . unemployment rates in Massachusetts in January 1934 were 32 percent for negroes and 19 percent for whites. These include only those totally unemployed. When the partially unemployed and those with only temporary employment on government projects are included, the rates become 50 percent for negroes and 34 percent for whites. In 1937, unemployment rates were 23.2 percent for negroes and 15.7 percent for whites.[11]

The magnitude of the economic stress experienced by blacks is masked partially by the fact that a large proportion were engaged in agricultural jobs and the figures cited above tell us nothing about farmers. For example, in 1920 there were 1.5 million black male workers in agriculture, and despite the urbanization of the 1920s the number decreased only slightly to 1.49 million by 1930.[12] Moreover, the majority—97 percent—of these workers were in the South.[13]

A study of the effects of the depression concluded that the hardest hit of all was the southern black sharecropper.

Already in bad shape because of boll weevil ravages and low cotton prices during the 1920's, Negro sharecroppers—indeed, sharecroppers in general—were reduced to starvation level by the further drop in farm prices. Often the money that sharecroppers received for their cotton crops was insufficient to pay the bill they had run up at the local store for "furnish." Cotton-farming conditions improved somewhat with the AAA, but often landlords used their government checks to buy tractors and stopped the sharecropping system. Then there was nothing for the Negro sharecropper to do but to move into an urban slum, from which he frequently commuted to the cotton fields as a day laborer during the picking season.[14]

Place of residence of blacks: 1920–1940

The year 1920 was a turning point in the nation's history since it was the first time that a majority of Americans were recorded as living in urban places. However, blacks and whites differed significantly in their rural-urban distribution. In 1920, nearly 54 percent of the nation's whites resided in urban places compared to only one-third of the nation's total black population. The rate of urbanization increased more rapidly for blacks during the 1920s, bringing the percent of blacks living in urban places to nearly 44 percent, while the percent of whites increased to 58 percent. The 1930s witnessed a slight decrease in the nation's proportion of urban whites; although urbanization continued among blacks during the depression years bringing the percentage of blacks living in urban places to 48.

Regional differences in the rural-urban character of whites and blacks were clearly visible during the 1920s and 1930s. The major differences followed the historic South and nonsouth patterns. For example, only one-fourth of southern blacks lived in urban places in 1920. The movement to southern cities continued, and by 1930, nearly 32 percent of the southern blacks lived in urban places. Despite national trends for the total population to the contrary, southern blacks continued their move to the region's cities during the depression years. By 1940, 36 percent of the South's black population lived in urban places. This movement reflected the dismal social and economic conditions in which the rural blacks were forced to live.

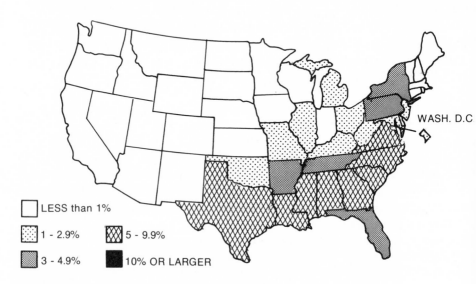

Figure 7-2. *Distribution of black population, 1930 (percent by state).*
Source: U.S., Department of Commerce, Bureau of the Census, *Statistical Abstract of the Unit*
States, 1947 (Washington, D.C.: Government Printing Office, 1947), Table 19, p. 20.

During this decade many southern landlords abolished sharecropping and forced many families either to become day laborers and/or move off the farm.

Blacks living in regions outside the South had been predominantly urban since 1880. Movement and migration intensified the urban character of nonsouth blacks until by 1920 nearly 87 percent of the Northeast's black population was urban. In the North Central region, 83 percent of the black population lived in urban places and 74 percent lived in urban places in the West. Nonsouth whites were far less urbanized than blacks in 1920, as they would be in each successive decade. By 1940 over 90 percent of blacks living in the Northeast were urban compared to 76 percent of their white counterparts. In the North Central region only 57 percent of the white population lived in urban places, in contrast to 89 percent of the region's blacks. Likewise, in the West the proportion of urban blacks was significantly greater than that of their white counterparts.

Extent of migration: 1930–1940

Prior to the publication of the 1940 census, many experts had believed that the northward migration of blacks had diminished considerably. However, the results of this census, which provided much greater detail about migration than previous censuses, indicated that migration had continued during the depression. It was not as extensive during the 1930s as it had been from 1915 to 1930, but the remarkable thing is that it kept on despite the lack of employment opportunities in the North.[15]

In the five years, 1935–1940, 8.15 percent (1.1 million) of the nation's blacks migrated to a different part of the country. Whites tended to be more geographically mobile, 12.3 percent moving during the same period. The vast majority of the migrating blacks came from rural farms (380,501) and urban areas of less than 100,000 population (280,805). Destinations were predominantly urban areas; however, rural farm destinations were common for large numbers of blacks on the move (374,137) as were rural nonfarms (265,761).

While the predominant character of black migration during the early decades of the century was rural-to-urban, by 1940 more than half (58 percent) the migrants living in urban areas had come from other urban areas. Forty-two percent of the urban-to-urban migrants came from cities with populations exceeding 100,000.

Migration to rural areas constituted an important part of the total pattern of black mobility during the late 1930s. Those moving to rural nonfarms came largely from urban origins (45 percent) while migrants to rural farm destinations were largely from rural farm origins (60 percent). Conversely, nearly one-fifth of the migrants (17 percent), or 64,900, living in rural farm destinations in 1940 had lived in urban areas in 1935.

Black migration during the latter half of the 1930s was characteristically selective of the popular urban industrial states of New York, New Jersey, Maryland, Pennsylvania, Ohio, Michigan, and Illinois. In addition to these urban industrial states, Florida and California attracted migrants. New York had the largest net black in-migration for the five-year period (25,400) followed by Florida (24,400) and California (20,000). Michigan (16,100), Illinois (9,300), and Ohio (8,500) also experienced relatively high black net in-migration during the prewar years.

The heaviest black net out-migration during this period was from southern agricultural states: Georgia (−30,800), Alabama (−26,400), and South Carolina (−24,100) experienced the largest net loss due to out-migration. Likewise, Mississippi (−17,900), North Carolina (−9,900), and Arkansas (−9,700) witnessed relatively heavy black out-migration.

More than one-third of the states experienced little net change in black population due to migration during the latter half of the 1930s. These states were primarily located in New England, the West North Central, Mountain, and Pacific Coast areas.

Among the nation's larger cities, i.e., those with 100,000 or more population in 1940, seventeen experienced a net black in-migration of 500 or more during the 1935–1940 period. New York City had the largest net increase (10,600) while Los Angeles (7,400) and Washington, D.C., (7,400) tied with the second largest black net in-migration of the major cities. Detroit and Indianapolis were also attractive to blacks during the prewar years each with a net in-migration between 1935 and 1940 of 1,600, but were surpassed by such cities as Baltimore (2,200) and Miami (1,900). Not all metropolitan destinations for blacks on the move, however, were located in the North: Baltimore, Chattanooga, Dallas, Houston, Memphis, and Miami experienced substantial black in-migration during the prewar period.

Twelve cities with populations of 100,000 or more in 1940 had a net black out-migration of 500 or more during the 1935–1940 period. Atlanta experienced the largest net out-migration (−3,250) followed by New Orleans (−2,600). Despite the attractiveness of southern California, West Coast cities were not uniformly popular to blacks. For example, Seattle experienced a net black out-migration of 719 for the five-year period. Other major nonsouthern cities lost blacks through net out-migration including Boston (−533) and St. Louis (−964). Despite examples to the contrary, the vast majority of cities experiencing net out-migration in the prewar years were in the South.

Earlier discussions have noted the fact that many popular destination cities in terms of net black in-migration were also places that had considerable out-migration. The greater depth in the 1940 census provided more detailed information about streams of migration. New York City, among others, was characterized by substantial out-migration during the prewar years. In that period, 1935–1940, nearly 20,000 blacks migrated to all parts of the nation. The largest proportion of the city's out-migrants (41 percent) remained in the state, while nearly one-third (29 percent) sought destinations in the South. Despite the great distance and difficulty of travel during the 1930s, nearly 4 percent of those leaving New York City went to California.

Considerable out-migration from Chicago occurred during the same period. Between 1935 and 1940, 12,100 blacks left the city that had earlier been hailed as the "Mecca of the North." The largest proportion of Chicago's out-migrants (29 percent) moved to places in Illinois. Eleven percent went to nearby Michigan, and 6 percent sought destinations in New York. The attractiveness of the South is evidenced by the fact that nearly one-fourth (23 percent) of Chicago's out-migrants moved to that region. Mississippi was the most attractive of the southern states for the ex-Chicagoans. Southern destinations were fairly evenly divided between rural and urban areas.

Causes of migration

Demographers and other students of migration have shown that people tend to migrate to improve their economic condition. To what extent did this motive affect black migration during the depression? Unfortunately, there were no empirical studies that permit comparisons of predepression, depression, and postdepression motives. As in the case of earlier migrations, the sizable movement of blacks off southern farms and into the cities of the South and other regions, the smaller movement out of northern cities to other metropolitan areas, and the return of some to the cities and farms of the South was not due to one single cause or motive, but to a combination of factors. Many of the causes and motives are difficult to evaluate, particularly counterstream movements, whereas others are easier to appraise, at least in a general way.

As in most migration, income differentials, real or imagined, played a major role in the depression; whether these differences had more influence among blacks than whites is not known. Educational opportunities and better medical care in many northern cities or a variety of personal factors may have tipped the balance in many individual cases, although, again, no one can tell precisely how effective such factors were in the decision to migrate.[16]

Fifteen years prior to the depression, the major factors causing the Great Migration were partially evident. The growing war in Europe with the eventual direct involvement of the United States resulted in a seeming unquenchable demand for labor in the factories and plants of northern cities. Clearly, this factor was of little significance during the 1930s when unemployment was the highest in the nation's history.

Economic conditions had become relatively worse for blacks in the South during the depression. Many whites who had lost their jobs or farms began to encroach on blacks in the heavy unskilled occupations and even in the service occupations—traditionally held only by blacks.[17]

What was, perhaps, a factor of major importance in motivating large numbers of people to relocate—black and white—was the greater availability of large-scale public relief in the cities. In the South, sharecroppers in the cotton belt suffered extreme economic privation during this period. Landlords, incapable of financing tenants, were forced to let them go with whatever they had made. Others were simply displaced from the land empty-handed. With no resources of any kind, and accustomed to depending on the landlord for providing basic necessities, "large numbers of tenant families were left stranded, bewildered, and helpless."[18]

Many rural counties throughout the South and other regions of the country had no relief or charitable organizations: in many areas where relief organizations were operative, corruption and discrimination kept large numbers from receiving their fair share—blacks in particular.[19] For many there was no alternative but to go where relief could be obtained. In one analysis of income, consumption, housing and public assistance among blacks during the depression, it was argued that "large-scale public relief in this country seems to provide one of the main explanations why Negroes have continued to move away from the farms during the last decade [the 1930s]."[20]

Migrants in search of economic relief faced numerous problems. Cities, counties, and states generally had residency requirements for eligibility for relief. Many migrants were ignorant of such residency requirements, while others moved despite their knowledge of eligibility rules, with the hope that there would be some way of getting around them.[21]

Social factors in the structure of southern agriculture contributed to the mobility of blacks during the depression as well as in previous periods. The degree of attachment to the land is important in this regard. Thus, the effect of those forces that tend to push an agricultural population off the land is dependent in part on the strength of the population's relationship to the soil. Data from the 1935 *Census of Agriculture* on the number of years spent on a given farm support the hypothesis that there was a relationship between mobility and tenure status. For example, in 1935, more than one-third of the black and nearly one-half of the white sharecroppers had been on their farms less than one year. The percentages for full owners were 5 and 7 percent, respectively. An analysis of the relationship between mobility- and tenure-group blacks show that they tended to stay on their farms somewhat longer than their white counterparts; however, because blacks tended to be concentrated in the lower tenure groups they were somewhat more mobile than whites as a group.[22]

President Roosevelt's attempts with the New Deal to address the problems in agriculture served to intensify the structural conditions that displaced black sharecroppers and wage earners. The Agricultural Adjustment Act (AAA) was adopted to enact programs to increase prices for agricultural products. This was achieved by providing payments to farmers who pledged not to grow a crop on more than an agreed upon portion of their land. Slight congressional attention was given to the programs' adverse effects on the farm workers and sharecroppers. Consequently, participating landowners and landlords had little or no use for tenants or workers. Landless farmers actually lost status as a result of the New Deal's cotton programs. Tenants were pushed off the land while many others were pushed down the tenure ladder from cropper to wagehand. This produced what was described as "a large army of unknown size . . . driven off the cotton lands to swell the legions of unemployed in towns and cities."[23]

Characteristics of migrants

Determining the characteristics of migrants—particularly blacks—during the 1930s is a difficult task. While the "raw" data exist from census enumeration, there was minimal cross-tabulating of black migration data with other socioeconomic information in the census reports. Such basic information as income, occupation, education, housing, etc., can be estimated only on the basis of general characteristics of areas with large migrant populations. At best, this approach can be suggestive of migrant characteristics; there is also the real danger of gross misrepresentation and erroneous generalizations.

The 1940 census does provide information on the sex of migrants for both black and white. These data offer the basis for comparisons and suggest some differences in the character of black and white migration during the latter 1930s. The sex ratio, i.e., the number of males per 100 females, of the total population in 1940 was 100.7. Migrants in both populations were characterized by substantially higher sex ratios than nonmigrants, revealing, in general, the greater propensity of males to move than females. The sex ratio among black nonmigrants was 95.6 compared to 103.9 for migrants.

In addition to differences between migrants and nonmigrants, there were significant variations in the sex ratio among the different types of migrants. For example, for blacks, the proportion of males was highest (109.3) among migrants who moved within a state and lowest (93.3) for migrants between noncontiguous states. Interestingly, the pattern is reversed for white migrants. For whites, the proportion of males is lowest (100.4) among in-state migrants and highest (111.8) among migrants between noncontiguous states. These ratios suggest that long-distance black migrants were more likely to be females while such migrants among whites tended to be males. Black immigrants from United States possessions and foreign countries were predominantly males with a sex ratio of 186.9. Among white immigrants also the number of males exceeded females but not by so wide a margin.

8. World War II

To study black migration, it is necessary to view it in context—chiefly the economic context of the areas involved. In this respect, 1940 was a signal year since significant changes in the southern economy would point to population redistribution of perhaps substantial proportions. Since 1940 the economic structure of the South has been changing at a pace more rapid than that of the rest of the nation.[1] One writer called the war years a "watershed" in recent black history. Certainly, as writers expressed at the time, the war years were a turning point. "There is bound to be," said one, "a redefinition of the Negro's status in America as a result of this war."[2]

Prior to 1940, the American South had the characteristics of an underdeveloped country: predominantly agricultural, with low living standards and wide discrepancies in social benefits. "History aside," wrote one author, "the region was an anomaly: a backward area contained within the borders of one of the most developed nations in the world."[3] But the war was the impetus for change, spurring industrialization and urbanization and bringing evident shifts in southern society.

> Gradually the scope and responsibility of the educational systems have expanded. Political traditions are crumbling, and the monolithic, Democratic South is no longer the deified, or, possibly, even the viable power it once was. Race relations have altered, and, in some respects, the changes have been more substantial in the South than the rest of the country.[4]

The result, then, was the transformation of the region into an integral part of the nation. So the questions are, did these social and economic changes influence the character of black migration and, if so, in what ways? Did the war have any significant impact on the distribution of the black population, particularly those living in the South?

For the nation as a whole the war imposed an obvious effect on population distribution and migration and, more important, on the meaning of migration. Migration in the decade before, in the early and mid-1930s, had been "depression migration," stimulated by sharp unemployment. But migration of the early 1940s was economic "boom" migration, motivated by equally sharp employment gains.

> Whereas in the thirties migration was largely negative—an attempt to escape from known misery—present (1942) migration is largely positive—a move with the expectation of steadier employment, better wages, or the acquisition of higher skill. And, whereas in the thirties migration was viewed with serious concern by the public, today it is received with general public approval.[5]

But a closer analysis of the data available for this period suggests such a description of migration applied only to whites. And not only that, but the characteristics of depression migration survived into the early 1940s for many black migrants. It was not until President Roosevelt issued Executive Order 8802 establishing the Committee on Fair Employment Practices in June 1941 that jobs began to open in defense industries for blacks, causing a turnaround to positive black migration.

The demographic setting

Reflecting national population trends, the black population of the United States grew at a rate during the 1940s that was twice that of the previous decade.[6] By 1950, when the total population showed an increase of 14.5 percent, the black population rose by nearly 17 percent. This was 10 percent of the nation's 150 million people. In 1940, when the national population amounted to 132 million,[7] blacks represented 12.8 million, or 9.8 percent.[8]

The South at the end of the 1940s kept its claim to the greatest share of the nation's black population, 68 percent. But the growth rate for this region was the lowest in the United States, much less than 1 percent a year—hardly comparable to the 12 percent annual increase that was the average for the West. Next came the North Central (4.5 percent), followed by the Northeast (3.9 percent).[9] Despite the rate of increase to the West, this region lagged behind the rest of the nation when it came to the numbers of blacks. Only 4 percent of the blacks were in the West in 1950. Fifteen percent were in the North Central and 13 percent were in the Northeast.[10]

Much of this redistribution of the black population represented the ongoing urbanization characteristic of all segments of American society. But the important difference for blacks was that the process was occurring considerably later than for the population as a whole. Not until after World War II did the number of blacks in urban areas exceed the rural black population—a shift that had been made among whites 30 years before.[11] Still, regional differences were sharp; blacks in the South remained predominantly rural by 1950, but in the North and West combined, 93 percent were urban residents.[12]

Volume of migration

In stark contrast to black migration during World War I when there was large-scale in-migration to northern industrial cities, blacks in the early 1940s comprised only a small proportion of the migration to areas heavy with defense industries.[13] This is one conclusion from a study of migration to 51 defense areas by the Works Progress Administration in October 1941. Of the areas the W.P.A. studied, half received 3 percent or less black in-migrants.[14]

The comprehensive picture drawn from the W.P.A. study showed in-migration to cities over 25,000 population amounting to approximately 2.2 million persons and 1 million workers in the period of a year after October 1940. For these 51 cities the overall migration rate was 4.3 percent.[15] The greatest proportion of black migrants was in Macon, Georgia, followed by Wichita Falls, Texas, and Atlanta, Georgia. Among northern cities the greatest proportions moved to Baltimore; Washington, D.C.; Pittsburgh, Johnstown, and Washington, Pennsylvania; and Battle Creek, Michigan. Even in these cities, though, blacks constituted no more than 11 percent of the migrants. And in 10 of the 51 cities studied by the W.P.A., black migrants accounted for less than one-half of 1 percent of all migrants for the year. (Appleton, Wisconsin, and Bloomfield, New Jersey, reported no black migrants.)

When the extent of migration is viewed in terms of the size of the population of the cities, the small amount of black migration during the early war years becomes evident. Macon, Georgia, center of large-scale military activity, had the largest proportion of black migrants, but this 20 percent in-migration rate hardly compared with the population of the city, which was about half black. The story was similar in Atlanta, where blacks made up 16 percent of migrants to the city, a rate of only 1.5 percent compared with 4.4 percent for whites.[16]

By 1942 wartime employment patterns began to change, partly as a result of increased social pressure for the implementation of fair employment practices with respect to blacks. While the 1940–1944 period is commonly cited for significant changes in black employment, most of the employment gains and consequent increases in migration occurred after 1942. In mid-1942 only 3 percent of war industries workers were black,[17] but two years later that proportion increased to more than 8 percent. After 1944, labor shortages and governmental pressure precipitated more affirmative hiring for blacks in previously white-only positions in aircraft, communications, explosives, industrial machinery, guns, plastics, and munitions industries.[18]

Dramatic increases in black employment were shown in analysis of 113 important war materials firms in Pennsylvania, New Jersey, and Delaware in 1942 and 1943. In the nine months that ended in October 1942, the proportion of black workers increased to 7 percent from 4 percent at a time when the total labor force in these selected firms increased about 18 percent. The black labor force posted a 120 percent gain. By March 1943, black employment had continued significant improvement. A shipyard in Pennsylvania, for example, employed more than 10,000 blacks in jobs at various levels of skill.[19]

Despite the definite improvements, hiring practices still reflected the persistent character of racial discrimination. Where white labor was plentiful, the pattern for blacks rang the too-familiar refrain of "last hired." Areas with labor shortages or otherwise tight labor markets created jobs that increasingly went to black workers. In Los Angeles, for example, 4 percent of the area's defense labor force was nonwhite (the vast majority of them black) in November 1943, a time of severe manpower shortage in Southern California. The labor shortage continued into the next year, resulting in an increase in the proportion of nonwhite workers to 6.5 percent of the area's defense labor force by November 1944.[20]

Job opportunities in the nation's defense industries in the North and West encouraged the black migration streams flowing from the South, reflecting an earlier era when World War I likewise triggered the Great Migration. As "color bars" began to ease, blacks increasingly joined whites in migration to industrial centers. From 1940 to 1942, approximately one million blacks moved to the nation's urban areas, especially to centers of defense industries. On the West Coast the increase was most significant. Not only did black population grow by tens of thousands, but in some cities "new migrants outnumbered the original Negro dwellers eight to one."[21] In the Portland, Oregon, area, the black population increased from 2,000 to 15,000 between 1940 and 1944. During the same time in San Francisco and the Bay Area, the black population grew to nearly 65,000 from less than 20,000.[22]

Significant increases in black population also occurred in many southern cities, especially in the shipbuilding centers like Hampton Roads, Mobile, Charleston, and Savannah, and border cities like Cincinnati, Baltimore, and Washington, D.C. The result of this migration was not only a regional relocation of the nation's black population, but a further concentration of blacks in tightly-restricted areas within the large industrial metropolitan centers.[23]

To alleviate the continuing manpower shortage of late 1942 and early 1943, the federal government developed several programs to subsidize both domestic and international migration.[24] One subsidy program administered by the Department of Agriculture intended to move farm families living on submarginal land in noncommercial rural areas to commercial farming areas. These new subsidy programs reversed the rural migration trend of the total population that had been encouraged and even assisted during the depression decade. The exact number of people relocated under the auspices of the Department of Agriculture and other federal programs is not known.[25] Likewise, the proportion of black migrants was not determined, but the areas from which they were drawn and their occupations suggest that a relatively high proportion were black. Most of the migrants came from several areas of the South, notably the Appalachian mountain region, the Ozarks, and the cotton-growing areas of the Old South.

Exportation of labor through subsidized migration programs was hardly popular, and local resistance could be found in varying degrees, especially in the cotton-farming regions. Since slavery, many of these areas enjoyed a surplus of manpower because of the established practice of keeping

workers year-round for cotton-chopping and then picking. Southern leg-
islators and congressmen contributed to the resistance by fighting subsidized out-migration of farm laborers.²⁶ But federally subsidized migration
escaped the protective devices thrown up by southern states during World
War I, when, as previously mentioned, labor recruiters for northern industry were burdened by heavy state licensing fees.

Further evidence of migration trends during the war years can be found
in the *Current Population Report* published by the U.S. Bureau of the Census
in 1947 and covering the period from April 1940 to April 1947.²⁷ During
this seven-year period, the extent of migration for blacks was comparable
to that for whites, approximately one person in five having moved to a
different county. But the distinction comes with the relative distances of
migration: about twice as many blacks moved to other states as moved
within their state of residence, and twice as many of these interstate migrants moved to states that were not adjacent to their own. A greater number of whites moved intrastate than moved between states, and of those
who did move out of state, the proportion moving to noncontiguous states
was not as pronounced as among black migrants.²⁸

The extent of black migration during the war was substantially greater
than in the last half of the 1930s, and it appears from available information
that black migration rates exceeded those for whites in the 1940–1947 period. This was particularly true for the long-distance migrants. But recall
that black migration increases did not occur at the outset of the war, but
only after the exhaustion of the white labor supply, the intensification of
the war, and the presidential order promoting affirmative hiring of blacks.
Thus it was 1942, or slightly later, that the significant increases in black
migration occurred.

Significantly, males overwhelmingly dominated the long-distance black
migration by almost two to one, or a sex ratio of 189.1. Compare this with
a sex ratio in 1947 of 93 males to every 100 females in the black civilian
population in the South, or with the ratio of 103.1 for black migrants as a
whole. The sex ratio for white migrants during the same time was 95.9,
and only 100.1 for those migrating between noncontiguous states (long-
distance migrants).

The wide sex ratio suggests problems not only for the migrant himself
but for his family and creates social problems in the destination communities. The migration of married male migrants meant a temporary—in
some cases, permanent—disruption of the family.

Causes of migration

Despite the powerful influence World War II exerted upon the South
and its people, black and white, the patterns of social behavior and race
relations that characterized the South before the war underwent remark-

Table 8–1. *Migration status and type of migration of the population, by urban-rural residence, color, and sex, for the United States civilian population, April 1947, and total population, April 1940 (percent not shown where less than 0.1)*

Migration status & type of migration, April 1940 to April 1947	Total	Sex		Color		Residences		
		Male	Female	White	Nonwhite	Urban	Rural/non-farm	Rural farm
Total civilian pop., April 1947	142,061,000	70,129,000	71,933,000	127,044,000	15,017,000	83,850,000	30,835,000	27,365,000
Born on or before April 1, 1940	122,633,000	60,218,000	62,415,000	110,099,000	12,534,000	73,353,000	25,122,000	23,152,000
Nonmigrants	96,565,000	47,439,000	49,126,000	86,864,000	9,701,000	58,323,000	19,411,000	12,755,000
Same house	52,136,000	25,425,000	26,711,000	47,065,000	5,071,000	31,444,000	9,642,000	11,056,000
Different house in same county	44,420,000	22,014,000	22,415,000	39,799,000	4,630,000	26,945,000	9,049,000	7,715,000
Migrants	25,469,000	12,491,000	12,978,000	22,740,000	2,729,000	14,452,000	6,655,000	4,341,000
Within a state	13,081,000	6,389,000	6,692,000	12,117,000	964,000	6,512,000	3,635,000	2,873,000
Between contiguous states	4,974,000	2,417,000	2,557,000	4,395,000	578,000	2,914,000	1,268,000	732,000
Between non-contiguous states	7,414,000	3,685,000	3,729,000	6,227,000	1,187,000	5,025,000	1,692,000	635,000
Persons abroad on April 1, 1940	599,000	288,000	311,000	495,000	104,000	518,000	35,000	26,000

SOURCE: U.S., Bureau of the Census, *Current Population Reports*, series P-20, no. 14, 1947 *Internal Migration in the United States: April, 1940 to April, 1947* (Washington, D.C.: Government Printing Office, 1947).

Table 8-2. Migration status of black population of the South, 1940-47

	Male	Female	Total	Sex ratio
Nonmigrant (Total)	3,186,000	3,491,000	6,677,000	91.3
Same house	1,688,000	1,908,000	3,596,000	88.5
Different house	1,498,000	1,583,000	3,081,000	94.6
Migrants (Total)	629,000	610,000	1,239,000	103.1
Within state	355,000	369,000	724,000	96.2
Between contiguous states	158,000	179,000	337,000	88.3
Between noncontiguous states	116,000	62,000	178,000	187.1
Abroad	1,000	1,000	2,000	
Total civilian black population in South, April, 1947	3,816,000	4,102,000	7,918,000	93.0

SOURCE: Ibid., Table 8, p. 21.

ably few changes as a result of the war. "The region was prepared to make all sacrifices necessary to win the war for the Four Freedoms," concluded a southern historian, "but it felt that external enemies, not Southerners, had committed the sins that made the war imperative. Germany and Japan were the targets of this bloody crusade, which Southerners believed could be won without injecting the Southern issue."[29]

Five years before the war a typical southern small town was described as a caste system within which the respective castes were occupied by the races. With little to suggest that any major changes occurred, it is likely that the descriptions were as appropriate in 1942 as they were in 1937. This caste system, as has been argued,[30] had replaced slavery as the essence of the old status order in the South, and so limited the forms of social contact between blacks and whites and defined whites as superiors and blacks as inferiors. For blacks, the majority of whom were living within such a social system, the caste barrier was the fact of life defining behavior. Their inferior caste resulted in social isolation to a degree and limited their personal development, making it more difficult or even impossible to compete for the highest social rewards and positions.[31] The frustration of such limitation was made all the more acute by whites with their sense of pride in achievements, superiority in management, and social responsibility.[32]

The caste system was at work in every aspect of life, from the most intimate interpersonal relationships to the distribution of economic and political power. It provided an explicit code of behavior by which each person knew how to act and what to expect in relations with the other caste group. The restrictions and controls were organized and predictable, and the black person who accepted and abided by them generally achieved a relatively high degree of security in relations with whites.[33] The alternative was punishment, ostracism, or perhaps even death.

Few places characterized the caste system in the South more appropriately than in the ownership and control of the land. With its occupational status of black tenants, the caste reinforced itself by making the purchase of farm land extremely difficult in the plantation areas. Landlords, unwilling even to sell land in small tracts, were particularly unwilling to sell to tenants. The one exception was fraudulent: the scheming during boom times of "selling" land to black tenants, outside due process of law, then taking the land back at the first opportunity in hard times.[34] These and other equally unjust practices gave rise to excessive labor turnover. Landowners who dealt more justly with their tenants in settlements attracted more stable workers.

But migration was not an exclusive characteristic of one caste, making it difficult to attribute the geographic mobility of black tenant farmers chiefly to their relegated social condition. Since white tenants also often moved, it is likely that economic factors contributed largely to the migratory behavior of all tenants.[35]

Although the search for economic opportunity must be considered a basic motivating factor in black migration of the South's Black Belt, a complex of interacting factors contributed to the relocation of black America. Mechanization in agriculture, especially in cotton production, had occurred for more than two decades, and must be regarded as one of the significant factors influencing black migration. Another factor was the growing problem of soil depletion, the significance of which lies in the concomitant reduction in economic opportunity for agricultural workers. In 1935, for example, the National Resources Committee estimated that 450,000 farms in the United States containing 75 million acres were in need of retirement. Sixty-three percent of the farms and 29 percent of the acreage were in the South.[36]

Still other factors pushing migrants out of the rural South in the late 1930s and early 1940s were crop restrictions and the transition from tenant farming to day labor. Under agricultural restrictions, landlords drove off the least productive workers—a practice usually more detrimental to blacks, since white tenants generally offered more resistance than blacks. Likewise reducing responsibility and security of former tenants, the change from tenancy to day labor encouraged mobility.[37]

Out-migration from the South during the early 1940s was not exclusively from the rural areas. In southern cities, economic conditions also contributed to black migration. But the migration of white tenant farmers to the towns and cities of the South in response to declining opportunities in agriculture fostered increased competition between blacks and whites for jobs in the cities. While a decade earlier there were jobs in southern cities known as "Negro jobs," at which whites would not work, the pressure created by young whites moving from rural areas effectively eliminated blacks from competition for these jobs. The decline in economic opportunities for southern blacks was obvious.[38]

Within the context of national and regional socioeconomic changes, the factors that previously had been of secondary importance with respect to migration became more significant. Greater educational opportunities in northern cities lured black migrants from crippling social conditions and destitute facilities of southern black schools. Echoing views of other southern black educators, Harvard-educated Alton Williams of Belle Glade, Florida, told a congressional committee of students in his classroom who spent as many as four days a week in the fields:

> Although we have laws in this state that a child must go to school until he is 16 years of age, yet those laws are not enforced. . . . In fact, only about a third of the children, school-age children in this particular area, are in school. You can go in these quarters anywhere and find, two to one, the children never have been registered in school. . . . [Many who are registered] lost months in the fall and in the spring. The greatest influx comes about November. . . . They start dropping out about April and by the first week in May the enrollment has gone way down.[39]

In addition to educational barriers encountered by blacks, caste, health, and sanitation problems were also major reasons for leaving the rural South. Few changes, if any, had occurred to improve living conditions among the destitute tenants. As further incentive, reports came home from northern cities of paved streets, running water, doctors, and hospitals—amenities that these southern poor had never enjoyed.

Strong discontent with existing social conditions, prompted by disenfranchizement, insecurity about property and even life, and inferior housing and transportation, acted as subtle but important factors encouraging migration. Seldom the primary motivation for black migrants, these social factors and others were important supporting influences, pushing migrants away from economic insecurities in the rural South coincidental with the pull of opportunities offered by the southern and northern industrial centers.[40]

Despite the fact that all the necessary conditions were present for a massive migration of blacks to urban centers of the North, the size and scope of the movement was far less than might have been expected. Chief among the factors inhibiting such a massive movement was racial employment discrimination. Discrimination, rampant in the beginning of the defense build-up in 1940, fostered disillusion on the part of blacks hoping to participate in the industrial revival. But the frustration that bore disillusionment gave way in some cases to pro-German and pro-Italian sentiments. Employers at the time were begging for workers, but blacks were turned away from any but the traditional Negro jobs. Training programs financed by the government sanctioned discrimination, and when government agencies issued orders to combat it, the orders were ignored.[41]

Some destinations, of course, were more attractive than others, a fact made significant by the differential attraction of cities for blacks and whites. While the reasons for migration are often numerous and interrelated, one factor that contributed notably to the attractiveness of a city for blacks was its unattractiveness for whites. Cities with low-wage industries, such as Baltimore, lost in competition for white workers to cities with reputations for higher wages. Those who came for lower pay came because the opportunity to work was sufficient attraction, and these people were often the black migrants.

Consequences of migration

To understand the consequences of migration it is important to realize that these consequences are felt by both the migrants and the nonmigrants, by the institutions and social structures of both the sending and receiving communities. The nature of the consequences depends on the size of the migrant stream, the speed with which the migrants move, their characteristics, and motivation for moving. Other influences include the size of the communities, their capacity to accommodate increases (or decreases in the cases of sending communities), and the attitudes of the residents toward people who constitute the migrant stream.

As migration to northern cities increased, the demand for housing likewise increased. The result was overcrowding, and houses originally designed as single-family dwellings were converted to tenements to allow several families to use the building. It was not uncommon to find families of ten or more living in one or two rooms.[42] In 1941, a study in Baltimore reported that a fifth of the population lived in one-fiftieth of the area of the city.[43] In one square mile there were more than 90,000 black residents.[44]

The demand for housing frequently meant weak enforcement of building and housing sanitation ordinances. In Detroit, for example, an inventory of real property revealed that of the dwellings occupied by blacks, more were found to be unsafe, unsanitary, or overcrowded than in satisfactory condition, and that half of all the dwellings occupied by blacks were substandard, compared with less than a fifth of dwellings occupied by whites.[45]

The problem of finding adequate housing for blacks moving into the cities was made more acute by strict segregationist policies and customs. Well-defined boundaries—railroad tracks, streets, buildings—limited the areas within which blacks could search for housing, despite the fact that housing was easily available elsewhere. As a rule, seldom-violated black residential areas were located in the most deteriorated neighborhoods previously occupied by whites, and the more suitable housing brought rents beyond the capabilities of most black migrants.[46] The shortage of adequate housing in black neighborhoods and the resulting problems were made all the more severe by inordinate rent hikes.

Partial, stop-gap measures were taken at the federal level by the United States Housing Administration to provide housing for workers as a defense measure. But the time lag required for administrative preparation and construction resulted in the majority of the projects being "too little, too late." In Trenton, New Jersey, a federal housing project was erected with a capacity of 118 families, all of whom were to be black. When it was completed, the units were filled and a lengthy waiting list was established.[47] In Detroit, the city housing commission had received more than 9,000 applications by May 1941 from black families looking for apartments in housing projects. Yet fewer than 2,000 of the applicants could be accommodated in projects that were either completed, under construction, or planned. For the remaining 4,500 eligible families, there was no provision.[48]

But more than just a matter of too little, too late, the argument can be made that housing projects were no solution at all to the problems of black migrants. The projects were located in already overcrowded black areas of cities, and space for most of the them could be obtained only by clearing almost as much housing as was replaced. So by removing homes to acquire the needed space, substantially more overcrowding resulted. And even as construction was in progress, waves of new migrants arrived in the cities, compounding the problem. The failure to integrate housing when the need was so great was a major contributing factor to the deterioration of the central cities, and this failure was a significant impetus to growing racial tensions that later would foment deadly riots.

Closely allied to the problems of migrant housing were public health problems. In all cities that bore the brunt of significant migration, there were ever-present threats of epidemics and other health emergencies. Rates of communicable diseases were out of all proportion to the size of the population, and there were frightening sporadic outbreaks of meningitis.[49] Moreover, significant increases also were found in tuberculosis and venereal disease. The situation at one point in Hartford, Connecticut, led the city's health officer to warn of a "condition that may explode into a conflagration."[50]

Prostitution, as well as other forms of vice, reportedly kept pace with population gains in most cities in the early 1940s. In Hartford, a report prepared to assess the impact on the city of the national defense program found a major disparity between police crime figures and what actually took place on the streets.

> The local police, in conference with the health officers, recently stated that there had been no increase in vice as a result of the industrial boom. This statement was made on the basis of comparative figures of

arrest. One has but to journey through the streets of certain areas to prove the contrary. Women walking the streets are being molested constantly by men. They feel unsafe without proper escorts.

White men are constantly coming into the area to seek Negro women companions. White women are setting up in the Negro area to consort with Negro men. They are not residents of the city. Rather, they have come to gather their share of the spoils.[51]

Still other symptoms of social disorganization showed in the higher homicide, juvenile delinquency, and arrest rates in the black areas of the cities. But the disproportionately high arrest and delinquency rates among blacks may be partially explained by municipal law enforcement personnel and policies. In Baltimore, for example, all the uniformed police and law enforcement personnel during the early 1940s were white. Police brutality reportedly was rampant in the black communities, with little or nothing ever done about it.[52]

The most dramatic and destructive consequence of the defense migration was the failure on the part of the receiving communities to accommodate black migrants in a nondescriminatory fashion. The results of this failure were four major racial outbreaks—one each in Harlem and Los Angeles and two in Detroit. The most destructive riot occurred in Detroit on June 20, 1943, the likely culmination of in-migration that swelled the city's population by more than a half million people in three years. Most of these migrants were from the South, 50,000 of them black,[53] and they were in competition for limited housing and frustrated at discrimination over jobs. The atmosphere was explosive, and when it blew on a hot Sunday afternoon 25 blacks and 9 whites were killed and $2 million in property was damaged.[54]

Chicago seethed with the discontent of 60,000 new black migrants between 1940 and 1944; while white men went to work, blacks waited in unemployment lines.[55] When Detroit and other cities broke under racial tensions in the summer of 1943, fear of a riot gripped Chicago, but despite scattered incidents that might have touched off a clash, the city escaped one. Civic leaders and institutions, black and white, worked through the mayor's office to dispel rumors, provide counseling, and control youth gangs, easing the city by these efforts through the early 1940s without the kind of disturbances that had followed the Great Migration.[56]

The war and resulting industrial expansion in the North and West created serious labor shortages in some segments of the South. Almost three million southerners moved outside the region to participate in the expansion beyond the Mississippi River and above the Mason-Dixon line. The southern farm population fell 3.2 million, compared with only 1.8 million from the farm population of the rest of the United States, and farm acreage decreased 7 percent during a time when acreage for the rest of the nation grew by 15 percent.[57] Although black migration during the early 1940s was much less pronounced than that of whites, southern whites openly decried black migration as a kind of personal affront or social insubordination. War jobs with good pay lured people away from domestic service, for example, which Charles S. Johnson, a black sociologist, called "one of the most intimate effects of the war in many households."[58]

Whatever the consequences for the communities, the migrants would never again be the same people they were before moving. For the rural blacks from the South, the war and its consequent migrations meant exposure to ideas and experiences they had never encountered. No one can say with certainty what the effects of that exposure were, but it is likely that traditional outlooks and perspectives were modified, if not radically changed. Even those who returned to their previous way of life must have retained some residue of their experiences.

9. The aftermath of World War II

Like the world war before it, World War II prompted a major shift in the black population of the United States.[1] The impact of migration on many northern cities was as great as, if not greater than, that of the earlier war. Paradoxically, a principal factor contributing to the intensity of the impact upon blacks was the lower rate of migration attributed to the discrimination they encountered during the early years of the war. The earlier arrival of great numbers of white migrants during the nation's dramatic shift from economic depression to war-time economy exhausted housing and other needed resources in the metropolitan areas. By the time blacks began to move in significant numbers, housing was scarce and living conditions had become difficult. Shortages of recreational facilities, consumer goods, and transportation were aggravated by the burgeoning demand of black and white newcomers. In many cities, white workers moving in for jobs in war industries met resentment from residents, and when black migrants began their influx they in turn became targets of this resentment.[2]

Despite the major problems of the nation, its cities and its people, the more profound domestic effects of the war were not really apparent during the war. It was only in the years after 1945 that these effects became increasingly evident. In 1945 and 1946, millions of soldiers came home, the whites looking forward to life as it was before the war, and the blacks hoping for something different. Both were to be disappointed. The period of demobilization was to be one of adjustment characterized by a host of social and psychological hurdles.

Black soldiers, particularly those from the South, could not have been expected to defend freedom and democracy abroad without the consequent reaction to discrimination at home. They were destined to give an impetus to considerable social changes in the postwar years. Moreover, black leaders and white liberals had been active during the war in efforts to bring about greater civil rights, particularly in employment opportunities.[3] The stage was set for a series of dramatic—if not revolutionary—demographic and social changes.

Postwar migration of black military personnel

When the war ended, it was time for the soldier to make plans for civilian life. The differences appear to be marked according to race. Attitudinal studies of enlisted men conducted by the army in 1944 surveyed the possible plans soldiers had about the area of the United States to which they intended to move or return after their release from the service. About 80 percent surveyed expected to return to their prior place of residence, but the black soldiers as a group indicated that only two-thirds of them were planning a return to the states from which they came. And the proportion of blacks that expected to migrate to different regions was nearly double that of the white soldiers.[4]

These postwar migration plans of black soldiers would have resulted in four streams of migration, the largest of which would substantially trace the predominant migration pattern of earlier years from the South to the Northeast. From the army's survey, a secondary movement from the South to the West Coast region would also have been expected. Moreover, the West North Central region would have lost population to the Northeast as well as to the West. And finally, a counterstream also would have been expected from the Northeast to the South.[5] While it can be expected that a significant proportion of these soldiers realized their plans, the lack of a follow-up study leaves the extent of these expectations unknown.

Volume of migration

The scope of black migration during the postwar years was not greatly different from the previous period. Approximately 5 percent of the nation's blacks migrated each year, compared with a 6 percent rate for whites. (The proportion of black persons who entered migration streams did increase slightly to 5.6 percent in 1950 from 4.7 percent in 1949.)[6]

But when region-of-birth and region-of-residence comparisons are made for their perspective of macromigration patterns, the population redistribution clearly runs northward and westward. In 1950 about one-fifth (18 percent) of the nation's 15.3 million blacks were living in regions of the country other than that in which they were born. Twenty-nine percent were residing outside their state of birth.[7] Characteristically, more than a fifth of the black population born in the South lived outside the region by 1950, compared with no more than 10 percent of blacks born in the other three regions of the nation. Accordingly, more than half of the black population of the Northeast, North Central, and West were born in other regions, while only 1 percent of southern blacks were born outside the region. But while the redistribution was unmistakably northward and westward during the 1940s, it would be misleading to view this shift as occurring evenly throughout the decade. The actual rates of migration fluctuated significantly from year to year in response to changing social and economic conditions and, in certain areas, were even reversed in the last year of the decade.

In all, 14 states had net black out-migration during the 1940s—four more than during the previous decade. With the exception of Delaware,

Maryland, and Florida, most southern states, led by Mississippi, had fewer black in-migrants than out-migrants. Interestingly, California, with net in-migration totaling 258,900, the largest of any state, saw as many migrants moving in as Mississippi saw moving out. Behind California were New York, Illinois, and Michigan in terms of attractive destinations.

Not only were blacks moving to states with greater urban populations in the North and West; they were moving by and large to the major metropolitan areas within these states. Ann Miller's analysis of 48 Standard Metropolitan Statistical Areas (SMSAs) with populations of 250,000 or more in 1960 indicates that four of these metropolitan areas had net black in-migration of 100,000 or more during the 1940s: New York City (211,000), Chicago (166,000), Detroit (130,000), and Los Angeles (112,000). Three other of Miller's 48 SMSAs, San Francisco, Philadelphia, and Washington, D.C., had net in-migration between 50,000 and 100,000, and eleven other metropolitan areas received between 10,000 and 50,000 migrants. Only three of the 48 SMSAs Miller studied experienced net out-migration, and all were in the South.[8]

Miller's findings are reinforced by census data on State Economic Areas (SEAs).[9] From 1949 to 1950, 43 percent of all black migrants in the United States chose metropolitan SEA destinations—a significantly larger proportion than reflected in the share of black residents in these areas. The majority of the migrants moving to metropolitan SEAs (58 percent) came from other metropolitan areas, and only 12 percent of the metropolitan migrants came from rural-farm SEAs. The remainder came from small towns. Nineteen percent of all black migrants moved to rural-farm SEAs, again less than the proportion of the black population residing in these areas. While the majority of rural-farm migrants moved from other rural-farm areas, it is interesting to note that one-fifth came from metropolitan areas.

Direction of migration

Black interstate migration during the war years and afterward was highly selective regionally, meaning that a large proportion of the migrants from each region tended to select the same region of destination. For example, in each of the South Atlantic states except Georgia, more than three-fourths of the black migrants moved to the Northeast. But with the exception of Alabama (from which the Northeast attracted less than one-fourth of the black migrants), there was virtually no attraction for migrants from other southern states to the Northeast.[10] The largest percentage of black migrants from the East South Central states went due north, from Mississippi, Alabama, Tennessee, and Kentucky, to communities principally in Illinois, Michigan, and Ohio. In similar fashion, the Pacific states pulled migrants mostly from Texas and Louisiana, and, to a lesser extent, Arkansas, Oklahoma, and Mississippi.[11]

Table 9–1. Net intercensal migration, 1940–1950, by sex, for the Negro population, 10 years of age and over, SMSA's

	SMSA		SMSA
	M	F	M&F
Akron, Ohio	3,821	4,001	7,822
Atlanta, Ga.	331	793	704
Baltimore, Md.	17,802	17,300	35,102
Birmingham, Ala.	− 2,133	− 747	− 2,880
Boston, Mass.	6,170	5,723	11,893
Buffalo, N.Y.	8,242	8,092	16,334
Chicago, Ill.	79,950	86,372	166,322
Cincinnati, Ohio–Ky.	6,928	8,839	15,767
Cleveland, Ohio	21,371	23,277	44,648
Columbus, Ohio	3,619	3,714	7,333
Dallas, Tex.	4,735	4,227	8,962
Dayton, Ohio	6,055	5,970	12,025
Denver, Colo.	3,524	2,646	6,170
Detroit, Mich.	64,238	66,034	130,272
El Paso, Tex.	749	480	1,229
Ft. Worth, Tex.	3,680	3,059	6,739
Houston, Tex.	12,451	12,607	25,058
Indianapolis, Ind.	3,333	3,755	7,088
Jersey City, N.J.	1,986	2,162	4,148
Kansas City, Mo.–Kan.	6,690	6,847	13,537
Louisville, Ky.	3,286	3,909	7,195
Los Angeles–Long Beach, Cal.	53,658	58,990	112,648
Memphis, Tenn.	591	1,690	2,281
Miami, Fla.	2,876	3,890	6,766
Milwaukee, Wis.	5,068	4,482	9,550
Nashville, Tenn.	985	904	1,889
Minneapolis–St. Paul, Minn.	1,407	1,184	2,591
Newark, N.J.	12,737	13,717	26,454
New Orleans, La.	4,781	7,169	11,950
New York, N.Y.	92,204	118,949	211,153
Norfolk-Portsmouth, Va.	9,977	8,490	18,447
Oklahoma City, Okla.	− 177	− 44	− 221
Philadelphia, Pa.–N.J.	41,196	44,532	85,728
Phoenix, Ariz.	2,102	2,155	4,257
Pittsburgh, Pa.	2,994	4,781	7,775
Portland, Ore.–Wash.	3,339	3,301	6,640
Rochester, N.Y.	1,682	1,618	3,300
St. Louis, Mo.–Ill.	17,747	20,898	38,645
San Antonio, Tex.	4,761	3,290	8,051
San Diego, Cal.	5,091	4,394	9,485
Seattle, Wash.	5,085	4,673	9,758
San Francisco, Cal.	49,990	48,789	98,779
Tampa-St. Petersburg, Fla.	1,512	1,338	2,850
Toledo, Ohio	3,839	3,783	7,622
Tulsa, Okla.	− 1,320	− 1,388	− 2,708
Wash., D.C.–Md.–Va.	30,496	34,863	65,359
Wichita, Kan.	1,220	1,297	2,517

SOURCE: Ann Ratner Miller, *Net Intercensal Migration to Large Urban Areas of the United States* (Philadelphia: University of Pennsylvania, 1964), Table II, pp. 129–208.

Although black out-migration from southern counties was the experience in every southern state, the largest and heaviest concentration of out-migrants came from the Mississippi Delta region in northwest Mississippi and southeast Arkansas. The data on the links between the various areas of origin and destination suggest there were basically three great streams of black migration in the United States during the 1940s. One connected the South Atlantic states with the Middle West or East North Central states, flowing north. The second stream was farther west, linking the Middle South states with the Middle West or East North Central states, again north and parallel to the Atlantic seaboard stream. The third stream went west, connecting the trans-Mississippi South with Los Angeles and San Francisco. In addition to the major streams, of course, there were numerous smaller streams and tributaries that formed a migration network.

Characteristics of black migrants

The major source of information on the characteristics of black migrants during this period is the 1950 decennial census. Just as the migration that occurred between 1949 and 1950 may not have been typical of the whole decade in terms of the volume and direction of the migrants, it should be clear that any interpolation from migrant characteristics provided by the census to other years in the decade could be inaccurate.

As an age group, young adults 20 to 24 years old composed the largest segment of interregional migrants in 1949–50. More often than not, a migrant would be between 14 and 29 years old (56 percent). Nearly one quarter of these interregional migrants were 13 years old or younger, nearly 16 percent between 35 and 44, 13 percent between 45 and 64, and only 4 percent 65 years old or older. Moreover, there were slight variations in the age structure of migrants among the various regions. For example, interregional black migrants moving to the South tended to be disproportionately overrepresented among teenagers (14–19 years old) and retirement age (65 and older). In the same way, migrants to the West tended to be slightly overrepresented among the middle-aged (30–64). It should be noted, though, that the age structure of the long-distance migrants, such as those moving from one region to another, is not necessarily representative of all migrants, particularly those migrating short distances.

Although these age characteristics are for only one year, it is clear that blacks moving from one region of the country to another were similar in age distribution to migrants in other streams and at other times. They tended to be young adults, but not to the complete exclusion of other groups—40 percent, after all, were middle-aged.

Not only were migrants younger, they also tended to be male more often than not. The sex ratio for black migrants was 107 in 1950, compared with 93 for the total black population. Pronounced variations, however, did occur for different age cohorts. The sex ratio for migrants between 35 and 44 years old, for example, was 126.7, but the ratio was only 89.2 for those 65 and over. None of the age cohorts over 20 years old had sex ratios of less than 100, with the exception of the elderly migrants.

Sex ratio variations also marked out-migrants from certain areas and in-migrants to other areas. It is perhaps significant that out-migrants and in-migrants from the various regions displayed pronounced differences in the proportion of men to women. Migrants to the Northeast from other regions had a sex ratio of 85.3, far less than the 101.9 ratio for those leaving the Northeast. In the North Central region, migrants coming in had a sex ratio of 101.7, compared with 114.8 for those from the region who were moving out.

Although the relationship between the sex ratio of migrants and the distance of migration is affected by many factors, the sex ratio generally increased with the distance of the move—men tended to migrate not only more, but also farther, than women. Thus, migration modified the ratio of men to women in various regions of the country, which is important because of the bearing on marriage rates and family formation. In turn, these rates also have a known relationship with fertility.[12]

Black migrants at the end of the 1940s were also better educated than the total black population. The significance of such educational selectivity is felt on local economies, because as better educated people move from one locale to another, they take with them their educational skills. Thus one effect is that originating communities lose the educational resources of their out-migrants and the receiving communities benefit. Of course, the relationship works both ways, since migrants of lower educational levels can depreciate educational levels of receiving communities and likewise raise the levels of originating communities.

The most pronounced educational difference between migrants and the larger black population was for people under 35. Twelve percent of the migrants between 25 and 29 years of age had attended college, compared with 7.6 percent of the total black population. A similar difference could be found for the 30 to 34 age cohort. But as migrant ages increased the differences decreased.

Regional redistribution of the black population through migration did result in some redistribution in the regional levels of education for the black population. For example, the Northeast profited from the migration, inasmuch as 15 percent of the migrants who left had attended college and 17 percent who moved in had comparable education, and inasmuch as 10 percent of the out-migrants had less than five years of schooling compared with less than 9 percent of the in-migrants. But not all regions fared as well. The South gained the poorly educated, and at the same time lost the better educated. In the West there was a slightly greater proportion of better-educated people moving into the region than leaving. Very little educational change occurred in the North Central region.

Table 9–2. *Educational attainment of nonwhite migrants, 1949–50*

North Central, 1949	Northeast No.	%	South No.	%	West No.	%	Out-migration Total	%	In-migration North Central No.	%
Total nonwhite	650	100	3915	100	1005	100	5570	100	4625	
Less than 5 yr.	40	6.2	485	12.4	20	2.0	545	9.8		7.6
5 to 8 yr.	135	20.8	1320	33.7	150	14.9	1605	28.8		29.6
High School	320	49.2	1455	37.2	575	57.2	2350	42.2		44.8
College	145	22.3	600	15.3	240	23.9	985	17.7		16.1
Not reported	10	1.5	55	1.4	20	2.0	85	1.5		1.9

Northeast, 1949	North Central No.	%	South No.	%	West No.	%	Total	%	Northeast No.	%
Total nonwhite	775	100	3880	100	390	100	5045	100	3675	100.0
Less than 5 yr.	45	5.8	465	12.0	15	3.8	525	10.4		8.7
5 to 8 yr.	160	20.6	1215	31.4	60	15.4	1435	28.4		30.1
High School	410	53.0	1555	40.0	195	50.0	2160	42.8		40.8
College	120	15.5	525	13.5	120	30.8	765	15.2		17.4
Not reported	40	5.1	120	3.1	120	0.	160	3.2		3.0

South, 1949	Northeast No.	%	North Central No.	%	West No.	%	Total	%	South No.	%
Total nonwhite	2775	100	3240	100	1660	100	7675	100	9350	
Less than 5 yr.	280	10.1	305	9.4	125	7.5	710	9.2		11.7
5 to 8 yr.	930	33.5	1150	35.5	435	26.2	2515	32.8		32.3
High School	1085	39.1	1265	39.0	850	51.2	3200	41.7		39.8
College	390	14.1	475	14.7	230	13.9	1095	14.3		13.8
Not reported	90	3.2	45	1.4	20	1.2	155	2.0		2.4

West, 1949	Northeast No.	%	North Central No.	%	South No.	%	Total	%	West No.	%
Total nonwhite	250	100	610	100	1555	100	2415	100	3055	
Less than 5 yr.	250		610		145	9.3	145	6.0		5.2
5 to 8 yr.	40	16.0	60	9.8	485	31.2	585	24.2		21.2
High School	95	38.0	395	64.7	710	45.6	1200	49.7		53.0
College	105	42.0	150	24.7	170	10.9	425	17.6		19.3
Not reported	10	4.0	5	.8	45	2.9	60	2.5		1.3

SOURCE: U.S., Bureau of the Census, *Census of Population: 1950*, Special Report PE no. 4D, *Population Mobility—Characteristics of Migrants* (Washington D.C.: Government Printing Office, 1951), Table 14, p. 331.

Causes of migration

The years immediately following the end of the war were a period of domestic and economic uncertainty. Fears of depression subsequent to industrial reconversion to production for civilian use were widespread. The federal government, also fearing large-scale unemployment, made every effort to ease the transition by reducing taxes, making money available for loans to business, and selling billions of dollars worth of surplus war material at bargain basement prices.[13] Actually, the fears of depression soon proved to be unfounded, and the nation entered a period of prosperity.[14]

Despite prosperity, serious economic problems also plagued the country in those postwar years. The chief problems were labor disputes and spiraling wage and price increases. During the war, labor had been able to maintain its standards of living largely through overtime pay. After the war, the unions demanded increases in regular wage rates in order to compensate for the expected loss in overtime. During the 18 months following V-J Day, there were a series of strikes in the automobile, steel, coal, and railroad industries. In most instances, the unions acquired significant wages with the resulting costs passed on to the consumer through higher prices.[15]

In the years immediately following the war, the American economy faced the threat of severe inflation. To make the threat an even greater likelihood, other inflationary factors emerged. For example, there was strong sentiment against continuing the unpopular price controls into the postwar years. Also, a large sector of American industry had been converted to the production of war material for the previous five years, and serious shortages in consumer goods had accumulated. These factors, which were only marginally offset by the temporary retention of some price controls and by the unemployment created by demobilization, combined to make the second half of the 1940s one of the most inflationary in American history.[16]

The economy of the South, like other regions, exhibited the postwar reconversion syndrome. In fact, those who planned the South's future were perhaps more apprehensive over peacetime adjustments than the economic planners in other regions.[17] The South had experienced unprecedented prosperity during the war. Yet, the type of industry developed there had less potential for peacetime reconversion than the industries elsewhere. Less than 1 percent of the war manufacturing awards in the South were in plants that manufactured vehicles; barely 1 percent in machinery and electrical equipment plants; and only 4 percent in iron and steel facilities. On the other hand, 20 and 31 percent, respectively, of the section's war awards were in munitions and chemicals, plants believed to have serious reconversion limitations.[18]

By the end of 1947, however, renewed confidence in the South's capacity to overcome reconversion limitations and to develop a viable peacetime economy appeared to be justified. In that year alone, more than one billion dollars had been expended in plants and equipment across the South. Employment, wages, and incomes were not far below wartime peaks, and the harvest of crops obtained almost unprecedented prices.[19] Despite the postwar economic upsurge, however, their relative position to nonsouthern regions was not significantly improved.[20] Moreover, within the South, pronounced disparities existed among the states in terms of personal income. For example, family—or individual—income in the state with the highest incomes was nearly three times as high as the corresponding income in the state with the lowest incomes.[21]

The postwar reconversion gave impetus to the changing occupational structure of the region. While the South was still a long way from catching up with the rest of the nation, the proportion of white-collar workers continued to increase and that of agricultural workers to decrease.[22] Despite the changes, one description of the occupational structure stated, "The more the South changes, the more it stays the same, persistently backward in comparison with other American regions."[23]

The backwardness of the South applied not only to its economy, but to its people as well. A sense of history and identity set the South apart. Unlike other regions of the United States, the conditions of the South prior to the war and during the postwar years can only be understood by considering its biracial nature.

> In its grand outlines the politics of the South revolves around the position of the Negro. It is at times interpreted as a politics of cotton, as a politics of free trade, as a politics of agrarian poverty, or a politics of planter and plutocrat. Although such interpretations have a superficial validity, in the last analysis the major peculiarities of Southern politics go back to the Negro. Whatever phase of the Southern political process one seeks to understand, sooner or later the trail of inquiry leads to the Negro.[24]

There is little question that the decade of the 1940s was a period of rapid social change for blacks in the South, as well as the nation. Yet the prewar disparity in income, occupations, and education between whites and blacks was so great that even major advances still left blacks second-rate citizens in most respects. Between 1940 and 1950 black occupational gains were substantially larger than gains of previous decades. But occupational gains were substantial for the total population as well. A study measuring changes in the occupational status of black males by using an intracohort analysis found that, while there was decreasing occupational dissimilarity between blacks and whites in the North during the 1940s, only insignificant increases in the South were observed for those in age groups 25–34 and 35–44. Actual increases in occupational dissimilarity were found for those 45–54 and 55–64.[25]

Blacks enjoyed substantial increases in income during the 1940s, but since whites also had increases, income disparities remained. By 1950, blacks and other non-Caucasian races had median incomes hardly more than half (54 percent) as large as median incomes for whites. Whereas in 1948, 13 percent of the nation's white families had incomes of $10,000 or more, only 2 percent of the black families enjoyed equally high incomes. The proportion of black families with such incomes declined by 50 percent from 1947 to 1948.[26] By 1950 the median income was only $1,569 for blacks.[27]

New industries in the South almost universally gave preference to white labor. Even the Atomic Energy Commission, an agency that had a reputation for a concern for advancing human welfare, blatantly violated any reasonable standard of equal opportunity by hiring fewer than 4 percent blacks in its 37,000 Oak Ridge work force. Moreover, the largest proportion of those hired were common laborers.[28]

At best, the 1940s were bittersweet years for blacks in the South, if not throughout the rest of the nation. What appeared toward the end of the war to be the beginning of the end of discrimination in the labor market was only a transitory period fostered by the conditions and necessities of war. The postwar years for blacks were years of larger paychecks and more white-collar jobs, but their relative position in the total socioeconomic structure remained all but unchanged. New strategies were needed to realize the American dream. The net result was that the economic structure in the South remained closed to blacks in many occupations and areas. The migration continued outward in large numbers and the migration to the South remained a dribble. Opportunities either did not exist or were very unattractive.

10. The fifties: the relocation of black America

The social setting

The 1950s have been characterized as a period of political conservatism and relative complacency in the United States. Most white Americans seemed content with things as they were. World War II was over, postwar prosperity had increased the nation's standard of living, and a tentative settlement had been achieved in the Korean conflict. For black Americans, however, it was a time of heightened tension, growing out of an increasingly strong determination to alter the structural barriers of discrimination and to overcome the racial status quo.

A partial solution to the problem of the structural inequities was to come about through migration. The steady migration of blacks to the North and West and their concentration in several important urban industrial communities gave them a new and often powerful voice in political affairs.[1] Although an important step, increased political participation alone was not sufficient to overcome the racial status quo of a half century. Other fronts were to be assaulted before a new social structure based on racial equality was to emerge. The courts, colleges, labor markets, housing markets, public conveyances, and other sectors of society became the battleground for civil rights.

Moreover, by 1950 black Americans were more prepared psychologically to launch a full-fledged campaign for first-class citizenship. Economic, political, and educational advances not only provided hope and strength but sparked ambition for further gains. The confidence of blacks had been stimulated during the war and in the postwar years by Presidents Franklin D. Roosevelt and Harry Truman and other national leaders acting in behalf of civil rights. Also, there was the Supreme Court's historic school desegregation decision of 1954, *Brown* v. *Topeka Board of Education*, which was the emotional turning point, marking the beginning of the structural changes being sought.

Progress was not uniform throughout the nation. The greatest strides seemed to be made in northern cities while the greatest resistance to change in the patterns of race relations was in the small towns and isolated rural areas of the South, where notions of white supremacy and segregation were deeply entrenched. These differential rates of social and economic progress in the various regions of the nation were the substance of the pushes and pulls which gave increasing motivation to southern blacks to pull up stakes and head north or west to join their friends and families who had been preceding them for more than a generation.

The demographic setting

By 1950 the population of the United States had slightly exceeded 150 million. The proportion of blacks in the total population was virtually unchanged from the three previous decades. Largely as the result of wartime and postwar migration from the South to the North and West, in some regions the proportion of blacks changed slightly from the previous decade. The black proportion of the South's population decreased from 24 percent in 1940 to 22 percent in 1950. At the other end of the migration streams, the North increased its black proportion of the population from 4 to 5 percent, while the West experienced an increase from 1 to 3 percent.[2] Despite substantial migration from the South, 68 percent of the nation's black population still lived there in 1950, a decrease of 9 percent from 1940. Twenty-eight percent of the black population lived in the North and 4 percent in the West.

From our earlier discussions, it is clear that much of the redistribution of the black population during the 1940s was an urbanward migration. Although in 1950 a larger proportion of whites than blacks was living in urban areas, the rate of increase was much greater for blacks. The percentage of change for blacks was almost double that of whites during the 1940s, so that by 1950 the proportion of each race in urban areas was almost equal: 64 percent for whites and 62 percent for blacks.

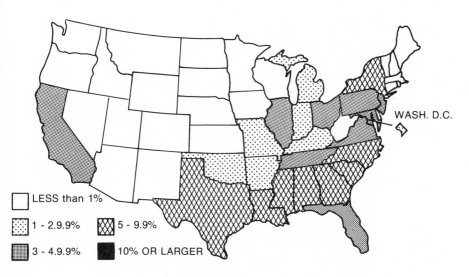

Figure 10-1. *Distribution of black population, 1950 (48 contiguous states; percent by state).*

SOURCE: U.S. Department of Commerce, Bureau of the Census, *Statistical Abstract of the United States, 1947* (Washington, D.C.: Government Printing Office, 1947), Table 19, p. 20.

Table 10–1. *Mobility status and type of mobility of the civilian population 1 year old and over, for the United States, April 1952–March 1960 (numbers in thousands)*

Period, color, & sex	Total civilian population	Same house non-movers	Different House in the U.S. (Movers)					
					Different county (migrants)			
			Total	Same county	Total	With-in a state	Between states	Abroad at beg. of period
March 1959 to 1960								
Both sexes, total	174,451	139,766	33,811	22,564	11,247	5,724	5,523	874
Percent	100.0	80.1	19.4	12.9	6.4	3.3	3.2	0.5
White	100.0	80.5	19.0	12.2	6.8	3.4	3.3	0.5
Nonwhite	100.0	77.2	22.4	18.4	4.0	2.1	1.9	0.4
April 1958 to 1959								
Both sexes, total	170,658	137,018	32,804	22,315	10,489	5,419	5,070	836
White	100.0	80.8	18.6	12.3	6.4	3.3	3.1	0.5
White	100.0	80.8	18.6	12.3	6.4	3.3	3.1	0.5
Nonwhite	100.0	75.8	23.8	19.6	4.2	2.5	1.7	0.4
March 1957 to 1958								
Both sexes, total	167,604	133,501	33,263	22,023	11,240	5,656	5,584	840
Percent	100.0	79.7	19.8	13.1	6.7	3.4	3.3	0.5
White	100.0	80.3	19.2	12.3	6.9	3.5	3.4	0.5
White	100.0	80.3	19.2	12.3	6.9	3.5	3.4	0.5
Nonwhite	100.0	74.6	25.1	19.8	5.3	2.3	3.0	0.3
April 1956 to 1957								
Both sexes, total	164,371	131,648	31,834	21,566	10,268	5,192	5,076	889
Percent	100.0	80.1	19.4	13.1	6.2	3.2	3.1	0.5
White	100.0	80.4	19.0	12.5	6.5	3.3	3.2	0.6
Nonwhite	100.0	77.5	22.2	17.8	4.4	1.8	2.5	0.3
March 1955 to 1956								
Both sexes, total	161,497	127,457	33,098	22,186	10,912	5,859	5,053	942
Percent	100.0	79.0	20.5	13.7	6.8	3.6	3.1	0.6
White	100.0	79.4	20.0	13.0	7.0	3.7	3.2	0.6
Nonwhite	100.0	74.9	24.8	19.9	4.9	2.7	2.2	0.3
April 1954 to 1955								
Both sexes, total	158,609	126,190	31,492	21,086	10,406	5,511	4,895	927
Percent	100.0	79.6	19.9	13.3	6.6	3.5	3.1	0.6
White	100.0	79.8	19.5	12.7	6.8	3.6	3.2	0.6
Nonwhite	100.0	77.4	22.4	18.0	4.4	2.2	2.2	0.2
April 1953 to 1954								
Both sexes, total	155,679	125,654	29,027	19,046	9,981	4,947	5,034	998
Percent	100.0	80.7	18.6	12.2	6.4	3.2	3.2	0.6
White	100.0	80.9	18.3	11.8	6.6	3.3	3.3	0.7
Nonwhite	100.0	78.8	20.8	16.0	4.8	2.4	2.4	0.4
April 1952 to 1953								
Both sexes, total	153,038	121,512	30,786	20,638	10,148	4,626	5,522	740
Percent	100.0	79.4	20.1	13.5	6.6	3.0	3.6	0.5
White	100.0	80.4	19.1	12.4	6.7	2.9	3.8	0.5
Nonwhite	100.0	71.9	27.9	21.7	6.2	4.2	2.0	0.2

SOURCE: U.S., Bureau of the Census, *Current Population Reports*, 1960 P-20, No. 118, Mobility of the Population of the United States: March 1960 to March 1961 (Washington, D.C.: Government Printing Office, 1960).

NOTE: In general, in this report, the "civilian population" includes members of the armed forces living off post or with their families on post but excludes all other members of the armed forces.

Major regional variations existed in the proportion of the black population living in urban areas. For example, 94 percent of the blacks living in the Northeast resided in urban areas. For those living in the North Central and West, 94 and 90 percent, respectively, lived in urban areas. In the South only 48 percent of the black population lived in urban areas.[3]

Volume of migration

The percentage of the black population that migrated each year during the 1950s ranged from a high of 6 percent for the year April 1952 to April 1953 to a low of 4 percent in the year March 1959 to March 1960. A smaller proportion of blacks moved between counties each year than did whites.[4]

As with previous decades, regional migration during the 1950s was predominately from the South to cities in the North and West. By 1960 there were 3.6 million blacks (nonwhites)[5] living in regions other than the ones in which they were born.[6] There were significant variations among the regions in the proportion of the black population born in regions other than the ones in which they were residing at the time of the 1960 census. For example, 1.5 million, or 47 percent, of the blacks living in the North Central region were born elsewhere. In contrast, only 1.4 percent of the South's black population were born outside that region.[7]

From 1955 to 1960, there were approximately 725,000 black migrants five years old and over who moved from one geographical division to another. In terms of gross migration, the greatest amount of movement occurred in the South Atlantic states, from which almost 190,000 blacks outmigrated and to which almost 95,000 in-migrated, resulting in a net loss to the division of slightly more than 95,000. The net loss through out-migration was even greater to the East South Central states. The East South Central division had the lowest ratio of in-migrants to out-migrants of any of the nine divisions in the nation, with respect to migration.

Table 10–2. Nonwhite native population by region of birth and region of residence with net gain or loss through interregional migration, 1960

Region	Living in the specified region			Net gain or loss through interregional migration
	Total	Born in other regions		
		Number	Percent	
United States	19,083,600	3,623,966	19.0	. . . .
Northeast	2,752,360	1,221,114	44.4	+ 1,091,713
North Central	3,310,706	1,559,541	47.1	+ 1,382,569
South	11,117,119	160,310	1.4	− 3,096,286
West	1,903,415	683,001	35.9	+ 622,004

SOURCE: U.S., Bureau of the Census, *Census of Population: 1960*, Subject Reports, Final Report PC(2)-2A *State of Birth* (Washington, D.C.: Government Printing Office, 1963) p. 3.

Table 10–3. Gain or loss from migration for divisions, 1955–60

Division	Nonwhite			White		
	In-migrants	Out-migrants	Net migration	In-migrants	Out-migrants	Net migration
New England	12.4	5.0	+7.4	4.5	5.3	−0.8
Middle Atlantic	5.8	2.8	+3.0	2.5	4.5	−2.0
East North Central	5.9	3.4	+2.5	4.2	5.7	−1.5
West North Central	7.6	6.4	+1.2	5.1	8.1	−3.0
South Atlantic	1.8	3.7	−1.9	9.5	6.3	+3.1
East South Central	1.9	6.9	−5.0	6.9	9.2	−2.3
West South Central	2.2	4.7	−2.4	6.5	7.4	−0.8
Mountain	10.3	8.0	+2.3	15.4	11.2	+4.2
Pacific	8.6	2.3	+6.3	10.8	5.1	+5.7

SOURCE: Ibid., Table 4, p. 15.

The most attractive group of states was found in the Far West. This division had a net black in-migration of more than 100,000 persons for the period 1955–1960. The strength of the division's attractiveness also is seen in the fact that there were 3.7 in-migrants for each out-migrant for any division.

Patterns of net migration for whites and blacks during the 1950s were quite dissimilar. In contrast to the black migration pattern, New England, Middle Atlantic, East North Central, and West North Central divisions experienced a net white out-migration. The South Atlantic division, which had one of the largest net black out-migration figures, experienced one of the larger net white in-migrations.

The volume of black migration which occurred during the 1950s is further indicated in greater geographical precision by changes in state of residence between 1955 and 1960. Only about two-thirds of the black population five years old and over were living in their state of birth in 1955 and 1960. In total, more than 850,000 blacks moved from one state to another during the five-year period, 1955–1960.

Major variations in attractiveness were found among the states. One indicator of migrant attractiveness is the number or proportion of the population living in a state but born in a different state. The least attractive states in the continental United States, i.e., those states with less than 10 percent of the state's black population born outside the state, were from the southern region. In South Carolina, only 3.8 percent of the state's black population was born in another state. Mississippi, Alabama, Georgia, Louisiana, and North Carolina, likewise, were among the least attractive.

The most attractive states for black migrants, i.e., those with more than 50 percent of the black population born in a different state, were distinc-

Table 10−4. *Place of birth by state of residence in 1955 and 1960, for nonwhite population 5 years old and over, by sex, for the U.S.*

Residence	Male	Female	Total	%
State of birth in 1955 and 1960	5,132,445	5,639,343	10,771,788	66.2
State of birth in 1960 but not 1955	73,770	73,815	147,585	0.9
State of birth in 1960, abroad in 1955, or not reported	55,836	26,637	82,473	0.5
Same state in 1955 and 1960 but born in different state	2,027,250	2,266,327	4,293,577	26.4
State of birth in 1955 but not 1960	289,229	310,532	599,761	3.7
Different states in 1955 and 1960, both different from state of birth	139,860	118,484	258,344	1.6
Not living in state of birth in 1960, abroad in 1955, or state not reported	75,893	31,018	106,911	0.7
Total native population, 5 yrs. and over	7,794,283	8,466,156	16,260,439	100.0

SOURCE: Ibid., Table 1, p. 2.

tively nonsouthern. In 16 states and the District of Columbia, more than half of the black residents had been born in a different state than the one in which they were residing in 1960.

Among the most attractive states for the decade were New York, Illinois, California, and Ohio, respectively. New York alone experienced a net black in-migration of 282,000 during the decade. Illinois had a net in-migration of almost 189,000, while California and Ohio experienced net in-migrations of 176,000 and 133,000.

The state with the largest amount of net out-migration was Mississippi. More than 323,000 blacks left Mississippi than arrived. The relative size of Mississippi's black out-migration during the 1950s was so great that Alabama, with the second largest net out-migration, had nearly 100,000 fewer net out-migrations for the same period. Also, North Carolina, South Carolina, and Georgia each had a net out-migration of more than 200,000 blacks. Yet it was not only the states of the Deep South that had net out-

Table 10–5. *State of birth of nonwhite population, 1960*

States with 15% or less of nonwhite population born in other states	%	50% or more born in other states	%
0.0–5%		Maine	53.7
South Carolina	3.8	New Hampshire	71.4
Alabama	5.0	Vermont	62.8
Mississippi	4.5	Connecticut	55.0
Hawaii	2.5	New Jersey	50.2
5.1–10%		Ohio	50.2
North Carolina	9.9	Indiana	51.3
Georgia	6.5	Illinois	55.8
Louisiana	7.5	Michigan	56.5
10.0–15%		Wisconsin	55.1
South Dakota	12.8	Nebraska	53.6
Kentucky	17.3	Kansas	50.2
Texas	12.7	District of Columbia	51.5
Montana	13.2	Colorado	61.5
		Nevada	58.7
		Oregon	51.3
		California	57.0

SOURCE: U.S., Bureau of the Census, *Census of Population: 1960*, Subject Reports, Final Report PC(2)-2A, *State of Birth* (Washington, D.C.: Government Printing Office, 1963), Table 14, p. 11.

migrations. Other states, including North and South Dakota, Montana, Wyoming, and Arizona experienced greater black out-migration than in-migration. Florida, a southern state, had one of the larger net gains in black population through migration.

The urban character of black migration during the 1950s is reflected in a wide variety of population statistics. It is estimated that more than 1.6 million more blacks migrated to metropolitan areas (SMSAs) than left during the decade.[8] The nonmetropolitan areas, on the other hand, experienced a net out-migration of approximately the same size. That blacks were more urban than whites during the 1950s is evidenced in their respective migration rates. For example, the net in-migration to metropolitan areas was 14 percent for blacks, compared with 7 percent for whites.

The cumulative effect of the urban migration of blacks became increasingly apparent over time, for it was not until 1960 that the black population had a larger percentage than whites classified as urban.[9]

The uneven rate at which the black population became urbanized regionally is exemplified by the different points in time at which the majority of the blacks came to reside in urban areas. In the Northeast, the majority of the black population was living in urban areas by the year 1870, compared to 1880 for the whites. In the North Central states, the majority of blacks were urbanized by 1890, while it was not until 1920 that whites were predominantly urban. The urban character of whites and blacks in the West was similar to the North Central, with the exception that the majority

Table 10–6. *Nonwhite net migration for regions, divisions, and for 48 contiguous states and District of Columbia, 1950–60*

Region–Division–State	Net migration Number	Rate	Region–Division–State	Net migration Number	Rate
Northeast	540,779	20.7	Dist. of		
New England	69,747	35.4	Columbia	53,756	14.7
Maine	1,998	50.1	Virginia	−71,452	−7.9
New			West Virginia	−40,337	−30.8
Hampshire	1,065	70.0	North Carolina	−206,897	−15.2
Vermont	NS	NS	South Carolina	−217,784	−20.7
Massachusetts	25,625	25.7	Georgia	−204,297	−15.3
Rhode Island	2,028	10.8	Florida	101,507	12.9
Connecticut	39,032	53.9	East South		
Middle Atlantic	471,032	19.5	Central	−619,928	−18.5
New York	282,072	23.3	Kentucky	−15,503	−6.5
New Jersey	112,084	27.0	Tennessee	−56,898	−8.8
Pennsylvania	76,876	9.7	Alabama	−224,201	−18.6
North Central	559,953	18.3	Mississippi	−323,326	−26.0
East North			West South		
Central	522,163	21.3	Central	−294,908	−9.2
Ohio	133,007	20.0	Arkansas	−149,814	−27.7
Indiana	44,629	19.5	Louisiana	−92,279	−8.0
Illinois	188,848	21.4	Oklahoma	−26,050	−10.6
Michigan	126,570	20.7	Texas	−26,765	−2.1
Wisconsin	29,109	45.6	West	346,664	18.5
West North			Mountain	22,374	7.0
Central	37,790	6.2	Montana	−2,012	−7.7
Minnesota	3,981	10.4	Idaho	512	5.5
Iowa	2,999	11.6	Wyoming	−983	−12.1
Missouri	28,378	7.7	Colorado	14,976	39.0
North Dakota	−2,006	−13.4	New Mexico	4,533	6.4
South Dakota	−4,526	−14.0	Arizona	−1,643	−1.1
Nebraska	3,991	12.2	Utah	982	6.2
Kansas	4,973	5.2	Nevada	6,009	38.0
South	−1,458,342	−11.2	Pacific	324,290	20.8
South Atlantic	−543,506	−8.3	Washington	18,051	21.6
Delaware	5,999	10.7	Oregon	6,002	19.6
Maryland	35,999	7.3	California	176,700	39.0

SOURCE: Gladys K. Bowles and James D. Tarver, *Net Migration of the Population, 1950–1960, by Age, Sex and Color.* U.S., Department of Agriculture (Washington, D.C.: Government Printing Office, 1965), Vol. II, Tables 1, 2, 3, pp. 1–33.

of blacks were living in urban areas by 1880. In the South, however, the urbanization of blacks and whites proceeded in a fairly uniform fashion and much slower than in other regions. It was not until 1960 that the majority of both whites and blacks made their homes in southern urban areas. Neither racial group preceded the other in its move to the cities in the South, in contrast to all other regions. Significant regional variations in the degree of urbanization continued to exist with more than 95 percent of blacks in the Northeast being urban, compared to only 58 percent in the South.

Table 10-7. Percent of urban population by region and race, 1870–1960

Region and race	1870	1880	1890	1900	1910	1920	1930	1940	1950	1960
United States										
White	27.5	30.3	38.4	43.0	48.7	53.4	57.6	57.4	64.3	65.5
Negro	13.4	14.3	19.8	22.7	27.4	34.0	43.7	48.6	62.4	73.2
Northeast										
White	44.2	50.6	62.5	69.0	74.0	75.7	76.9	76.1	78.7	79.1
Negro	54.0	62.7	71.5	78.3	82.6	86.7	89.0	90.1	94.0	95.6
North Central										
White	20.5	23.8	32.7	38.2	44.7	51.6	56.9	57.3	62.6	66.8
Negro	37.2	42.5	55.8	64.4	72.6	83.4	87.8	88.8	93.8	95.7
West										
White	25.3	30.7	37.9	41.2	49.2	53.0	59.6	58.8	69.7	77.6
Negro	44.6	50.8	54.0	67.4	78.6	74.0	82.5	83.1	90.3	92.7
South										
White	13.3	13.1	16.9	18.5	23.2	29.6	33.4	36.8	48.9	58.6
Negro	10.3	10.6	15.3	17.2	21.2	25.3	31.7	36.5	47.7	58.5
Secessionist South										
White	8.8	8.8	12.8	14.9	20.4	26.4	33.0	35.5	48.7	59.2
Negro	8.3	8.5	12.9	14.7	18.8	22.7	29.1	33.7	44.6	55.4
Nonsecessionist South										
White	23.8	24.3	27.6	27.4	29.9	35.8	39.2	40.2	49.7	56.5
Negro	26.2	29.4	38.4	42.1	44.3	49.4	54.7	60.8	71.6	79.3

Source: Daniel O. Price, *Changing Characteristics of the Negro Population,* U.S., Bureau of the Census, 1960 Census Monograph (Washington, D.C.: Government Printing Office, 1969), p. 11.

The usual perception of the black urban population is generally northern in character, conjuring images of New York, Chicago, and Detroit. Of the 42 cities with 100,000 or more population and with 20 percent or more black population in 1960, a disproportionate number were in the South. Among the top half with the highest percent of black population, only two, Gary and Newark, were outside the South.[10] Of the 18 cities with more than 100,000 blacks in 1960, 8 were in the South, while the rest were in other regions. The largest concentrations of urban blacks were outside the South by 1960, but a disproportionate number of the urban areas with large proportions of blacks were in the South.

Characteristics of migrants

The age structure of migrants is not uniform among all types. For example, the intercounty migrants do not have the same age structure as interstate, interdivisional, or interregional migrants. Each migrant group varies in this and other demographic characteristics.

The age of black interstate migrants (between contiguous and noncontiguous states) during the 1950s was similar to that of migrants in other times. They were younger than the total population by nearly five years.

The median age of the black population was 29.1 and the median age of black interstate migrants was 24.6. Very little difference in age is found between migrants to contiguous states, as compared to the migrants to noncontiguous states.

The model age group of the migrants was 20 to 24, which included 19 percent of the migrants. The pronounced age selectivity of migration is revealed by the fact that only 7.4 percent of the total black population was of comparable age. More than half the migrants were less than 25 years of age, compared to only about 44 percent of the total black population. Moreover, migrants were overrepresented in each of the five-year age cohorts, from age 15 through 34. In all of the remaining cohorts, the migrants were underrepresented.

The ratio of males to females and its importance for family formation and other types of behavior has been discussed in previous chapters. The relative distribution of males to females in a population is one of the limiting factors for the marriage rate which, in turn, is reflected in the fertility.

Most long-distance migrants were males. Black migrants during the 1950s reflected this general pattern. For example, the sex ratio of the black population over five years of age in 1960 was 93.5. The sex ratio for black interstate migrants for the period 1955–1960 was significantly higher at 102.3. The greater selectivity of males among long-distance migrants is evident in the comparison of the sex ratio for interstate migrants between

Table 10–8. *Age for interstate nonwhite migrants, 1960 (25% sample)*

Age	Population reporting on 1955 residence	Interstate migrants		
		All migrants	Contiguous states	Noncontiguous states
5 to 9 years	14.9	13.5	14.4	13.2
10 to 14 years	12.4	8.5	9.5	8.1
15 to 19 years	9.3	10.4	10.7	10.2
20 to 24 years	7.4	19.2	16.1	20.5
25 to 29 years	7.3	14.6	12.4	15.4
30 to 34 years	7.6	10.0	9.5	10.2
35 to 39 years	7.5	7.1	7.5	6.9
40 to 44 years	6.7	4.6	5.3	4.4
45 to 49 years	6.2	3.5	4.4	3.2
50 to 54 years	5.3	2.6	3.0	2.4
55 to 59 years	4.7	2.1	2.5	1.9
60 to 64 years	3.5	1.3	1.6	1.2
65 to 69 years	3.0	1.0	1.2	0.9
70 to 74 years	2.0	0.7	0.9	0.6
75 to over years	2.2	0.8	0.9	0.7
Median age	29.1	24.6	24.8	24.5
Total Number	17,070,117	1,063,321	305,695	757,626

SOURCE: U.S., Bureau of the Census, *Census of Population: 1960*, Subject Reports, Final Report PC(2)-2B, *Mobility for States and State Economic Areas* (Washington, D.C.: Government Printing Office, 1963), Table 2, p. 1.

Table 10–9. Sex ratio of migrant and nonmigrant black population, 1960

	Number	Sex ratio
Total Population, 1960		
Male	8,473,768	93.55
Female	9,057,922	
Interstate migrants		
Male	536,669	102.3
Female	525,652	
Contiguous state migrants		
Male	153,282	100.5
Female	152,413	
Noncontiguous state migrants		
Male	384,387	103.0
Female	373,239	

SOURCE: Ibid.

contiguous states, 100.5, with the ratio for migrants between noncontiguous states, 102.9.[11]

Each migration stream is generally distinctive in its sexual composition. For example, the sex ratio of the black migrants to the Middle Atlantic division was a low 89, while the ratio of those migrating to the Pacific division was a high 106.4. The other geographic divisions fell between these two extremes.

One study has recognized the difference in the sex ratios of black interregional migrants.[12] This analysis of the census also indicates that males tend to constitute a disproportionately large part of the total of long-distance migrants, with the notable exception of the rather long trek from the South Atlantic and East South Central divisions to the New England, Middle Atlantic, and East North Central divisions. In these divisions black women greatly outnumbered men. Of special importance was the reverse flow of blacks back into the South (more than 120,000) from the North and West. The sex ratio in this case was well above the average.[13]

In reports on the educational attainment of migrants,[14] findings indicate that the rate of migration for both white and nonwhite populations of both sexes tend to vary directly with the level of educational attainment, i.e., the higher the level of education, the higher the migration rate.[15] Evidence for this pattern is given in Tables 10–11 and 10–12, which indicates that while nearly 60 percent of the total black population 25 years old and over had less than eight years of formal education, only 42 percent of the black interstate migrants failed to exceed that level of schooling. Likewise, the proportion of interstate migrants that had four or more years of college was more than twice as great as the total adult population.

Table 10–10. Sex ratio of nonwhite migrants by place of residence in 1955 and 1960

Place of Residence 1955	Place of residence 1960								
	New England	Middle Atlantic	East N. Central	West N. Central	South Atlantic	East S. Central	West S. Central	Mountain	Pacific
Total	96.9	89.0	93.9	93.9	93.4	90.6	91.9	102.6	106.4
New England	91.4	113.4	120.5	151.1	134.0	103.4	214.9	140.8	114.1
Middle Atlantic	114.9	88.1	99.0	155.2	109.6	123.9	187.9	158.7	118.8
East North Central	149.5	100.6	92.6	137.5	137.1	107.0	145.9	127.7	122.2
West North Central	140.7	99.1	96.8	90.6	149.4	106.7	115.0	118.0	106.2
South Atlantic	93.4	76.9	89.1	140.0	91.4	123.5	151.8	158.0	130.8
East South Central	88.9	69.7	83.7	93.6	119.8	89.6	103.0	106.6	102.3
West South Central	127.8	102.7	88.0	103.0	155.0	105.4	90.2	106.9	97.2
Pacific	173.7	133.9	138.1	115.5	147.9	187.4	121.0	99.2	124.3
Atlantic	141.5	131.1	112.3	111.4	165.2	141.0	121.6	136.6	101.2
Abroad	153.5	106.0	159.0	137.4	246.9	180.0	153.8	119.2	110.4
Not reported 1955	139.5	123.5	122.8	129.3	157.5	138.8	152.4	136.0	163.2

SOURCE: U.S., Bureau of the Census, Census of Population: 1960, Subject Reports, Final Report PC(2)-2D Lifetime and Recent Migration (Washington, D.C.: Government Printing Office, 1963), Table 3, pp. 12–15.

Table 10–11. *Educational attainment of the nonwhite population 25 years old and over, intercounty and interstate migrants, 1960 (by percent)*

Educational attainment	Nonwhite population		Intercounty migrant		Interstate migrant	
	Male	Female	Male	Female	Male	Female
No school completed	6.77	4.62	4.75	3.32	2.93	2.10
Elementary school, less than 5 years	20.89	14.98	15.42	10.94	11.84	8.34
Elementary school 5–8 years	35.19	36.92	30.02	31.25	28.44	29.85
High school 1–3 years	17.09	20.22	19.65	21.33	20.97	23.12
High School, 4 years	12.16	15.29	15.60	18.87	19.05	21.37
College, 1–3 years	4.37	4.38	7.01	6.98	8.04	7.87
College, 4 years or more	3.51	3.55	7.52	7.25	8.69	7.31
Total (numbers)	4,684,174	5,187,248	455,036	426,607	262,894	255,912
Total, both sexes	9,871,422		881,643		518,806	

SOURCE: U.S., Bureau of the Census, *Census of Population: 1960*, Subject Reports, Final Report PC(2)-2B, *Mobility for States and State Economic Areas* (Washington, D.C.: Government Printing Office, 1963), Table 6, pp. 14–15.

It is also true that as the distance of migration increases, the differentials become even sharper.[16] For example, Table 10–11 presents migration data for intercounty and interstate migrants. At each level of education above elementary school, the interstate migrants have a larger proportion than the intercounty. Likewise, at each educational level below high school, the intercounty migrants have a larger proportion than the interstate migrants.

There also are significant variations in the various migrant streams. For example, from Table 10–12, it may be seen that migrants into the South, both black and white, male and female, had lower levels of education than migrants into other regions. Migrants to the West, on the other hand, tended to be of higher educational attainment than migrants into other regions.

The heavy out-migration of blacks from the South, combined with the educational selectivity, resulted in a "brain drain" for the region. The South was disadvantaged in at least two respects: one, the public investment in education for the out-migrants was lost to the region; two, the region was left with blacks of lower levels of educational achievement, who were less able to make positive economic contributions.[17]

The popular stereotype of the migrant has been one of a single person setting off alone from the farm or small town to seek his fortune in the big city.[18] Of course there were many such migrants, but more than 60 percent of the black interstate migrants were married. Slightly over 30 percent were single. Some reinforcement for the stereotype was provided by the fact that migrants were somewhat overrepresented among the single persons in comparison to the total black population 14 years and over. On the

Table 10–12. Median years of school completed by region of residence in 1955 and 1960 by color and sex

Color, sex, and region of residence in 1960	Region of Residence in 1955			
	Northeast	North Central	South	West
Northeast				
White				
Male	9.8	13.7	12.9	12.9
Female	9.8	12.8	12.6	12.7
Nonwhite				
Male	9.0	9.9	9.1	12.5
Female	9.3	12.0	9.3	12.7
North Central				
White				
Male	13.3	9.7	12.3	12.6
Female	12.6	10.0	12.2	12.5
Nonwhite				
Male	9.9	8.9	9.0	12.2
Female	12.1	9.3	12.7	12.3
South				
White				
Male	12.6	12.3	9.5	12.5
Female	12.4	12.2	9.7	12.4
Nonwhite				
Male	9.3	9.3	5.6	9.9
Female	9.6	9.5	8.1	9.8
West				
White				
Male	12.7	12.4	12.4	12.1
Female	12.4	12.4	12.3	12.2
Nonwhite				
Male	12.4	10.0	9.7	9.3
Female	12.3	12.1	9.7	9.5

SOURCE: Daniel O. Price, *Changing Characteristics of the Negro Population*, U.S., Bureau of the Census, 1960, Census Monograph (Washington D.C.: Government Printing Office, 1969), Table VI-7, p. 209.

other hand, migrants were underrepresented among the widowed. Only 5 percent of the migrants were widows, while nearly 10 percent of the black population was of comparable marital status. This was probably a result of the age differences between the two groups. About equal proportions of migrants and of the total black population were divorced.

Of course, the manner in which migration data are obtained could conceal the true character of marital status. For example, a migrant who arrived at his destination as a single person and married before the census enumeration, would be counted as married rather than single. But it may be that the movement of families is increasing. As the population becomes better educated and occupations become more specialized, the result is a rising tendency for corporations to move workers from one place to an-

Table 10–13. Marital status of the nonwhite population, intercounty and interstate migrants, 1960 (by percent)

Marital status, 14 yrs. and over	Nonwhite population		Intercounty migrant		Interstate migrant		Total % both sexes	IC* % both sexes	IS**% both sexes
	Male	Female	Male	Female	Male	Female			
Single	30.1	21.98	36.65	25.88	36.08	24.47	25.85	31.35	30.2
Married, spouse present	53.20	48.53	42.69	47.50	44.58	48.83	50.76	40.05	46.6
Married, spouse absent	9.66	11.99	14.88	14.23	14.22	15.00	10.88	14.56	14.6
Widowed	4.58	13.88	3.06	8.82	2.49	7.95	9.44	5.89	5.1
Divorced	2.44	36.16	2.70	3.55	2.60	3.73	3.05	3.12	3.1
Total (column)	6,273,795	6,872,196	718,299	695,160	426,454	416,786			
Total, both sexes	13,145,991		1,413,465		843,240				

SOURCE: U.S., Bureau of the Census, *Census of Population: 1960*, Subject Reports, Final Report PC(2)-2B *Mobility for States and State Economic Areas* (Washington, D.C.: Government Printing Office, 1963), Table 7, pp. 16–18.
*Intercounty
**Interstate

other and for heads of families to look for employment in an area much less geographically restricted. This would give rise to a greater tendency for whole families to be among the migrants than previously.[19]

The importance of occupation as an indicator of social status in American society is well known. Moreover, as the educational differentials among migrants would lead us to suspect, there were occupational and employment differences between black migrants and the total black population. One such difference was in the proportion of the population in the labor force. The interstate migrants contained a larger proportion in the labor force than did the total black population.

One of the more pronounced differences occupationally was the disproportionately larger number of the male migrants who were professional, technical, or kindred workers. Among interstate male migrants, the relative proportion of professionals was nearly two and one-half times as large as their counterparts in the total population. While 8.6 percent of black interstate male migrants were professional or technical workers, only 3.8 percent of the total black male population was so employed.

An analysis of migration rates of the black population 25 to 34 years of age, in terms of occupational differences, found that among males the migration rate of professional and technical workers was more than twice as great as that of most other occupational groups.

Causes of migration

It is important to distinguish between the causes of migration and the migrant's motivation for moving. The migrants themselves were some-

Table 10–14. *Migration status and occupation, 1935–40 and 1955–60*

Time period and migration status	% of employed males engaged in white-collar occupations
1935–40	
Nonmigrants	20.1
In-migrants	11.0
South—Total	
South—Urban	12.3
South—Rural	7.8
1955–60	
Nonmigrants	21.1
In-migrants	28.3
Other SMSA	
Nonmetropolitan areas	15.7

SOURCE: Karl E. Taeuber and Alma F. Taeuber, *Negroes in Cities* (Chicago: Aldine Publishing Co., 1965), p. 140.

times unaware of their own motives. Responses such as "I just felt like moving," "It just seemed like the thing to do," and "I don't know, I just wanted to get out of . . . " are not uncommon, particularly among the lower income migrants.[20] Generally, when asked, they cite two, three, or more reasons for moving.

Theoretical problems also complicate the issue of migrant motivation. A case in point is the approach taken by most economists and other social scientists, who view the decision to migrate as a rational one, based on calculated gains and losses, a decision made by the migrant himself. In reality, the rational element in the decision is only partial and depends upon the migrant's personality, access to information, emotional factors, and the independence of the individual.[21] It also assumes that the migrant himself made the decision.

Though we may identify in broad terms those factors which predispose a given population to migration, this does not in itself explain the variety of responses made to these pressures. For example, how does one explain the absence of migration in the presence of all the push factors usually associated with heavy out-migration? In the final analysis, understanding the causes of migration remains dependent upon both objective and subjective elements in the situation of the migrant and on his awareness of them.[22]

Such an approach creates problems for those trying to understand black migration during the 1950s. Motivation must be inferred on the basis of objective demographic data, most of which were obtained by the census. These inferences, of course, are subject to the limitations generally associated with this type of exercise. The true meaning of the migration for the migrants cannot be documented. The limitations do not, of course, invalidate the push-pull model of migration. They do, however, limit our ability to identify all the factors associated with push and pull forces.

Black migration during the 1950s, as in other periods, was the product of a complex array of interactive forces which affected not only the migrants but also the sending and receiving communities. The chief push forces were technological change in southern agriculture, retarded economic conditions in the South, and the heightened tension between whites and blacks resulting in harsh social and political realities for blacks. The pull from regions outside the South was pressure to join family and friends already living in the North and West, the hope and the promise of a better life. Not to be discounted as a pull factor was the greater maturity of black institutions in the North and the assistance they were providing to the black community.

Economic conditions. Perhaps the major push factor for blacks in the 1950s was the technological change occurring in southern agriculture. Biological, chemical, and mechanical innovations required tremendous outlays of capital, but resulted in major labor savings. The old South was characterized by a large labor force, small land holdings, poor soils, and a climate that was conducive to heavy damage from insects, pests, and diseases. Thus, the initial emphasis in research and technological change in the South was placed upon biological and chemical improvements that enabled the region to increase the productivity of agricultural land.[23] By the 1950s, mechanical innovation had begun to result in extensive substitution of machinery for manpower. Commercial farming developed rapidly. Many farmers reorganized production, improved marketing efficiency, and greatly reduced their need for labor. These changes affected rural black farm workers more than it did whites.[24]

Some evidence of these trends is offered by a study of the impact of the adoption of tractors and mechanical cotton-pickers upon migration. Tractors were adopted by some growers before World War II, resulting in a shift from sharecropping toward a more flexible daily wage labor. More were adopted after the war, partly in response to the general tightening of labor as many black workers and families migrated to the North to search for jobs in war industries. Some cotton growers were reluctant to adopt tractors since their use would reduce earnings enough to force many of their tenants to seek employment elsewhere—thus leaving them without the labor necessary for weeding and picking.[25] The results of the study concluded that even the limited adoption of tractors drove black tenants away from their home counties.

But more than the tractor, mechanical cotton pickers had a severe impact on the agricultural South. The adoption of mechanical pickers began in 1943, when the first machines were marketed. While their widespread adoption was slowed by the same general considerations that hindered tractor adoption, two factors facilitated recent adoption of mechanical pickers in large numbers:

> One of these is the fact that by the early 1950s many cotton growers had acquired tractors (and the more mechanical equipment acquired or available to the farmer, the greater the temptation to realize the economies possible with such equipment); the other factor has been the development (beginning in the early 1950s) of chemical weed-killers. Even though the weed-killers do not destroy weeds as efficiently as hand-hoeing, they do permit the economies of tractor use and mechanical pickers to be fully realized: this combination sounded the death knell of the Negro hand-laborer.[26]

An analysis of 17 cotton-growing counties in Arkansas during the 1950s gave support to the assumption that mechanical pickers displaced large numbers of black tenants. In these counties, the number of tenant farmers declined by two-thirds—from more than 21,000 to about 6,500—by the end of the decade. In the same time, mechanical cotton pickers increased at least sevenfold.[27]

The potential impact of adopting mechanical pickers is indicated by the fact that the small-sized picker can harvest an acre of cotton in 6 man-hours, compared to 74 man-hours of hand labor.[28] In actual fact, not all the mechanical pickers were of the smaller variety. Moreover, most tenant laborers were supporting four or more other family members (the median size of black families in these counties was over five). It is not difficult to understand how an increase of a hundred mechanical pickers in a county could lead to the out-migration of hundreds or even thousands of persons.[29] The magnitude of the impact upon the out-migration of tenant labor is revealed by the fact that in 1958, 27 percent of the Mississippi Delta cotton crop was harvested by mechanical pickers. By 1964, six years later, the percentage had increased to 81. The obvious consequence of this increased mechanization was a staggering reduction in black tenancy in the Delta and other southern areas that grow cotton.[30]

Relocation was unquestionably difficult for these ex-tenant farmers. Few or no opportunities in agriculture existed without considerable capital. The only possible opportunities were in the urban areas. Some evidence suggests that most of these out-migrants went to urban areas in the South.[31] The result was increased competition for unskilled work in the southern cities and increased pressure from some to move on to areas outside the South. This type of economically impelled movement best characterizes the migration of the 1950s. Initially it was from the rural, agricultural areas of the South to the nearby small towns and cities, which were mostly temporary destinations. As the supply of unskilled increased in these communities, it was inevitable that a sizable proportion would have to seek employment in the larger industrial cities in the South as well as in the North and West. The result was the considerable black interregional migration discussed earlier.

Technological innovations in agriculture were only one part of the economic pressures in the South which increased out-migration. General economic conditions caused a movement away from areas in which the economic status of black people was poor to areas in which their status was somewhat better.[32] Of course, the disparity between the South and other regions in terms of income[33] and the disparity between whites and blacks with respect to income has been widely documented.[34] These disparities, given a precipitating event or events of sufficient magnitude, translate into "push" factors that, in turn, convert relatively stable populations into migrants.

Indicative of these disparities are the median incomes of black and white individuals in 1950 and 1960. In 1950, for example, the median individual income of white males in the United States was $2,572. The individual income for black males was only about half as much, or $1,341. In the South, individual income for blacks was not only absolutely but relatively lower as well. The median individual income for white males in the South in 1950 was $2,065, compared to $1,033 for blacks, exactly one-half. By 1960 incomes were up, but black males in the South were relatively worse off than they were ten years earlier. Their individual earnings were only about half (46 percent) as large as their white counterparts, a relative decline of 3 percent during the decade.[35]

Black males fared considerably better in the Northeast, earning 74 percent as much as whites, and in the North Central regions as much as 80 percent. Although by 1960 the median incomes for black males in these regions increased, their relative position to whites worsened as it had in the South. But this was not the case for black females, who had median incomes almost equal to their white counterparts in both regions. Still, income levels for women, white and black, were less than $1,800 in the Northeast and less than $1,400 in the North Central region.[36]

Of course, black workers in the South, men and women, were aware that their earnings were significantly lower than those being paid outside the South. Close family ties and frequent communication with those who had left were sources of information about conditions elsewhere. Black newspapers, black magazines, movies, television, and the ommipresent "grapevine" also facilitated the flow of information. Of course, the reliability of the information was another question, and it was not infrequent that the promise of job openings in Cleveland, East St. Louis, or some other city proved to be misinformation, causing individuals and whole families to become dependent on the charity and resources of kin or friends or some sort of public assistance. Others, failing to find the jobs they sought, or finding the conditions of ghetto living too strange or difficult, returned South, not always to their original home, but to some nearby city where the promise of a job was not so remote.

Social factors. The social and political realities of being black in the South in the 1950s also constituted a significant push factor. Perhaps the overriding issue of the decade was the 1954 Supreme Court decision on school desegregation. Since Reconstruction, the social structure of the South had been buttressed by both social and legal sanctions. But with the *Brown* decision, the legal reinforcement of that structure had been severely weakened, thus creating a sense of crisis throughout the South.[37] Although the reaction to the decision was varied, a few states in the Deep South reacted with shock and anger, which soon hardened into defiant resistance. Two months after the decision, a White Citizens' Council was formed in Indianola, Mississippi, which, in turn, served as a model for the organization of many such councils throughout the South. Likewise, the Ku Klux Klan renewed its efforts.[38] The principal objective of these organizations was to bring pressure on the South's political system, and to force public officials to denounce the Supreme Court's decision.

Strategies of resistance took many forms. One form of resistance was economic reprisals against blacks: "A Negro who sought to enter his child in a 'white' school might find it difficult to keep his job, to have his teaching contract renewed, to extend his mortgage, or to get credit at the bank. A Negro tenant who favored integration ran the risk of being evicted."[39] In some areas, public schools were closed to avoid integration and violence. In Little Rock, Arkansas, public schools were closed during the entire 1957–58 term. Likewise, Prince Edward County, Virginia, closed its public schools in 1959, although private schools continued to operate for white children with state monies.[40] These actions inflamed the relationships between the racial groups and convinced many black people that the North or West offered better social conditions, such as better education for their children and at least the prospect of less blatant discrimination.

Thus, the mechanical innovations in agriculture, the relative economic deprivation in the South, and the hostile social and political climate for blacks were the major push factors bringing pressure on the black populations to relocate. Unquestionably, there were numerous other personal reasons why some black individuals moved during the 1950s. However, without these harsh conditions, it is doubtful that such a sizable interregional black migration would have occurred.

Conditions in the North and West—the "pull" factors. The major pull factors of the North and West in the 1950s were economic, social, political, and familial. Personal and family incomes were higher in the North and West, but so was the cost of living. Central city tenement housing was inordinately expensive, while suburban housing was rarely available at any price for black families. Despite these limitations, the migration streams continued to flow.

One important and revealing study of the determinants of black migration during the 1950s in 90 SMSAs sought to discover the relative importance of economic conditions and the size of a community's black population. The findings indicate that high levels of unemployment provided a stimulus to out-migration, but differences among low levels of unemployment did not seem to affect in-migration. The most striking conclusion was that while economic factors were statistically significant they nevertheless played a relatively minor role in the overall direction of black migration. The bulk of the migrants moved in response to differences in the size of the black population in the SMSAs studied. This was true in both the South and the non-South, but particularly so outside the South.[41]

Of course, the attractiveness of large cities with sizable black communities, and the subsequent neglect of cities with small black communities, was not new in the 1950s. A decade earlier the same patterns were observed in explaining the attractiveness of larger urban areas for black migrants in the prewar years.

> The primary explanation seems to be that in rural areas of the West, white settlers decided that there were not to be any Negroes. The same seems to have been true in most rural areas of the Northeast and in most small towns of the entire North. The closer neighborhood controls in smaller communities seem to have blocked the Negro from moving in when he was no longer protected as a slave. Even apart from actual pressure there must have been imagined pressure: individuals in a lower caste, like the Negroes, are always on the lookout for discrimination and intimidation and probably felt that it was not safe to venture into the loneliness of a small community. At any rate, it soon became a popular belief among Southern Negroes that the only outlet from the Southern Black Belt was to the cities and preferably to the big cities, where Negro neighborhoods were already established. Negro migration thus early tended to become migration between fairly large-sized Negro communities or to be stopped altogether.[42]

In addition to the greater physical protection afforded by the larger black communities, there seemed to be greater economic security as well. The migrant not only had to find a place to live, but also had to ensure himself and his family some means of support until he obtained employment. These needs are commonly met by relying upon kinfolks or friends already living in the destination community. Thus, the larger the black community, the greater the potential source of assistance during the migrant's period of initial adjustment.

Unfortunately, this pattern of destination selection by black migrants was somewhat problematic, and, to a degree, continues to be. For example, to the extent that size of the black community exceeded economic considerations in the selection of a destination, persistent pockets of very low income blacks tended to be created and perpetuated as the number of persons in these communities expanded beyond the economic opportunities open to them.[43] Likewise, other problems resulted from such patterns of migrant destination selection, such as inadequate and insufficient housing and overcrowding. These problems precipitated other behavioral and health problems.

Another pull factor that affected blacks was the promise of upward social mobility that the cities offered. They held greater educational opportunities than rural areas for blacks and whites. Education was viewed as the avenue for "getting ahead" and thus was highly valued, especially for the children and young people. High school diplomas became increasingly essential and sought after, and sacrifice to send children on to college was not uncommon. In addition, the increasing sophistication of black institutions, particularly those in the large northern cities, also became attractions for potential migrants. Institutions such as the church, schools and colleges, business and professional associations, labor and political organizations, the Urban League, and the National Association for the Advancement of Colored People began flourishing in the urban black belts. These social institutions provided the breeding ground for a new kind of citizen and a new kind of leadership trained in the values and skills of the middle class.[44] Southern blacks were not ignorant of the activities of these organizations and institutions and the hope they offered for better conditions. And, it was this hope that inspired many black individuals and families to leave the South to participate in the making of a new life.

It has often been charged that one of the chief attractions for blacks in the North was, and continues to be, the relatively larger welfare benefits available there. Although an interesting hypothesis and one that has retained a degree of popular appeal, even a casual review of intercensal black migration rates and welfare outlays reveals little evidence to support such an hypothesis. The highest rates of black migration to New York were at a time when there was no such thing as relief, and the poor were dependent on private charity. When public relief and welfare did become a reality, population increases due to in-migration were much smaller.[45] The welfare hypothesis, likewise, overlooks the fact of legal residence requirements imposed by most states for eligibility to such programs.

Summary of causes. The picture that emerges of black migration in the 1950s is one in which blacks moved away from areas in which their economic opportunities were severely limited and toward areas where these opportunities were relatively more plentiful. Yet, the cities selected as destinations were already faced with serious problems stemming from the segregation practices which prevented blacks from availing themselves of housing beyond the boundaries of designated black communities and ghettos. The coming of the migrants intensified many of these problems. At the same time, the increasing size of the black communities, together with their concentration, began to alter the political structure in many cities that promised a greater black voice in urban, state, and national affairs.

Consequences of migration

It would be difficult to overstate the consequences of black migration to the North. But it would be even more difficult to isolate and identify the consequences of the migration which occurred only in the 1950s. For the most part, those consequences are still unfolding. While some of the effects of the migration were distinct enough to observe, many of the consequences have gone undetected for a variety of reasons. Of one thing we can be sure: few metropolitan areas in the North and rural areas in the South have been unaffected by the patterns of black migration. In the areas of in-migration, as well as out-migration, the political, economic, social, and personal lives of all the residents have been affected, directly or indirectly, by the migration. Some of the more significant consequences for the migrants themselves and the areas of origin and destination can be discussed.

Efforts to understand the consequences of black migration and the assimilation of the migrants into urban life have often yielded conflicting results. Perhaps one of the major controversies surrounding black migrants to metropolitan areas is whether or not they will experience the same pattern of adjustment and assimilation that has characterized other immigrant groups. Many social scientists have tried to analyze what has happened to black migrants in terms analogous to the experiences of the Irish, Italians, Poles, and other immigrant groups. The basic argument is captured in Irving Kristol's article, "The Negro Today Is Like the Immigrant Yesterday."[46] Kristol reminds his readers of how much of the derogatory and discriminatory language directed at black newcomers also was experienced by the Irish a few generations earlier. A number of historians of American immigration and assimilation, like Oscar Handlin, also have taken the position advocating the similarity of experiences of alien and black newcomers.[47]

Others argue that there are important differences between the aspiring, foreign-born white and the aspiring, domestic-born black migrants, that blacks differed from European immigrant groups in that they did not develop the "same kind of clannishness, they did not have the same close family ties, which in other groups created little communities for ethnic businessmen and professionals to tap."[48] Foreign-born immigrants coming to America began at the bottom. They gradually moved up the ladder as they acquired skills, capital, land, and eventually, acceptance.[49] The black family was not thought to be strong enough to create those extended clans that elsewhere were most helpful in establishing the necessary foundation for upward mobility. The lack of trust and business reciprocity among blacks effectively prevented the establishment and growth of black enterprise. Blacks were dependent on non-blacks for jobs and their economic survival. This dependency, in the context of racial antagonism, also effectively prevented most blacks from "moving up the ladder."

In many ways the consequences of migration for the migrants during the 1950s were similar to those of earlier periods. Despite the fact that migration is often undertaken as a solution to a personal or family need, the act of migrating is itself traumatic, creating stress which includes conflict upon arrival at the destination community. These problems may have deleterious effects upon the migrant's personality and adjustment.[50] This ability to adjust is often related to the extent to which formal institutional provision for medical, psychiatric, social, and welfare assistance is available. Few such provisions were available for blacks in the 1950s outside those offered by the church. Since the pastoral duties of the clergy include comforting and assisting those who call on the church for help, the role of the church was characterized as one of assimilating blacks into urban life.[51] Accordingly, many first generation migrants chose the warmth and interpersonal closeness of the storefront church, while their children and others chose the huge, elaborate, and often impersonal black urban church (the average size of the black urban church at the time was around 800 members). The church continued to perform important functions in the organized social life of the black community and to communicate and reinforce dominant family values and behaviors.[52]

Marital and family disruption was a frequent cause of migration, and it is also a common consequence which stemmed from a variety of unanticipated pressures brought on by the stress of urban living. It has been argued that "it is the move to the city that results in the very high proportion of mother-headed households."[53] From 1949 to 1962, the percentage of white families headed by a woman changed very little (8.8 to 8.6 percent). But among black families, the proportion increased from about 19 to 23 precent.[54].

The revolution of rising expectations, associated in large part with migration to urban areas, also has been destructive of black families. The rural life of tenant farmers and sharecroppers was well defined and precluded realizing any upward social mobility. Those same aspirations which motivated black families to leave the small towns and rural areas of the South in order to gain more of a share in the "American Dream" were also left largely unfulfilled in the metropolitan ghettos of the North. These unfulfilled expectations frequently resulted in negative consequences for marriage and family solidarity.

The key to successful postmigration adjustment was acquiring an acceptable job. The types of job opportunities and level of wages, however, varied from city to city and area to area. During the 1950s, New York was behind Detroit and Chicago in wages because it did not have the same concentration of auto plants, steel mills, stockyards, and other heavy industry in which powerful and progressive unions had achieved high wages and strict equality in pay between blacks and whites.[55] The lack of heavy industry in New York exaggerated all problems. The garment industry, which attracted a substantial number of Jewish males as sewing machine operators, was not attractive to black males. Discrimination against outsiders, and particularly black outsiders, effectively prevented black males from any substantial participation in the trade skills.[56]

The success of black women in obtaining work was much greater than their male counterparts. "It was the woman who could get whatever work was available even in the worst times. It was the man who was seen as a threat and subject to physical violence. It was the woman who came in touch with the white world, and for whom favors, if any were forthcoming, were more common."[57]

The differences in success of men and women in obtaining employment retarded the adjustment process for migrants by limiting their incomes. It threatened also the stability of marital and family relationships by depriving the males of the opportunities to fulfill their societal roles as "breadwinner" and "head of the family."

Despite the obstacles encountered, a significant proportion of the migrant population obtained "white-collar" occupations. A comparison of the occupational status of black in-migrants to the city of Chicago for the two time periods, 1935–1940 and 1955–1960, indicate an occupational upgrading of in-migrants relative to non-migrants.

As Table 10–14 indicates, even the highest status in-migrants in the thirties, those from the urban South, had relatively lower incomes compared to nonmigrants than the lowest status migrants in the 1950s, those from nonmetropolitan areas. It also is clear that black persons migrating to Chicago during the same time from other metropolitan areas were significantly more capable of acquiring white-collar occupations than migrants from nonmetropolitan areas.[58] One of the consequences has been changes in the vital rates for the black population. On the basis of "demographic transition theory," social scientists would predict that with the rapid migration of blacks away from farms to the urban and industrialized areas, along with the concomitant increments in educational attainment and occupational status, fertility would gradually decline. Yet, an analysis of black fertility from 1920 to 1964 indicates the birth rate fell slowly during the early

1920s and then fell precipitously during the latter half of that decade and during the depression, to a low of 25 in 1936. The latter half of the 1930s and the early 1940s saw the crude birth rate of the black population make a modest recovery. After the war, the birth rate increased rapidly and continued to climb until the late 1950s, when a peak was reached in 1956 at 35. The crude birth rate of the urbanized black population in 1958 was as high as the crude birth rate of the primarily rural black population of the early 1920s.[59] This pattern parallels the changes in the white race.

A number of factors were related to these substantial increases. It is suggested that a major factor may have been changes in fecundity stemming from improved health care and improved sanitary conditions associated with urban life. The National Center for Health Statistics reported that between 1935 and 1960 there was a major trend toward the hospitalization of birth deliveries among blacks. In 1935, about 19 percent of all births among blacks occurred in hospitals. By 1950, this increased to almost 60 percent and reached 87 percent by 1963.[60] Improved health conditions also were indicated by decreases in death rates between 1935 and 1955.

It also may be argued that while increasing fecundity tended to raise the birth rates of the black population, increasing urbanizations should have a counterbalancing effect. Yet another point of view contends that urbanization may have no effect at all on fertility, raising or lowering fertility rates depending "upon the balance between changes in fecundity and the control of fertility."[61]

Black migration during the 1950s was also important in terms of its consequences for the relative distribution of whites and blacks in metropolitan areas and their respective residential locales. Writing of Philadelphia in the 1890s, W. E. B. DuBois states that the new immigrants "get the worst possible introduction to city life" by settling, or being forced to settle, in well-defined localities in or near the slums.[62] This perception of the black migrant has persisted through the years to become the dominant view of migrant settlement patterns. Historically, such has been the pattern for black migrants. Blacks, as had white immigrant groups before them, found their chief ports of entry to cities in the inner slum areas, where they took up residence in ghettos or small enclaves.[63] The process of settlement for both white and black immigrant groups was characterized by segregation. There were, however, at least two major differences in the settlement patterns of the two groups. First, blacks were initially more segregated than white ethnic groups. Second, black segregation increased while the white ethnic migrant groups experienced residential desegregation.[64]

Evidence of the continued intensity of black residential segregation was obtained for 207 cities within which there were more than a thousand occupied housing units with a non-white head in 1960.[65] Among the 207 cities were virtually all the large cities of the country. Indices were obtained for each city which represented the percentage of blacks that would have to move from one block to another to effect an even, unsegregated residential distribution. The average index value of black segregation for the 207 cities was 86.2, with regional variations ranging from 76.2 in New England to 91.1 in the South Atlantic states. It was found that, on the average, the segregation index scores for cities outside the South was below the total; the average for southern cities was higher. Moreover, segregation indices for 109 cities for which the required data were available for the periods 1940, 1950, and 1960 indicate that segregation increased between 1940 and 1950 in the eight geographic divisions they examined (New England, Middle Atlantic, East North Central, West North Central, West, South Atlantic, East South Central, and West South Central). Between 1950 and 1960, segregation decreased slightly in the five northern and western divisions but actually increased in the three southern geographic divisions.[66]

Thus, it is clear that the migration of blacks during the 1950s was similar to the migration of earlier periods in that blacks moving to the North and West "landed" in the black neighborhoods of the destination communities. Contrary to the pattern of settlement in previous periods,[67] which portrayed blacks moving to the worst area of the destination cities, an analysis of the residential settlement patterns of the migrants during the 1950s reveals that there was not any area that might be considered a "migrant zone." Black migrants generally distributed themselves throughout the city where the black population was distributed.[68]

There was a slight tendency for migrants to locate in "newly invaded" areas more often than non-migrants, perhaps because housing opportunities are more numerous in areas in which the normal residential turnover among the black population is supplemented by a net out-movement of whites characteristic of transition neighborhoods. Whites living in predominantly black neighborhoods move with greater frequency than whites living in predominantly white neighborhoods. This could change since "Negro migrants of relatively high socioeconomic status comprise a large and increasing share of all in-migrants, particularly in Northern and border cities. Hence, it should not be surprising that such migrants seek residence in all accessible areas of the city compatible with their status rather than settling only in concentrated Negro areas."[69]

The consequences of the migration of the 1950s combined with that of earlier periods became increasingly important for the political structure and political processes of the destination communities. These consequences exhibited rather pronounced variations from one place to another. For example, the participation of blacks in politics in New York can be contrasted with Chicago:

In New York, Negroes are more evidently aggressive than in Chicago. In New York, the Negro press and civic leaders level a steady stream of criticism against the city regarding school segregation, inadequate school facilities, alleged police brutality, slum conditions in Harlem and various discriminatory acts. Legal suits against the city seeking the correction of alleged racial injustices are more common in New York than in Chicago. The number and strength of voluntary associations dealing with race issues are higher in New York. Negroes holding public office in New York are more likely to take strong—and often public—stands on race issues.[70]

The increasing voting strength of blacks made an impact on most destination communities, particularly in the area of the administration of justice. Black political power became increasingly capable of restraining mayors and police chiefs from discriminatory practices. A voice in educational administration was also becoming evident, although this alone was not the solution to the ills of education in black communities.[71] Yet the increasing size of the black population, strategically concentrated as it was by the design of exclusion from most outlying areas and metropolitan suburbs, was forming a political foundation which could no longer be ignored.

There were, of course, other consequences of the migration. Some of these were in the communities of origin, most of which were small southern towns and rural areas. For many areas, the migration meant not only fewer black people, but a significantly smaller labor force, fewer consumers, and, for some areas, a smaller tax base. In certain respects, the out-migration of blacks from the rural areas placed those that remained in a better bargaining position. As a consequence of population loss, increasing supplies of housing brought reductions in rents; decreasing supplies of labor brought better wages in those jobs that were not easily handled by machines; and the threat of continued out-migrations evoked promises of better treatment for those who remained. The promises of better treatment, however, proved to be inconsistent with the stark reality of the existing racial and economic structure in many areas. Efforts in the latter part of the fifties to alter that structure met with resistance that precipitated the "direct action" which would increasingly become the modus operandi of the civil rights movement.

11. The sixties: a decade of social change

The social setting

Social change for the black population of the United States in the 1960s was rapid and dramatic—at times so extensive that the decade is popularly characterized as revolutionary, particularly in the area of race relations. The decade witnessed the "Negro Revolution," so described because, although there had been numerous instances of direct action by blacks in the past two centuries to achieve freedom and equal opportunities, this was the first time that direct action took the form of a national movement. The movement penetrated even the strongest bastions of prejudice and discrimination.

Linked inseparably to this revolution was another of rising expectations, which brought about a keener sense of dissatisfaction despite improvements in income, education, and occupations. Blacks began to look more at the differences between themselves and their white counterparts than simply at improvements in their own standard of living. In this context the concept of "relative deprivation" became a meaningful way of assessing social progress for blacks and other minorities.

Perhaps nowhere were expectations so stymied as in the nation's central cities. At the same time the absolute size of the population in metropolitan areas was declining, the economic and racial composition of residents in the central cities changed significantly. The general pattern of the 1950s and 1960s was that of upper and middle-income whites moving to the suburbs and leaving the cities to low-income blacks. The central cities simultaneously lost some of their aggregate wealth and markedly increased their nonwhite populations, which resulted in greater education, welfare, and transportation needs, while the tax bases declined. Industry subsequently relocated to the suburbs, eroding the tax bases of the cities even further.

In 1970, a greater proportion of blacks were urban dwellers than were whites. More than half of the black population lived in 50 cities, 15 of which held a third of this population. The combined effects of the flight by whites to the suburbs and the influx of blacks into the core cities produced black majorities in six sizable cities by 1970—all but one in the North.[1]

During the sixties there were important influences on race relations from outside American society. By the beginning of the 1960s, for example, the movement for independence in Africa was well in progress. In the twenty years following World War II, at least 30 black African nations achieved independence.[2] Blacks in America followed with interest the efforts of black Africans, and some American blacks, such as the Black Muslims, identified closely with the African nationalists.

These international and domestic conditions set the stage for the "Negro Revolution," or as it was better known, the civil rights movement. The principal features of the civil rights movement have been recounted in detail by several scholars.[3] The dramatic and impressive events of the movement included the sit-ins at lunch counters in Greensboro, North Carolina, the efforts of Freedom Riders and the resulting violence in Birmingham, Alabama, the integration of the University of Mississippi, and the later heinous attempts in Birmingham to crush the movement by scattering marchers with fire hoses and police dogs, cattle prods, mass arrests, and bombings.

Perhaps the greatest peaceful demonstration for civil rights in the United States, the March on Washington in August, 1963, brought a quarter of a million people together, black and white, in an eloquent plea for equal rights for American blacks. The reaction by Congress to this march and other events in the several years leading up to it was the 1964 Civil Rights Act, the strongest such measure in the nation's history. Using the commerce powers given to Congress, the law ordered an end to segregated public accommodations, such as discrimination by hotels and restaurants, but the broader implications applied to employers, institutions of higher learning, and social services.

It was evident that this federal legislation was insufficient to dictate or encourage the changes needed in many parts of the country, particularly in the South, where groups organized to speed civil rights. In the summer of 1964 about a thousand students, mostly from the North and enlisted under the banner of the Student Nonviolent Coordinating Committee (SNCC), established widespread voter registration efforts for southern blacks. It was known as the Mississippi Summer Project, and its byproduct was the Freedom Democratic party, created to embarrass the Democratic party at the 1964 Convention by challenging the all-white Mississippi party delegation. One far-reaching consequence of this incident was the tactical split between black moderates and militants—gradualists on one hand, who hoped integration might work and who preferred to negotiate with the white power structure, and activists on the other, mostly young people who could not trust the white establishment and concluded there was no alternative but to fight for "black power."

Few better indications of national stress in the country's failure to respond to black needs and demands could be found than riots that seared cities in the summers between 1964 and 1967. A decade of progressive court rulings and legislation and nonviolent demonstrations failed to match the rising expectations of blacks.[4] They did not compare black ghetto situations with immigrant slums, but instead to the society around them. Ghetto attitudes were shaped and encouraged by

> films and television [that] open[ed] to large numbers a view of wealth that seems so easy to come by because it is enjoyed with such ease and

taken so much for granted. What the family shows on TV portray is not the hard-working father of the lower middle class, the American ideal until the 1950s, but increasingly upper middle-class families where lush family consumption is portrayed, but never the hard work necessary to afford it.[5]

But race riots were not new. They had occurred before in such cities as Chicago in 1919 and Detroit in 1943. Race-related violence had also occurred in the early 1950s in Georgia, Alabama, and North Carolina. But the radical violence of the 1960s was different: riots were more numerous and more destructive in terms of lives lost and property damaged. New York's Harlem in 1964, the Watts district of Los Angeles in 1965, Chicago and other cities in 1966, Detroit and Newark in 1967—all exploded in violent racial conflict. This wave of riots subsided in the early months of 1968, but the problems and conditions that gave rise to the violence and destruction persisted. And ghetto resentment and frustration continued unabated.

The demographic setting

In 1960 the total population of the United States was 179 million. Eleven percent were black—18.9 million. By 1965 the total population had increased to 193 million, and the black population, remaining at the same relative proportion, had increased to 20.9 million. By the end of the decade, 1969, the nation's population had passed the 200 million mark and the black population numbered more than 22 million.

At the beginning of the decade, more than 59 percent of the nation's black population lived in the South. As a result of the continued substantial out-migration, this percentage had declined to slightly over half (53 percent) at the end of the decade. Corresponding increases occurred in the proportion of blacks living in other regions during the same period. For example, in 1960 only a third (34 percent) of the nation's blacks lived in the North compared to about 39 percent in 1969. The West had 6 percent of the black population in 1960 and 7 percent by the end of the decade.

The changing distribution of the black population at large brought about a slight change in relative proportion in various regions. For example, blacks constituted 21 percent of the South's population in 1960, but by 1970 the proportion had declined to 19 percent. During this decade the relative proportion in the North increased from 7 to 9 percent and in the West from 4 to 5 percent.[6]

The increasing urbanization of the black population during the decade is reflected in the fact that in 1960 more than two-thirds resided in metropolitan areas and more than half lived in the central cities. Only 32 percent lived in nonmetropolitan areas. By 1970, however, nearly three-

Table 11–1. *Percent distribution of the black population by region, 1960 and 1970*

Region	1960 Population (1000s)	Percent	1970 Population (1000s)	Percent
United States	18,872	100.0	22,581	100.0
South	11,312	59.9	11,970	53.0
North	6,474	34.3	8,916	39.5
Northeast	3,028	16.0	4,344	19.2
North Central	3,446	18.3	4,572	20.2
West	1,086	5.8	1,695	7.5

SOURCE: U.S., Bureau of the Census, *Historical Statistics of the United States, Colonial Times to 1970*, Bicentennial Edition, Part I. (Washington, D.C.: Government Printing Office, 1975),Table A 172–194, p. 22.

fourths (74 percent) of the black population resided in metropolitan areas, 58 percent in the central cities. Only 26 percent lived in nonmetropolitan areas. The more significant change was the decrease in the proportion of whites living in central cities: from 31 percent to 28 percent during the decade. Likewise, there was an increase from 36 percent to 40 percent of the white population living outside central cities in metropolitan areas, reflecting the increasing suburbanization of whites.

Thus, the overall pattern of population distribution was one of continued net black out-migration from the South to the North and West with increasing concentration within the central cities. Whites, however, continued their flight to the suburbs, which had begun in the early postwar years.

Volume of migration

It should be noted here that measuring migration with place-of-birth data is a crude method for determining the extent of migration. However, it is useful information to the extent that its limitations are recognized. It enables the determination of cumulative migration, and then only if the migration does not include return migration. It does not take account of intermediate moves between birth and the time of the census enumeration. Nor does it include the migrants who died before the census.

In 1970 nearly one-fifth (19 percent, or 3.9 million) of the black population of the United States was living outside the region of birth. But broken down on a regional basis, there is a major difference between the South and the other regions of the country, since a considerably smaller proportion (76 percent) of southern-born blacks remained there in 1970 as compared with more than 90 percent of the natives of nonsouthern regions living in the region of their birth.

Of those blacks living in the Northeast in 1970, one-third (33 percent) were born in the South. Thirty-six percent of the North Central's black

Table 11–2. *Black native population by region of birth and region of residence with net gain or loss through interregional migration, 1970*

Region	Total	Born in other regions Number	Born in other regions Percent	Net gain or loss through inter-regional migration
		Living in the specified areas		
Northeast	3,623,229	1,245,314	34.4	1,060,429
North Central	4,119,293	1,576,835	38.3	1,343,645
South	11,131,531	221,792	2.0	−3,188,218
West	1,514,537	846,156	55.9	784,144
United States	20,388,590	3,890,097	19.1	

SOURCE: Ibid., Table 2, p. 2.

population and nearly half of that in the West likewise were native southerners. These figures compare with only 2 percent of the South's 1970 black population born outside the South.

A more refined measure of migration, as discussed in previous chapters, is obtained by using place-of-residence at a fixed past date. A measure of the extent of interregional migration is obtained from the census simply by comparing region of residence in 1965 and 1970.

Two-thirds (66 percent) of the more than 12 million blacks five years of age and over were living in their state of birth in both 1965 and 1970. The stable portion of the black population was the same in 1970 as it was a decade earlier (66 percent for 1955–60). The only difference in the interstate mobility rates for the United States from 1960 to 1970 was a slight increase in the proportion of return migrants, i.e., those living in their state of birth in 1970. There also was a proportionate increase in the black migrants abroad reflected in the increased number of blacks in the armed forces serving in Vietnam and other countries.

During the five-year period, 1965–70, there were 1.9 million black migrants who changed their county of residence. The number of interre-

Table 11–3. *Black population, percent, region of birth by region of residence, 1970*

Region of Birth	Northeast	North Central	South	West	Total
	Place of residence, 1970				
Northeast	92.8	1.7	4.1	1.3	100.0
North Central	1.6	91.6	3.0	3.8	100.0
South	8.3	10.6	76.2	4.9	100.0
West	1.4	2.5	4.5	91.5	100.0
Total	17.8	20.2	54.6	7.4	

SOURCE: U.S., Bureau of the Census, *Census of Population: 1970*, Subject Reports, Final Report PC(2)-2A, *State of Birth* (Washington, D.C.: Government Printing Office, 1973), Table 3, p. 3.
    *Rounding error

Table 11–4. *Black population by region of residence and region of birth in 1970*

Region of residence 1970	Northeast	North Central	South	West	Total
(Both sexes)					
Northeast	65.6	1.2	32.9	0.3	100.0
North Central	1.1	61.7	36.7	0.5	100.0
South	1.0	0.7	98.0	0.3	100.0
West	2.3	7.0	46.6	44.1	100.0
Total	12.6	13.6	70.2	3.6	100.0

SOURCE: Ibid.

gional migrants for the same period was 660,000—34 percent of all black migrants. The largest proportion of interregional migrants were those whose 1965 residence was in the South. Out-migration from the South during the latter half of the 1960s accounted for more than 57 percent of all interregional migration among blacks. Interestingly, the Northeast and North Central regions had approximately 110,000 out-migrants each and the West had 61,000.

Interregional in-migration varied somewhat from region to region. Perhaps the most interesting feature was the size of the streams to the South.[7] Nearly 162,000, or one-fourth, of all black interregional migrants in the United States during 1965-70 went to the South. This constituted a larger stream of migrants than was attracted to the Northeast or the West. The largest number of black interregional migrants went to the North Central regions. More than 200,000 blacks from the other three regions migrated there during the five-year period, with more than 80 percent coming from the South alone. The West was the third most attractive region for black

Table 11–5. *Place of birth and state of residence in 1965 and 1970 of the black population 5 years old and over by sex, for the U.S.*

Residence	Male	Female	Total	Percent
State of birth in 1965 and 1970	5,651,655	6,417,307	12,068,962	66.4
State of birth in 1970 but not 1965	119,045	123,700	242,745	1.3
State of birth in 1970, abroad in 1965, or state not reported	292,525	293,766	586,291	3.2
Same state in 1965 and 1970, but born in a different state	1,895,225	2,235,224	4,130,449	22.7
State of birth in 1965, but not 1970	298,539	300,928	599,467	3.3
Different states in 1965 and 1970, both different from state of birth	158,588	139,396	297,984	1.6
Other than state of birth in 1970, abroad in 1965, or state not reported	140,575	117,597	258,172	1.5
Total	8,556,152	9,627,918	18,184,070	100.0

SOURCE: U.S., Bureau of the Census, *Census of Population: 1970*, Subject Reports, Final Report PC(2)-2D, *Lifetime and Recent Migration* (Washington, D.C.: Government Printing Office, 1973), Table 1, pp. 1–6.

Table 11–6. *Region and residence in 1970 of black migrants by region of residence in 1965*

Region of residence 1965	1970				
	Northeast	North Central	South	West	Total
Northeast	70.9	6.0	18.3	4.8	100.0
North Central	6.1	60.0	21.0	13.6	100.0
South	10.8	14.7	66.0	8.4	100.0
West	5.7	10.9	23.0	60.4	100.0
United States	21.6	19.1	46.6	12.6	100.0
Interregional migration	146,017	203,179	161,703	149,658	660,557

SOURCE: U.S., Bureau of the Census, *Census of Population: 1970*, Subject Reports, Final Report PC(2)-2B, *Mobility for States and the Nation* (Washington, D.C.: Government Printing Office, 1973), Table 42, p. 303.

interregional migrants in absolute size. Nearly 150,000 migrants, 63 percent of whom came from the South, went to the West. The least attractive region was the Northeast, but only slightly less so than the West. More than 146,000 blacks from other regions moved into the Northeast during the five-year period. As with the other regions, the largest proportion by far were from the South.

That black people were moving to the South is not surprising, since they had been moving there in ever-increasing numbers for almost two centuries, despite the predominant pattern of out-migration from the region. Yet, increasing attention has been focused on these streams with southern destinations. It is important to note, however, that the apparent increase in the number of blacks who moved to the South from the North and other regions is due in large measure to the fact that there were ever-increasing black populations outside the South from which a pool of migrants would be drawn. Demographers refer to this as the population-at-risk. As the size of the population-at-risk increases, it follows that there probably will be more migrants if similar rates remain. Indeed, such was the case for blacks moving South.

But determining whether black migration to the South increased or decreased during the 1960s depends upon the method of measuring the migration flow. For example, there are at least three ways in which black migration to the South can be viewed, each with correspondingly different results. One measure of migration is in simple, absolute numerical terms, similar to those presented above on interregional migration. There was an increase in the number of blacks moving to the South between 1960 and 1970. Between 1955 and 1960, for example, there were just over 98,000 blacks moving from the North to the South. In the later corresponding period, 1965–1970, there were more than 126,000 such migrants—an increase of 28,000 migrants for the decade. But a simple mathematical approach to the question neglects the important matter of population growth in the North, i.e., the population-at-risk. While for some purposes it may be useful to know that there was an absolute numerical increase in the size of the migration stream from 1960 to 1970, it does not provide the best measure of migration.

A more meaningful and more easily interpreted measure of the back-flow is that which takes into account the population-at-risk. This measure provides a rate of black migration to the South. A rate measures migration, not in absolute terms but in terms per hundred, thousand, or ten thousand. The rate of black migration from the North (Northeast and North Central regions) to the South for the period 1955–1960 was 152 for every 10,000 black persons five years of age and over living in the North in 1960. For the corresponding period, 1965–70, there were 142 migrants, a decrease of 10 migrants per 10,000 population for the decade.

Still another measure of black migration to the South is one that uses the black migration to the North as the base for calculating the size of the backflow migration stream rather than the population-at-risk. The justification for such an approach rests principally on the theoretical notion that "for every migration stream there is a counterstream."[8] Historically, the major black migration streams are determined in part by comparing the size of the major stream to that of the counterstream. The larger the major stream relative to the counterstream, the more "efficient" is the major stream in redistributing a population. Contrariwise, the smaller the major stream relative to the counterstream, the less efficient is the major stream. When such comparison is made for black migrants moving North and South, it is clear that the size of the southward stream has been increasing relative to the size of the northward stream. In the period 1955–60, the North-to-South migration stream was about a third (32 percent) as large as the South-to-North stream, whereas, ten years later it was approaching half (44 percent) as large. Thus, from this perspective one may conclude that black migration to the South increased during the decade compared with black migration to the North.

The question of the extent of black migration to the South during the period 1960–70 is subject to different measures and interpretations with correspondingly different results. From one perspective black migration to the South during the 1960s increased, but from another it decreased. Regardless of the perspective, it is clear that the South was not only the area of origin for thousands of black out-migrants, but it was also the destination for many. The streams of black interregional migration in the United States form a complex web of major population movements and countermovements linking each region with every other region.

Interstate migration data provide a more refined perspective on migration patterns than regional data. The greater geographical specificity offered by the state data aid in pinpointing sending and receiving areas. Patterns of in- and out-migration for individual states exhibited the same general patterns revealed in the divisional migration streams. From Table 11–7 it may be seen that for the period 1965–70 almost all the Deep South states experienced black net out-migration. In two of these states—Mississippi and Alabama—the out-migrants exceeded the in-migrants by more than 10,000 per year for the five-year period. But not all states in the South, as defined by the census bureau, experienced net out-migration. Delaware, Maryland, and Texas noted net in-migrations. In fact, only two states showed larger net in-migration of blacks than Maryland.

The net out-migration occurred in several states outside the South. In the Northeast, Maine, New Hampshire, and Vermont lost more blacks than they gained through migration. In the North Central region, the Dakotas and Nebraska also experienced small net out-migrations. Likewise, in the West, Montana, Idaho, Wyoming, New Mexico, and Hawaii were characterized by net out-migrations. But no state outside the South except New Mexico, had a net out-migration that exceeded a thousand.

New York had the largest number of in-migrants of any state in the North. It also had the largest number of out-migrants, resulting in a relatively small net in-migration. Other traditionally attractive states continued to receive large numbers of migrants in the 1960s, but many also experienced large out-migrations, similar to the New York pattern. Such northern states as Massachusetts, Connecticut, New Jersey, Pennsylvania, Ohio, Indiana, Illinois, Michigan, and Missouri were destinations for large numbers of black migrants. Among these attractive states only Michigan and Connecticut kept out-migration comparatively low. Missouri, like New York, attracted more than 25,000 migrants. But the out-migration was so large that the state gained only about 250 black persons.

The most attractive state in the nation was also one with considerable holding power: California, which attracted 133,200 blacks—an average of 26,000 per year in the 1965–70 period. The total number of out-migrants was less than 50,000 for the same period, giving the state a net in-migration of more than 83,000 for the period.

It was noted earlier that net migration is frequently small relative to gross migration, or the turnover for a particular area. The ratio of net migration to turnover is referred to as a measure of the"effectiveness" of migration.[9] The higher the ratios for an area, the fewer the number of moves required to effect a given amount of population redistribution.[10] Frequently there may be a great deal of migration between two areas, but because of the similarity in the size of the stream and counterstream the migration has little net effect on population redistribution.

The ratio of effectiveness for each state appears in Table 11–7. There are two types of ratios; positive, which reflect the effectiveness of a net in-migration to the specified state, and negative, which reflect the effectiveness of the migration from those states with net out-migration. From the table it may be observed that the most effective (positive) in-migration occurred in Michigan, as indicated by a ratio of 52.2. Other states with rela-

Table 11–7. *Black migration by state, 1970*

State	In-migrants	Out-migrants	Net migration	Effective-ness ratio
Northeast				
Maine	1,240	1,762	−522	−17.3
New Hampshire	925	1,089	−164	−8.1
Vermont	188	279	−91	−19.4
Massachusetts	18,842	11,141	7,701	25.7
Rhode Island	3,526	2,795	731	11.6
Connecticut	17,212	8,856	8,356	32.1
New York	86,266	79,213	7,053	4.3
New Jersey	56,634	31,698	24,936	28.2
Pennsylvania	38,387	36,205	2,182	2.9
North Central				
Ohio	51,447	33,590	17,857	21.0
Indiana	26,603	17,426	9,177	20.8
Illinois	68,951	56,281	12,670	10.1
Michigan	82,721	25,992	56,729	52.2
Wisconsin	13,445	5,535	7,910	41.6
Minnesota	5,180	2,733	2,447	30.9
Iowa	3,773	3,260	513	7.3
Missouri	25,902	25,649	253	0.4
North Dakota	1,497	1,795	−298	−9.0
South Dakota	743	933	−190	−11.3
Nebraska	4,730	4,990	−260	−2.7
Kansas	13,429	12,181	1,248	4.9
South				
Delaware	5,753	3,863	1,890	19.6
Maryland	64,624	23,874	40,750	46.0
D.C.	38,307	57,183	−18,876	−19.7
Virginia	40,783	49,231	−8,448	−9.3
W. Virginia	3,009	9,300	−6,291	−51.1
N. Carolina	42,677	68,564	−25,887	−23.3
S. Carolina	24,338	47,800	−23,462	−32.5
Georgia	39,132	58,775	−19,643	−20.0
Florida	44,440	49,906	−5,466	−5.8
Kentucky	11,011	16,266	−5,255	−19.3
Tennessee	24,458	40,035	−15,577	−24.1
Alabama	19,838	73,692	−53,854	−57.6
Mississippi	18,095	74,462	−56,367	−60.9
Arkansas	9,928	33,393	−23,465	−54.2
Louisiana	21,875	56,203	−34,346	−44.0
Oklahoma	11,982	12,946	−964	3.9
Texas	56,549	51,540	5,009	4.6
West				
Montana	865	1,359	−494	−22.2
Idaho	797	865	−68	−4.1
Wyoming	574	1,005	−431	−27.3
Colorado	13,113	8,349	4,764	22.2
N. Mexico	4,107	5,253	−1,146	−12.2
Arizona	6,996	6,901	95	0.7
Utah	2,310	1,155	1,155	33.3
Nevada	3,294	3,066	228	3.6
Washington	13,324	9,774	3,550	5.6
Oregon	4,244	2,513	1,731	25.6
California	133,200	49,882	83,318	45.5
Alaska	4,135	4,117	18	0.2
Hawaii	4,051	4,757	−56	−0.6

SOURCE: U.S., Bureau of the Census, *Census of Population: 1970*, Subject Reports, Final Report PC(2)-2B, *Mobility for States and the Nation* (Washington, D.C.: Government Printing Office, 1973), Table 45, pp. 321–25.

tively high migration effectiveness were Maryland, California, and Wisconsin. Those states with the most effective (negative) out-migration were Mississippi, with −60.9, followed by Alabama, Arkansas, West Virginia, and Louisiana. For each of the states mentioned above, black migration resulted in substantial population redistribution during the latter 1960s.

There were two states, Missouri and Pennsylvania, that had relatively high population turnover, but the result was a very small redistribution of the population. The ratio of effectiveness for Missouri was a positive 0.4 while the ratio for Pennsylvania was 2.9. Florida had a negative ratio of effectiveness of −5.8 that resulted from a large black out-migration and an almost equally large in-migration. New York had a low ratio of effectiveness and a large turnover.

Characteristics of migrants

As in earlier periods, black migrants of the late 1960s generally were younger, slightly more often male and single, and tended to be better educated than the total black population. Nearly 58 percent of the migrants were less than 25 years old, compared with 48 percent in the total black population. Moreover, four-fifths of the migrants were less than 35 years old, compared with only 62 percent of the total black population. As in the previous decade, the largest five-year age cohort in the migrant population was the group 20 to 24 (22 percent). The same age cohort represented only 9 percent of the total black population.

Table 11–8. Age for interstate black migrants, 1970 (by percent)

		Interstate migrants		
Age	Reporting residence 1965	All migrants	Contiguous state	Non-contiguous state
Total no.	20,129,816	1,071,881	292,833	779,048
5 to 9 years	13.7	13.7	13.6	13.6
10 to 14 years	14.0	10.3	10.5	10.1
15 to 19 years	12.1	12.2	12.1	12.2
20 to 24 years	8.7	21.6	18.9	22.5
25 to 29 years	7.0	13.9	12.9	14.3
30 to 34 years	6.2	8.3	8.4	8.3
35 to 39 years	6.0	5.7	6.3	5.4
40 to 44 years	5.9	4.0	4.6	3.7
45 to 49 years	5.5	2.7	3.2	2.5
50 to 54 years	4.9	2.0	2.3	1.8
55 to 59 years	4.4	1.5	1.8	1.3
60 to 64 years	3.8	1.2	1.3	1.1
65 to 69 years	3.2	1.1	1.2	1.0
70 to 74 years	2.2	0.7	.8	.6
75 years and over	2.7	1.1	1.3	.9

SOURCE: Ibid., Table 1, pp. 1–4.

Among interstate migrants the number of males outnumbered females five years old and older by a ratio of 101.5. The sex ratio for the total black population five years old and older in 1970 was 89.6. Moreover, migrants moving longer distances (to noncontiguous states) reflected a greater sex ratio, 102.7, compared with 98.3 for migrants to contiguous states.

Because marital status is in large part a function of age, it follows from the observation that migrants tended to be younger, that we could expect a larger proportion of the migrant population to be single and a smaller proportion widowed. Compare, for example, that more than 35 percent of the interstate migrants at least 14 years old were single with the fact that less than a third (32 percent) of the total black population were not married. Or, note that more than 9 percent of the total black adult population was widowed, compared with only 4.3 percent for the interstate migrant population.

Very little difference existed between the total adult population and interstate migrants with respect to the proportion married with spouse present. But slightly more migrants than the total population were married with spouse absent.

Differences by sex may be noted in marital status. There is a substantially larger proportion of males among the single populations of both the migrant group and the total population. And the difference in marital status between the migrant males and the total male population is greater than the difference between the migrant females and the total female population.

As in earlier periods, education selectivity of migration continued into the 1960s, with black migrants better educated than the total black population. One-third of the black population 25 years old and older had only an elementary school education of seven years or less, but among migrants less than one-sixth had less education. Nearly one-third of the migrants

Table 11–9. *Sex ratio of black population and of migrants*

	Number		Sex ratio
	Male	Female	
Population, 5 years and over	9,514,569	10,615,247	89.6
Interstate migrants, 5 years and over	539,972	531,909	101.5
Contiguous states	145,167	147,666	98.3
Noncontiguous states	394,805	384,243	102.7
Intercounty migrants	966,798	955,068	101.2

SOURCE: Ibid., Table 2, pp. 5–11.

Table 11–10. Marital status for black interstate migrants, 14 years old and over, 1970 (by percent)

		Interstate migrants		
	Reporting residence 1965	All migrants	Contiguous state	Non-contiguous state
Single	31.7	35.0		
Male	35.5	40.2	36.6	41.2
Female	28.3	29.6	28.6	30.0
Married, S.P.*	44.5	44.2		
Male	48.3	43.2	45.5	42.1
Female	41.3	45.1	46.1	44.5
Married S.A.**	10.3	12.6		
Male	8.5	11.8	11.6	11.5
Female	11.8	13.1	12.2	13.5
Separated	7.2	7.2		
Male	5.2	5.0	5.8	4.7
Female	8.9	9.3	8.8	9.6
Other	3.0	5.3		
Male	3.2	6.7	6.4	6.8
Female	2.8	3.9	3.7	4.0
Widowed	9.2	4.3		
Male	0.1	1.7	2.5	1.5
Female	13.4	6.8	7.2	6.8
Divorced	4.2	3.8		
Male	3.2	2.8	2.8	3.0
Female	5.0	4.6	4.5	4.7
Total (numbers)				
Male	7,008,659	423,559	112,315	311,244
Female	8,117,455	412,012	115,223	296,789
Total, both sexes	15,126,114	835,571		

SOURCE: Ibid., Table 3, pp. 12–15.
*Spouse present
**Spouse absent

(30 percent) had four years of high school, compared with 21 percent for the total population.

The pattern of education selectivity continued at the higher education level. While only a tenth of the total black population had ever attended college, nearly one-fourth of the migrants had completed at least one year.

On the whole, interstate migrants were slightly better educated than intercounty migrants. Migration was selective on those with higher levels of education, and those migrating greater distances tended to be slightly better educated than those migrating short distances.

As would be expected, the higher educational levels of the migrants were reflected in their occupations. A larger proportion of migrants held white-collar jobs than did the total population, and in the professional occupations there were 1.75 migrants for every one professional in the total population. As for craftsmen and operative occupations, the proportions were nearly equal. Continuing this tapering pattern, the proportion of mi-

Table 11–11. *Educational attainment of the black population 25 years old and over, intercounty and interstate migrants, 1970*

Educational attainment 25 yrs. and over	Total black pop.		Intercounty migrants		Interstate migrants		Total %	Inter-county %	Inter-state %
	Male	Female	Male	Female	Male	Female			
Elementary: 0–7 years	1,735,228	1,716,034	96,189	83,730	39,015	37,087	33.3	21.5	16.8
Both sexes	3,451,262		179,919		76,102				
Elementary: 8 years	478,003	611,417	30,561	33,538	14,207	16,757	10.5	7.6	6.8
Both sexes	1,089,420		64,099		30,964				
High School: 1–3 years	1,076,380	1,492,316	95,795	101,197	48,818	54,235	24.7	23.5	22.8
Both sexes	2,568,696		196,992		103,053				
High School: 4 years	946,270	1,257,833	113,905	119,221	69,771	68,825	21.2	27.8	30.6
Both sexes	2,204,103		233,126		138,596				
College: 1–3 years	283,924	326,927	42,920	40,310	26,728	24,782	5.9	9.9	11.4
Both sexes	610,851		83,230		51,510				
College: 4 years	102,453	164,047	21,164	26,715	13,410	17,125	2.6	5.7	6.7
Both sexes	266,500		47,879		30,535				
College: 5 years or more	90,946	93,987	20,673	12,997	13,821	8,456	1.8	4.0	4.9
Both sexes	184,933		33,670		22,277				
Total, reported 25 yrs. and over	4,713,204	5,662,561	421,207	417,708	225,770	227,267	100.0	100.0	100.0
Both sexes	10,375,765		838,915		453,037				

Source: Ibid., Table 5, pp. 22–25.

grants occupied as laborers and service workers was consistently less than the total black population.

It should be noted that employment patterns are subject to rapid changes, and it should not be assumed that employment for black migrants in 1970 reflected the pattern of employment for the total decade. But several aspects are noteworthy. First, a larger proportion of the migrants than of the total black population were in the labor force—66 percent and 58 percent, respectively. This difference probably can be attributed largely to the fact that more than 12 percent of the interstate migrants were in the armed forces as opposed to only 1.3 percent of the total population. The unemployment rate for the black migrant population was 4 percent in 1970, but slightly more than 5 percent for interstate migrants.

In line with occupational, age, marital status, sex, and educational characteristics, the 1960s were similar to previous periods in that migrants generally received higher incomes than did the total black population. Migration, of course, has been one of the few systematic ways for blacks to improve their income, and the gains resulting from migration in the 1960s were as great as during the two previous decades.[11] But since the most promising people migrate, perhaps the economic value of migration has been exaggerated. The fact that migrants were better educated and had a larger proportion in white-collar positions would strongly suggest that higher earnings should occur.

The median family income for interstate black migrants in 1969 was $6,850, compared with $6,129 for black families as a whole. The median family income for intercounty migrants was $6,692. Nonmovers earned slightly less than median income for the total black population, with $6,086.

In summary, black migrants during the 1960s generally exhibited the same characteristics as their counterparts of earlier periods. As a group the migrants were younger than the total population, with a slight tendency toward a larger number of males. Reflecting their youthfulness, a

Table 11–12. *Median income for black families, intercounty and interstate migrants, 1970*

Family income 1969	Total black family head	Intercounty migrants	Interstate migrants	Intercounty %	Interstate %	All migrants %
Under $3,000	1,150,829	82,255	44,141	19.3	18.1	23.7
$3,000–$6,999	1,638,150	141,369	80,631	33.2	33.1	33.7
$7,000–$9,999	914,929	86,192	51,559	20.3	21.2	18.8
$10,000–$14,999	782,804	78,563	45,980	18.5	18.9	16.1
$15,000–$24,999	332,575	32,691	18,484	7.7	7.6	6.8
$25,000 and over	45,001	4,409	2,708	1.0	1.1	0.9
Total	4,864,288	425,479	243,503	100.0	100.0	100.0
Median income	$6,129	$6,692	$6,850			

SOURCE: Ibid., Table 20, pp. 181–94.

larger proportion of the migrants were single and fewer of them widowed. Educationally, migrants excelled, compared with the total black population. Of course, this would be attributed in part to the differing age structures of the two populations. Consistent with the higher educational attainment of the migrants were higher level occupations and higher incomes. Thus, selectivity of black migrants continued into the last decade for which we have comprehensive national data.

The consequences of migration

The consequences of black migration during the 1960s, as in earlier periods, reflected the continued problems of an increasingly urbanized and largely disadvantaged minority group in an increasingly urbanized, highly technological, racially segregated, and competitive society. In many ways, the problematic consequences of migration for the migrants were similar to those of most immigrant groups, i.e., finding suitable housing, obtaining employment, and securing needed health and educational services. But the problems blacks faced in their pursuit of these human essentials in the 1960s were compounded by race consciousness. Segregation was increasing rather than decreasing. Schools and neighborhoods were more distinctly segregated than a decade earlier. Black income was still only three-fifths of the white income, and nearly one-third of the nation's black population was poor in 1969.[12]

Relatively few studies have focused specifically on the postmigration adjustment of the black migrants during the 1960s, but those that have been conducted suggest that living conditions were largely unchanged from what they had been in the 1950s. But the expectations of blacks had grown far beyond those of the 1950s, thus creating increased frustration and dissatisfaction, particularly among the residents of the larger ghettos of the nation's major metropolitan areas. It was called the "psychological urban problem."

> As more affluent suburbs spring up, with neat lawns and good schools, the apparent gap between the quality of life in the central city and at the periphery increases. The suburbanites, adjusting rapidly to residential comfort, become more discontented with the conditions that surround the places where they work in the central city, even though these conditions are also (on the average) improving. Those city dwellers who cannot, for reasons of income or race, move to the suburbs, grow increasingly envious of those who can; the prices of worldly success are held up before their eyes but out of their reach.[13]

One of the prizes sought by blacks migrating to metropolitan areas was employment. A mid-decade study of the employment problems faced by blacks and other disadvantaged migrants to Indianapolis concluded that most of the jobs for black males lasted only three to nine months and those for black females lasted only one to three months. Jobs that were available generally paid poorly. Over four-fifths of the black females received $1.45 per hour or less, and 70 percent of their male counterparts earned no more than $1.70 per hour. Thus, the migrant was found in a low wage-earning position at a time when above normal expenses had been incurred in moving.[14]

The focus of the Indianapolis study was the "disadvantaged urban migrant" and was not representative of all black migrants. In fact, a somewhat different picture of black rural-to-urban migrants is presented in the 1967 Survey of Economic Opportunity (SEO).[15] Migrants were defined in the SEO as persons who had ever lived 50 miles or more from their 1967 residences. Earlier residences classified as rural included a town or village, in the open country but not on a farm, or on a farm. Occupational categories were the same as those used by the 1960 census. Their findings tend to refute the idea that black as well as white rural-urban migrants contribute unduly to the lowest status occupations.

> Rural-urban migrants comprised varying shares of the occupational classes among race-sex groups; in few occupations were their shares significantly different in terms of the SEO sample size, from the share they comprised of urban employed people. The only clear-cut evidence of excessive shares in lower status occupations was found among female private household workers, both white and Negro.[16]

Moreover, the relative occupational achievement helps account for the fact that rural-urban migrants were about as likely to be impoverished as the urban population of urban origin.[17]

Additional insight is gained into the occupational consequences of black migration during the 1960s from a Johns Hopkins University study in 1970 comparing the migration experiences of blacks and nonblacks.[18] In the report, based on retrospective life histories collected from a national sample of nonblack and black men who reached the ages of 30 through 39 in 1968, the study shows that those locations where the occupational returns for the individual are not high are more likely to be left. While in both black and nonblack samples it was clear that younger respondents were more likely to leave locations, age had a positive effect on increments in occupational status. In other words, while younger people tend to move more, the older movers gain more in job status by doing so. For blacks and nonblacks, the better educated migrants gain more in job status when they move. Among other findings on the occupational consequences of migration, the study reported that black migrants whose fathers had a higher occupational status gain more in status when they move than migrants with fathers of lower occupational status. The migrant who was an incumbent of low-status occupation just prior to making a geographical move, was found to gain more by migrating than an individual who occupied a high-status position initially.

In the same study, the respondents were asked if they "had a job" waiting or "know of a job." Interestingly, only among the black migrants did a significant number reply affirmatively. The interpretation of this finding was that because of the difficulties blacks encounter in finding jobs, having some information is of more use to them than to nonblacks, who may not encounter as much discrimination in being hired.

The consequences of migration for the migrant's earning power also were documented. With respect to income, the same phenomenon was found as was observed for occupational status, i.e., the lower one's income prior to migrating, the more one tended to gain by making a move. Moreover, for blacks, the greater the migrating distance north and west the greater the income increments obtained. These findings point both to the importance of different wage structures in different parts of the United States and the additional increments in income that could accrue to an individual by selecting his destination wisely.

The Johns Hopkins study also was revealing of the consequences of migration for the household composition of the migrant. Compared with white migrants, blacks were less likely to leave households in which members of an older generation were present and more likely to move into households with such persons at his destination. This kin-network effect also was seen in the case of young migrants as well as older ones. At the same time, a difference between blacks and nonblacks was found in family formation and dissolution and migration. Nonblacks were more apt to get married in conjunction with migration than blacks, and blacks were more likely to leave their wives in the year in which they moved. In other words, among nonblacks, it was family formation that was primarily associated with migration; among blacks, family dissolution.

Reduced fertility was an additional by-product of the rural-to-urban migration of southern black couples. From the 1967 SEO data, it was found that within four of the five age groups—20 to 24 years, 25 to 29 years, 30 to 34 years, 35 to 39 years, and 40 to 44 years—urban black in-migrants from the rural South had greater fertility than the indigenous urban black population. But the fertility of the migrant couples in all age groupings was significantly less than their nonmigrant counterparts remaining in the rural South.[19]

12. Epilogue: the 1970s

The pattern of black migration described in the previous chapters has been for many decades a large-scale movement of black Americans from the rural and urban South to the metropolitan centers of the North and West.

In the late 1960s and early 1970s, evidence began to develop that this pattern was changing. The rate of migration to the North declined while the movement to the South increased.

Between 1970 and 1975, 238,000 blacks moved outside the South while 302,000 moved to the South with a net gain of 64,000 black population for the South.[1] The most significant change was in the Northeast where for every one migrant moving to the Northeast, two were moving to the South. The North Central region had a balance of movement, that is, about the same number moved out as moved in. The West region continued to attract black migrants. The ratio was about four persons moving to the West for each one moving to the South.

Obviously, the dream of the North as a place of milk and honey, where racial discrimination did not exist, where jobs and good housing were to be had by all, was dying. The ghettos of the North and West during the 1960s were festering with discontent which erupted in the riots of the late 1960s, such as Watts. The violence has been displaced by what can be characterized as a quiet (for now) desperation. Many people both black and white are fleeing from the central cities.

During the 1960s the South was changing also. Schools were integrated, civil rights increased, industrialization and other changes had improved the lot of black people—at least in degree. As a result the amount of return migration has increased and probably the amount of primary migration has increased also.

This dramatic reversal of previous long-term trends has raised important questions such as: Why are black people moving to the South? Who is moving? Where are they going? In 1972, a group of researchers under the direction of Rex R. Campbell at the University of Missouri-Columbia started to examine the migration of black people to the South. Interviews were completed in five southern metropolitan areas: Atlanta, Georgia; Houston, Texas; Greensboro, North Carolina; Mobile, Alabama; and Tampa-St. Petersburg, Florida, and two nonmetropolitan areas, one in Mississippi and the other in North and South Carolina. One intriguing fact supported by our research and that of Larry Long's[2] is that the majority is return migration. Most of the people moving to the South were either born or had lived previously in the South.

Notes

Chapter 1

1. William Petersen, *Population* (New York: Macmillan Co., 1975), p. 280.
2. Calvin Goldscheider, *Population, Modernization, and Social Structure* (Boston: Little, Brown & Co. 1971), p. 299.
3. Ibid., p. 301
4. William Petersen, "A General Typology of Migration," *American Sociological Review* 23 (June 1958): pp. 256–66.
5. Goldscheider, *Population, Modernization, and Social Structure*, p. 300.
6. Phillip Curtin, *The Atlantic Slave Trade* (Madison: Univ. of Wisconsin Press, 1969), p. 3.

Chapter 2

1. Jerome Dowd, "Slavery and the Slave Trade," *Journal of Negro History* 2 (Jan. 1917): 1.
2. Ibid, p. 6.
3. Basil Davidson, *The African Slave Trade* (Boston: Little, Brown & Co., 1861), p. 180.
4. Leslie Fischel and Benjamin Quarles, *The Negro American* (Glenview, Ill.: Scott, Foresman & Co., 1967), p. 4.
5. Noel Deerr, *The History of Sugar* (London: 1949–1950), vol. 2, p. 283 as cited in Phillip Curtin, *The Atlantic Slave Trade* (Madison: Univ. of Wisconsin Press, 1969), pp. 17–18; Robert W. Fogel and Stanley L. Engerman, *Time on the Cross* (Boston: Little, Brown & Co., 1974), p. 15.
6. Fogel and Engerman, *Time on the Cross*, p. 15.
7. Daniel P. Mannix, *Black Cargoes* (New York: Viking Press, 1962), p. 3.
8. Ibid., p. 54.
9. Ibid, p. 55.
10. Fischel and Quarles, *Negro American*, pp. 3–4.
11. Samual McKee, *Labor in Colonial New York; 1664–1766* (New York: Columbia Univ. Press, 1935), p. 311.
12. Reynolds Farley, *The Growth of the Black Population* (Chicago: Markham Pub. Co., 1970), pp. 15–16.
13. Davidson, *African Slave Trade*, p. 79.
14. Curtin, *Atlantic Slave Trade*, p. 11.
15. Ibid, pp. 4–8.
16. Donald L. Wiedner, *A History of Africa South of the Sahara* (New York: Random House, 1962), p. 67; Robert Rothberg, *Political History of Tropical Africa* as cited in Curtin, *Atlantic Slave Trade*, p. 13; Basil Davidson, *Black Mother* (Boston: Little, Brown & Co., 1961), p. 79; Curtin, *Atlantic Slave Trade*, p. 12; Fogel and Engerman, *Time on the Cross*, p. 15.
17. Lorenzo J. Green, *The Negro in Colonial New England* (New York: Atheneum, 1969), pp. 72–73.
18. Curtin, *Atlantic Slave Trade*, pp. 89–92.
19. Ibid, p. 72. For discussion on this topic see also David B. Davis, *The Problem of Slavery in Western Culture* (Ithaca: Cornell Univ. Press, 1966); Arthur Zilversmit, *The First Emancipation: The Abolition of Slavery in the North* (Chicago: Univ. of Chicago Press, 1967); Donald L. Robinson, *Slavery in the Structure of American Politics, 1756–1820* (New York: Harcourt Brace Jovanovich, 1971); Herbert S. Klein, *Slavery in the Americas* (Chicago: Univ. of Chicago Press, 1967); Carl R. Degler, *Neither Black Nor White: Slavery and Race Relations in Brazil and the United States* (New York: Macmillan Co., 1971); Elizabeth Donnau, *Document*

Illustrative of the History of the Slave Trade to America Pub. No. 409 (Washington, D.C.: Institute of Washington, 1955).

20. Curtin, *Atlantic Slave Trade*, p. 74.
21. Fogel and Engerman, *Time on the Cross*, pp. 13–18.
22. Mannix, *Black Cargoes*, pp. 55–56.
23. Greene, *Negro in Colonial New England*, pp. 72–73.
24. Ibid, p. 73.
25. Farley, *Black Population*, p. 17.
26. Greene, *Negro in Colonial New England*, pp. 389–99.
27. Farley, *Black Population*, p. 17.
28. Greene, *Negro in Colonial New England*, pp. 89–90.
29. Farley, *Black Population*, p. 18.
30. Mannix, *Black Cargoes*, p. 68.
31. Davidson, *Black Mother*, pp. 102–4.
32. Wiedner, *History of Africa*, p. 70.
33. Davidson, *Black Mother*, p. 106.
34. Ulrich B. Phillips, *American Negro Slavery* (Gloucester, Mass.: Appleton-Century-Crofts, 1959), p. 43.
35. Ibid., p. 43.
36. Ibid., pp. 52–53.
37. Ibid., pp. 61.
38. Mannix, *Black Cargoes*, p. 90.
39. Ibid., pp. 104–5.
40. Ibid., pp. 105–6.
41. Phillips, *American Negro Slavery*, p. 37.
42. Curtin, *Atlantic Slave Trade*, p. 275; Mannix, *Black Cargoes*, p. 123; Wiedner, *History of Africa*, p. 67.
43. Mannix, *Black Cargoes*, p. 117.
44. Ibid., pp. 127.
45. Ibid., pp. 127–28.
46. Ibid., pp. 166–67.
47. Ibid., p. 167. See also Curtin, *Atlantic Slave Trade*, p. 157.
48. Mannix, *Black Cargoes*, pp. 167–68.
49. Ibid., p. 168.
50. Curtin, *Atlantic Slave Trade*, p. 269.
51. Davidson, *African Slave Trade*, pp. 80–81.
52. Ibid., pp. 175–79.
53. Curtin, *Atlantic Slave Trade*, p. 269.
54. Ibid.
55. Davidson, *Black Mother*, p. 278.
56. Ibid.
57. Fogel and Engerman, *Time on the Cross*, pp. 59–77.
58. See Avery Craven, *The Growth of Southern Nationalism*, 1848–1861 (Baton Rouge: Louisiana State Univ. Press, 1953).
59. Mannix, *Black Cargoes*, p. 55.
60. E. Franklin Frazier, *The Negro in the United States* (New York: Macmillan Co., 1957) pp. 3–31.
61. Melville J. Herskovits, *The Myth of the Negro Past* (New York: Harper and Brothers, 1941), pp. 276–79.
62. Cited in Frazier, *Negro in the United States*, p. 10.
63. Ibid., p. 11.
64. Ibid., pp. 14–19.
65. Ibid., p. 20.
66. Ibid., pp. 20–21.

Chapter 3

1. See John Elliott Cairnes, *The Slave Power: Its Character, Career and Probable Designs: Being An Attempt to Explain the Real Issues Involved in the American Contest* (New York: Harper and Row, 1969).

2. Robert W. Fogel and Stanley L. Engerman, *Time on the Cross* (Boston: Little, Brown & Co., 1974), pp. 47–49.

3. Ulrich B. Phillips, *American Negro Slavery* (Gloucester, Mass.: Appleton-Century-Crofts, 1959), p. 187.

4. John Hope Franklin, *From Slavery to Freedom* (New York: Alfred A. Knopf, 1965), p. 174.

5. Ibid.

6. Ibid., pp. 184–86, 175.

7. Kenneth Stampp, *The Peculiar Institution* (New York: Alfred A. Knopf, 1956), p. 253.

8. Ibid., pp. 253, 255.

9. Frederic Bancroft, *Slave Trading in the Old South* (Baltimore: J. H. Furst Co., 1931), p. 368.

10. Ibid., p. 367.

11. Phillips, *American Negro Slavery*, p. 191.

12. Ibid., p. 190.

13. U. S., Bureau of the Census, *Negroes in the United States, 1920–1932* (Washington, D.C.: Government Printing Office, 1935), pp. 10–11, 14–15.

14. E. Franklin Frazier, *The Negro in the United States* (New York: Macmillan Co., 1966), p. 38; Fogel and Engerman, *Time on the Cross*, p. 44.

15. Frazier, *Negro in the United States*, p. 39.

16. Fogel and Engerman, *Time on the Cross*, p. 46.

17. Frazier, *Negro in the United States*, p. 39.

18. Fogel and Engerman, *Time on the Cross*, p. 47.

19. Bancroft, *Slave Trading*, p. 393.

20. Fogel and Engerman, *Time on the Cross*, p. 47.

21. Bancroft, *Slave Trading*, p. 394.

22. Fogel and Engerman, *Time on the Cross*, p. 47.

23. Bancroft, *Slave Trading*, p. 237.

24. Ibid., p. 250.

25. Ibid., p. 382.

26. Ibid., pp. 384–85.

27. Stampp, *Peculiar Institution*, p. 251.

28. Ibid.

29. Bancroft, *Slave Trading*, pp. 299–300n.

30. Ibid., p. 63.

31. Phillips, *American Negro Slavery*, p. 193.

32. Ibid., p. 192.

33. Ibid., p. 193.

34. Bancroft, *Slave Trading*, p. 276.

35. Ibid.

36. Phillips, *American Negro Slavery*, p. 195.

37. Bancroft, *Slave Trading*, p. 277.

38. Stampp, *Peculiar Institution*, p. 262.

39. Bancroft, *Slave Trading*, p. 277n.

40. Ibid., p. 279.

41. Ibid., p. 282; Phillips, *American Negro Slavery*, p. 194.

42. Bancroft, *Slave Trading*, p. 285.

43. Ibid., p. 288.

44. Phillips, *American Negro Slavery*, p. 201.

45. Ibid., pp. 101–2.

46. Bancroft, *Slave Trading*, p. 291.

47. Ibid.

48. Franklin, *Slavery to Freedom*, p. 183.

49. Ibid., p. 177.

50. Fogel and Engerman, *Time on the Cross*, p. 5.

51. Ibid.
52. Franklin, *Slavery to Freedom*, p. 178.
53. Stampp, *Peculiar Institution*, p. 252.
54. Ibid.
55. Franklin, *Slavery to Freedom*, p. 178.
56. Ibid.
57. Ibid.
58. William Petersen, *Population*, p. 307.
59. Wilbur H. Siebert, *The Underground Railroad From Slavery to Freedom* (New York: Russell and Russell, 1967), p. 358.
60. Ibid., pp. 113–14.
61. Gara, Larry, *The Liberty Line: The Legend of the Underground Railroad* (Lexington: Univ. of Kentucky Press, 1961).
62. Siebert, *Underground Railroad*, p. 25. See also Frederick Douglass, *Narrative of the Life of Frederick Douglass, An American Slave* (Cambridge: Belknap Press of Harvard Univ. Press, 1960), pp. 55–56.
63. Stampp, *Peculiar Institution*, p. 118.
64. Gerald W. Mullin, *Flight and Rebellion: Slave Resistance in Eighteenth Century Virginia* (New York: Oxford Univ. Press, 1972), pp. 105–12.
65. Ibid., pp. 106–7.
66. Stampp, *Peculiar Institution*, p. 114.
67. Siebert, *Underground Railroad*, p. 236.
68. Ibid., p. 237.
69. Franklin, *Slavery to Freedom*, pp. 225–56.
70. Stampp, *Peculiar Institution*, p. 110.
71. Douglass, *Frederick Douglass*, p. 142.
72. Franklin, *Slavery to Freedom*, pp. 250–56.
73. Stampp, *Peculiar Institution*, p. 110.
74. Siebert, *Underground Railroad*, p. 195.
75. Ibid.
76. See Mary Frances Berry, *Black Resistance—White Law* (New York: Appleton-Century-Crofts, 1971), for details of federal laws supporting slaves.
77. Siebert, *Underground Railroad*, p. 341.
78. Franklin, *Slavery to Freedom*, p. 212.
79. Ibid., pp. 214–15.
80. Ibid., p. 215.
81. Ibid., pp. 220–21.
82. Ibid., p. 216.
83. August Meier and Elliott M. Rudwick, *From Plantation to Ghetto* (New York: Hill and Wang, 1966), pp. 67–68.
84. John W. Barton, "Negro Migration," *Methodist Quarterly Review* 74 (Jan., 1925): 84.
85. Franklin, *Slavery to Freedom*, p. 231.
86. Leon F. Litwack, *North of Slavery* (Chicago: Univ. of Chicago Press, 1961), p. vii.
87. Meier and Rudwick, *Plantation to Ghetto*, p. 69.
88. Barton, "Negro Migration," pp. 84–85.
89. Litwack, *North of Slavery*, pp. 113–14.
90. Ibid., pp. 115, 116.
91. Ibid., p. 161.
92. Ibid., p. 162.
93. Ibid.
94. Ibid., pp. 162–65.
95. Carter G. Woodson, *A Century of Negro Migration* (New York: Russell and Russell, 1969), p. 35.
96. Franklin, *Slavery to Freedom*, p. 231.
97. Woodson, *Century of Migration*, p. 42.
98. Ibid., p. 44.
99. De Tocqueville, *Democracy in America*, vol 2, pp. 292–94 as cited in Woodson, *Century of Migration*, p. 44.
100. Franklin, *Slavery to Freedom*, p. 232.

Chapter 4

1. Bell Irvin Wiley, *Southern Negroes, 1861–1865* (New Haven: Yale Univ. Press, 1938), p. 3.
2. Ibid.
3. Ibid., p. 4.
4. Ibid., pp. 4–5.
5. Ibid., p. 5.
6. Ibid.
7. Ibid., p. 7.
8. Benjamin Quarles, *The Negro in the Civil War* (Boston: Little, Brown and Co., 1953), p. 64.
9. Franklin, *Slavery to Freedom*, p. 269.
10. Ibid.
11. Ibid., p. 271.
12. Ibid., p. 273.
13. Quarles, *Negro in the Civil War*, p. 94.
14. Wiley, *Southern Negroes*, p. 87.
15. Ibid., pp. 90–94.
16. Ibid., p. 91.
17. See Quarles, *Negro in the Civil War* for a general discussion of Lincoln's approach to the problem of emancipation.
18. Wiley, *Southern Negroes*, pp. 91–92.
19. U.S., Bureau of the Census, *Historical Statistics of the U.S., 1789–1945* (Washington, D.C.: Government Printing Office, 1949). p. 27.
20. Carter G. Woodson, *A Century of Negro Migration* (New York: Russell and Russell, 1969), pp. 117–18.
21. Fleming, *The Civil War and Reconstruction in Alabama*, as cited in Woodson, *Century of Migration*, p. 119.
22. Woodson, *Century of Migration*, p. 118.
23. Ibid., p. 119.
24. Ibid., pp 119–20.
25. Thompson, *Reconstruction in Georgia*, p. 69, as cited in Woodson, *Century of Migration*, p. 120.
26. Alrutheus Ambush Taylor, *The Negro in the Reconstruction of Virginia* (New York: Russell and Russell, 1969), p. 92.
27. Joseph A. Hill, "The Recent Northward Migration of the Negro," in *The Trend of Population*, ed. Ernest W. Burgess, American Sociological Society Series, vol 18, (Chicago: Univ. of Chicago Press, 1924), p. 35.
28. Ibid., pp. 35–36.
29. Meier and Rudwick, *Plantation to Ghetto*, p. 134.
30. Norman Coombs, *The Black Experience in America* (New York: Twayne Publishers, 1972), pp. 151–52.
31. Woodson, *Century of Migration*, pp. 124–25.
32. Ibid., pp. 123–24.
33. Ibid., p. 120.
34. Taylor, *Reconstruction of Virginia*, p. 93.
35. Franklin, *Slavery to Freedom*, p. 322.
36. Ibid., pp. 322–23.
37. Taylor, *Reconstruction of Virginia*, pp. 93–102.
38. W. O. Scroggs, "Interstate Migration of Negro Population," *Journal of Political Economy* 25 (Dec. 1917): 1035.
39. Meier and Rudwick, *Plantation to Ghetto*, pp. 148–49.
40. Taylor, *Reconstruction of Virginia*, pp. 103–4.
41. Ibid., p. 102.
42. C. Vann Woodward, *The Strange Career of Jim Crow* (New York: Oxford Univ. Press, 1955), p. 22.
43. St. Clair Drake and Horace R. Cayton, *Black Metropolis* (New York: Harper and Row, 1962), p. 44.
44. Robert C. Weaver, *The Negro Ghetto* (New York: Harcourt, Brace and Co., 1948), p. 12.

45. Taylor, *Reconstruction of Virginia*, p. 102.
46. C. Vann Woodward, *Origins of the New South, 1877–1913* (Baton Rouge: Louisiana State Univ. Press, 1951), p. 105.
47. Woodward, *New South*, p. 106.
48. Ibid., p. 107.
49. Francis Butler Simpkins, *A History of the South* (New York: Alfred A. Knopf, 1963), p. 298.
50. Milton Meltzer, *In their Own Words, A History of the American Negro, 1865–1916* (New York: Thomas Y. Crowell Co., 1965), vol. 2, p. 100.
51. Meier and Rudwick, *Plantation to Ghetto*, p. 156.
52. Simpkins, *History of the South*, p. 302.
53. Walter L. Fleming, "'Pap' Singleton, The Moses of the Colored Exodus," *American Journal of Sociology* 215 (July 1909): 77–78.
54. Arna Bontemps and Jack Conroy, *Anyplace But Here* (New York: Hill and Wang, 1966), p. 2.
55. Fleming, "'Pap' Singleton," p. 61.
56. Bontemps and Conroy, *Anyplace But Here*, pp. 61–62.
57. Ibid., p. 60.
58. Ibid.
59. Ibid., p. 58.
60. Woodson, *Century of Migration*, p. 135.
61. U.S., Department of the Interior, *Compendium of the Tenth Census (June 1, 1880)* (Washington D.C.: Government Printing Office, 1880), p. 349.
62. Woodson, *Century of Migration*, p. 142.
63. Bontemps and Conroy, *Anyplace But Here*, p. 58.
64. Ibid.
65. Homer C. Hawkins, "Trends in the Black Migration from 1863 to 1960" *Phylon* 34 (June 1973): 141.
66. Fleming, "'Pap' Singleton," pp. 61–65.
67. From U.S., Senate Report No. 693, 64th Cong., 2nd Sess., pt. 2 as quoted in Milton Meltzer, ed., *In Their Own Words: A History of the American Negro*, vol. 2 (New York: Thomas Y. Crowell Co., 1965), p. 101.
68. Woodson, *Century of Migration*, pp. 135–36.
69. Scroggs, "Interstate Migration," p. 1035.
70. Meltzer, *In Their Own Words*, vol. 2, p. 94.
71. August Meier, *Negro Thought in America, 1880–1915* (Ann Arbor: Univ. of Michigan Press, 1963), p. 62.
72. Bontemps and Conroy, *Anyplace But Here*, p. 63.
73. Ibid.
74. Woodson, *Century of Migration*, p. 141.
75. Bontemps and Conroy, *Anyplace But Here*, p. 67.
76. Ibid., p. 63.
77. Woodson, *Century of Migration*, p. 142.
78. Scroggs, "Interstate Migration," p. 1037.
79. Ibid., p. 1041.
80. Bontemps and Conroy, *Anyplace But Here*, p. 61.
81. Ibid., p. 65.
82. Ibid.
83. Ibid.

Chapter 5

1. Francis A. Walker, "Statistics of the Colored Race in the United States," *Publications of the American Statistical Association* 2 (Sept.–Dec., 1890): 97, as quoted in Reynolds Farley, *The Growth of the Black Population* (Chicago: Markham Pub. Co., 1970).
2. Farley, *Black Population*, p. 24.
3. Ibid., p. 25.

4. Carter G. Woodson, *A Century of Negro Migration* (New York: Russell and Russell, 1969), p. 120.
5. Ibid., p. 121.
6. George Brown Tindall, *South Carolina Negroes, 1877–1900* (Columbia: Univ. of South Carolina Press, 1952), p. 170.
7. Ibid.
8. Ibid.
9. Ibid.
10. Ibid., pp. 170–71.
11. Ibid., pp. 170–74.
12. C. Vann Woodward, *Origins of the New South, 1877–1913* (Baton Rouge: Louisiana State Univ. Press, 1951), p. 107.
13. Ibid., p. 108.
14. Ibid., p. 111.
15. Ibid., p. 112.
16. August Meier, *Negro Thought in America, 1880–1915* (Ann Arbor: Univ. of Michigan Press, 1963), p. 59.
17. Woodson, *Century of Migration*, p. 146.
18. Ibid.
19. Ibid.
20. Mozell C. Hill, "The All-Negro Communities of Oklahoma: The Natural History of a Social Movement." *The Journal of Negro History*, 31 (July 1946): 254–68.
21. Ibid., p. 257.
22. Allan H. Spear, *Black Chicago: The Making of a Negro Ghetto, 1890–1920* (Chicago: Univ. of Chicago Press, 1967), p. 5.
23. Ibid., p. 6.
24. Ibid., p. 13, Table 2.
25. Charles S. Johnson, "How Much is the Migration a Flight from Persecution?" as quoted in Meier, *Negro Thought in America*, p. 62.
26. W. E. B. DuBois, "The Negro as He Really is," *Worlds Work* 2 (June 1901): 864, as quoted in Meier, ibid.
27. Farley, *Black Population*, pp. 45–46.
28. Arna Bontemps and Jack Conroy, *Anyplace But Here* (New York: Hill and Wang, 1966), pp. 140–44.
29. Farley, *Black Population*, p. 46.
30. Meier, *Negro Thought in America*, p. 61.
31. St. Clair Drake and Horace R. Cayton, *Black Metropolis* (New York: Harper and Row, 1962), p. 53.
32. Henry Bauford Parkes, *The United States of America: A History* (New York: Alfred A. Knopf, 1968), p. 468.
33. Thomas Jackson Woofter, Jr., *Negro Migration: Changes in Rural Organization and Population of the Cotton Belt* (New York: W. D. Gray, 1920), pp. 105–6.
34. Ibid., pp. 117–18.
35. Ibid., p. 149.
36. W. O. Scroggs, "Interstate Migration of Negro Population," *Journal of Political Economy* 25 (Dec. 1917): 1040.
37. Emmett Scott, *Negro Migration During the War* (New York: Oxford Univ. Press, 1920), p. 9.
38. Woofter, *Negro Migration*, pp. 105–6.
39. Ibid., p. 117.

Chapter 6

1. Tyson, *Negro Migration in 1916–1917* (Washington, D.C.: U.S. Department of Labor), p. 121, as cited by Henderson H. Donald, "The Negro Migration of 1916–1918," *Journal of Negro History* 6 (Oct. 1921): 402.
2. T. Lynn Smith, "The Redistribution of the Negro Population," *Journal of Negro History* 51 (July 1966):158.

3. Allan H. Spear, *Black Chicago: The Making of a Negro Ghetto, 1890–1920* (Chicago: Univ. of Chicago Press, 1967), p. 139.

4. Daniel O. Price, *Changing Characteristics of the Negro Population*, U.S. Bureau of the Census, 1960 Census Monograph (Washington, D.C.: Government Printing Office, 1969), p. 11.

5. Ibid., p. 12.

6. Ibid.

7. Reynolds Farley, *Growth of the Black Population* (Chicago: Markham Pub. Co., 1970), p. 22.

8. Letter of Authorization by the Secretary of Labor, W. B. Wilson, in U.S., Department of Labor, *Negro Migration in 1916–1917: Reports by R. H. Leavell, T. R. Shavely, T. J. Woofter, Jr., W. T. B. Williams and Francis D. Tyson* (Washington, D.C.: Government Printing Office, 1919), p. 7, quoted in Smith, "Negro Population," p. 158.

9. Smith, ibid.

10. Henderson H. Donald, "The Negro Migration of 1916–1918," *Journal of Negro History* 4 (Oct. 1921): 404.

11. Benjamin Brawley, *A Social History of the American Negro* (London: Collier-Macmillan Ltd., 1970), p. 347.

12. Smith, "Negro Population," p. 158.

13. Ibid.

14. Emmett J. Scott, *Negro Migration During the War* (New York: Oxford University Press, 1920), pp. 55–58.

15. Charles E. Hall, *Negroes in the United States, 1920–1932* (New York: Arno Press, 1969), p. 48.

16. Ibid.

17. T. Lynn Smith, *The Sociology of Rural Life* (New York: Harper and Brothers, 1947), p. 177.

18. Ibid., p. 164.

19. Ibid., p. 54.

20. Charles S. Johnson, "The Black Worker in the City," *Survey*, March 1925, p. 642.

21. Ibid., p. 55.

22. Ibid., p. 54.

23. Ibid., p. 48.

24. Ibid., p. 93.

25. G. E. Haynes, "Negro Migration," *Opportunity*, Oct. 1924, p. 273.

26. Ibid., Sept. 1927, p. 273.

27. Ibid.

28. Arna Bontemps and Jack Conroy, *Anyplace But Here* (New York: Hill and Wang, 1966), p. 160.

29. John Hope Franklin, *From Slavery to Freedom* (New York: Alfred A. Knopf, 1965), pp. 464–65.

30. Spear, *Black Chicago*, p. 131.

31. St. Clair Drake and Horace R. Cayton, *Black Metropolis* (New York: Harper and Row, 1962), p. 58.

32. Gunnar Myrdal, *An American Dilemma* (New York: Harper and Brothers, 1944), p. 193.

33. Ibid.

34. Everett S. Lee, "A Theory of Migration," in J. A. Jackson, *Migration* (London: Cambridge Univ. Press, 1969), pp. 286–87.

35. Donald, "Negro Migration of 1916–1918," p. 410.

36. Robert B. Grant, *The Black Man Comes to the City* (Chicago: Nelson Hall Co., 1972), pp. 31–32.

37. Ibid., pp. 33–36.

38. Johnson, "Black Worker," p. 643.

39. Ibid.

40. Ibid.

41. Franklin, *Slavery to Freedom*, p. 494.

42. Ibid., p. 482.

43. James Weldon Johnson, "The Making of Harlem," *Survey*, March 1925, p. 637.

44. Ibid., p. 635.

45. August Meir and Elliott Rudwick, *From Plantation to Ghetto* (New York: Hill and Wang, 1970), p. 236.

46. Thomas Jackson Woofter, Jr., *Negro Migration: Changes in Rural Organization and Population of the Cotton Belt* (New York: W. D. Gray, 1920), p. 121.
47. Scott, *Negro Migration During the War*, p. 19.
48. *Montgomery Advertiser*, 21 Sept. 1916, cited in *The Negro in Chicago*, Chicago Commission on Race Relations (New York: Arno Press, 1968), p. 85.
49. Ibid., p. 84.
50. Scott, *Negro Migration During the War*, p. 20.
51. Woofter, *Negro Migration*, p. 121.
52. Dewey Palmer, "Moving North: Migration of Negroes," *Phylon* 28 (1967): 61.
53. Woofter, *Negro Migration*, p. 138.
54. Ibid., pp. 138–39.
55. Scott, *Negro Migration During the War*, pp. 26–27.
56. Ibid., pp. 28–29.
57. Charles Spurgeon Johnson, *The Negro in American Civilization* (New York: Henry Holt and Company, 1930), p. 22.
58. Palmer, "Moving North," p. 58.
59. Ibid., p. 59.
60. John Henrik Clarke and Amy Jacques Garvey, *Marcus Garvey and the Vision of Africa* (New York: Random House, 1974) p. 427.
61. Johnson, "Black Worker," pp. 651, 654.
62. *Encyclopedia Americana*, 1968 ed., s.v. "George Gershwin."
63. Franklin, *Slavery to Freedom*, p. 496.
64. Langston Hughes, "I Too," *Survey*, March 1925, p. 683.

Chapter 7

1. David A. Shannon, *Between the Wars: America, 1919–1941* (Boston: Houghton Mifflin Co., 1965), p. 109.
2. Bernard Sternsher, ed., *The Negro in Depression and War* (Chicago: Quadrangle Books, 1969), p. 6.
3. Lester V. Chandler, *America's Greatest Depression, 1929–1941* (New York: Harper and Row, 1970), p. 1.
4. Ibid.
5. Shannon, *Between the Wars*, p. 109.
6. Ibid., p. 110.
7. Chandler, *America's Greatest Depression*, p. 6.
8. Shannon, *Between the Wars*, p. 110.
9. Chandler, *America's Greatest Depression*, p. 6.
10. Shannon, *Between the Wars*, p. 193, and E. Franklin Frazier, *The Negro in the United States* (Toronto: Macmillan Co., 1957), pp. 559–605.
11. Chandler, *America's Greatest Depression*, pp. 40–41.
12. *Fifteenth Census of the United States: 1930, Population*, vol. 5, pp. 74–75 as cited in Richard Sterner, *The Negro's Share* (Westport, Conn.: Negro Universities Press, 1971), p. 352.
13. Sterner, *Negro's Share*, p. 11.
14. Shannon, *Between the Wars*, pp. 193–94.
15. Gunnar Myrdal, *An American Dilemma* (New York: Harper and Brothers, 1944), vol. 1, p. 197.
16. Sterner, *Negro's Share*, p. 19.
17. Myrdal, *American Dilemma*, p. 197.
18. David A. Shannon, ed., *The Great Depression* (Englewood Cliffs, N. J.: Prentice-Hall, 1960), p. 33.
19. Myrdal, *American Dilemma*, p. 197.
20. Sterner, *Negro's Share*, p. 20.
21. Ibid.
22. Ibid., p. 13.
23. Norman Thomas, *The Plight of the Sharecroppers* (New York: League for Industrial Democracy, 1934), pp. 19–25.

Chapter 8

1. John C. McKinney and Linda Brookover Bourque, "The Changing South: National Incorporation of a Region," *American Sociological Review* no. 36 (June 1971):399–411.
2. Gunnar Myrdal, *An American Dilemma* (New York: Harper and Brothers, 1944), p. 997.
3. Leonard Reissman, "Social Development and the American South," *Journal of Social Issues*, Jan. 1966, p. 101.
4. McKinney and Bourque, "Changing South," p. 399.
5. Harold B. Myers, "Defense Migration and Labor Supply," *Journal of American Statistical Association* 37 (March 1942): 69.
6. Reynolds Farley, *The Growth of the Black Population* (Chicago: Markham Pub., 1970), p. 3.
7. U.S., Bureau of the Census, *Census of the Population: 1960*, Subject Reports, Final Report PC(1)-1A, *Number of Inhabitants: United States Summary* (Washington, D.C.: Government Printing Office, 1961), p. 4.
8. U.S., Bureau of the Census, *Historical Statistics of the United States, 1789–1945* (Washington, D.C.: Government Printing Office, 1949), p. 25.
9. Farley, *Black Population*, p. 42.
10. U.S., Bureau of the Census, *Current Population Reports*, Series P-23, no. 42, *The Social and Economic Status of the Black Population in the United States, 1971* (Washington, D.C.: Government Printing Office, 1972), p. 13.
11. Farley, *Black Population*, p. 42.
12. Ibid.
13. *Social and Economic Status of the Black Population*, p. 18.
14. U.S., Congress, House, Select Committee on National Defense Migration, *Hearings*, 77th Cong., 2nd sess., 1942 (Washington, D.C.: Government Printing Office, 1942), p. 10321.
15. Ibid.
16. Ibid., pp. 10449–633.
17. Robert C. Weaver, *Negro Labor: A National Problem* (New York: Harcourt, Brace and Co., 1946), p. 79.
18. Ibid.
19. Ibid., p. 82.
20. Ibid., p. 83.
21. Ibid., p. 91.
22. Ibid.
23. Ibid.
24. Paul H. Landis, "Internal Migration by Subsidy," *Social Forces* 22 (Dec. 1943): 183–87.
25. Ibid., p. 183.
26. Ibid., p. 184.
27. U.S., Bureau of the Census, *Current Population Reports*, Series P-20, no. 14 *Internal Migration in The United States: April, 1940 to April, 1947* (Washington, D.C.: Government Printing Office, 1947).
28. Ibid. p. 2.
29. Francis Butler Simkins, *A History of the South* (New York: Alfred A. Knopf, 1963), p. 564.
30. John Dollard, *Caste and Class in a Southern Town* (New Haven: Yale Univ. Press, 1937), pp. 62–63.
31. Ibid., pp. 64–66.
32. Ibid., p. 65.
33. Allison Davis, *Deep South* (Chicago: Univ. of Chicago Press, 1941), p. 57.
34. Ibid., p. 293.
35. Ibid., p. 342.
36. National Defense Migration, *Hearings*, p. 771.
37. Ibid.
38. T. J. Woofter, Jr., "Southern Population and Social Planning," *Social Forces* 14 (Oct. 1935): 18.
39. National Defense Migration, *Hearings*, pp. 12773–4.
40. Ibid., p. 772.
41. Richard M. Dalfiume, "The Forgotten Years of the Negro Revolution," in *The Negro in Depression and War*, ed. Bernard Sternsher (Chicago: Quadrangle Books, 1969), p. 299.

42. National Defense Migration, *Hearings*, p. 6090.

43. Ibid.

44. Ibid., p. 6072.

45. Ibid., p. 7246.

46. Ibid., p. 5955.

47. Ibid., p. 5844.

48. Ibid., p. 7247.

49. Ibid., p. 6072.

50. Ibid., p. 5465.

51. Ibid.

52. Ibid., p. 6072.

53. Benjamin Quarles, *The Negro in the Making of America* (New York: Collier Books, 1964), p. 227.

54. Ibid.

55. St. Clair Drake and Horace R. Cayton, *Black Metropolis* (New York: Harper and Row, 1962), p. 90.

56. Ibid., pp. 92–93.

57. Calvin B. Hoover and B. U. Ratchford, *Economic Resources and Policies of the South*, as quoted in Simkins, *History of the South*, pp. 567–68.

58. Charles S. Johnson, *Social Forces* 23 (Oct. 1944), as quoted in Simkins, *History of the South*, p. 568.

Chapter 9

1. Benjamin Quarles, *The Negro in the Making of America* (New York: Collier Books, 1964), p. 228.

2. Robert C. Weaver, *The Negro Ghetto* (New York: Harcourt Brace and Co., 1948), p. 82.

3. August Meier and Elliott M. Rudwick, *From Plantation to Ghetto* (New York: Hill and Wang, 1966), pp. 222–23.

4. Abram J. Jaffe and Seymour L. Wolfbein, "Postwar Migration Plans of Army Enlisted Men," *Annuals of the American Academy of Political and Social Science* 238 (March 1941): 18.

5. Ibid., p. 19.

6. U.S., Bureau of the Census, *Current Population Reports*, Series P-20, *Mobility of the Population for the United States: April 1950 to April 1951* no. 39 (Washington, D.C.: Government Printing Office, 1952), Table 1, p. 9.

7. U.S., Bureau of the Census, *Census of Population: 1950*, vol. 4, Special Reports, *State of Birth* (Washington, D.C.: Government Printing Office, 1953), Tables 5 and 9.

8. Ann Ratner Miller, *Net Intercensal Migration to Large Urban Areas of the United States* (Philadelphia: University of Pennsylvania Press 1964), pp. 129–208.

9. U.S., Bureau of the Census, *Census of Population: 1950*, vol. 4, Special Reports, pt. 4, chap. D, "Population Mobility-Characteristics of Migrants," (Washington, D.C.: Government Printing Office, 1957), p. 6.

10. John Fraser Hart, "The Changing Distribution of the American Negro," *Annuals*, Association of American Geographers, 50 (Sept., 1960): 402.

11. Ibid.

12. Reynolds Farley, *The Growth of the Black Population* (Chicago: Markham Pub. Co., 1970), pp. 166–87.

13. Henry Bauford Parkes, *The United States of America: A History* (New York: Alfred A. Knopf, 1968), p. 677.

14. Ibid.

15. Ibid.

16. Daniel Snowman, *America Since 1920* (New York: Harper and Row, 1968), p. 117.

17. Francis Butler Simkins, *A History of the South*, (New York: Alfred A. Knopf, 1963), p. 586.

18. Frederick L. Deming and Weldon A. Stein, *Disposal of Southern War Plants* (Washington, D.C.: National Planning Assn., 1949), cited in ibid.

19. Ibid., pp. 587–88.

20. Joseph J. Spengler, "Southern Economic Trends and Prospects," in John McKinney and

Edgar Thompson, eds., *The South in Continuity and Change* (Durham, N.C.: Duke Univ. Press, 1965), p. 109.
21. Ibid., pp. 110–11.
22. Richard L. Simpson and David R. Norsworthy, "The Changing Occupational Structure of the South," in McKinney and Thompson, *The South*, p. 223.
23. Ibid.
24. V. O. Key, *Southern Politics in State and Nation*, p. 5, cited in McKinney and Thompson, *The South*, p. 339.
25. Nathan Hare, "Recent Trends in the Occupational Mobility of Negroes 1930–1960: An Intracohort Analysis," *Social Forces* 44 (Dec. 1965): 169.
26. U.S., Bureau of the Census, *Current Population Reports*, series 23, no. 42, *The Social and Economic Status of the Black Population in the United States, 1971* (Washington, D.C.: Government Printing Office, 1972), pp. 29–31.
27. U.S., Bureau of the Census, *Census of the Population: 1950, Current Population Reports*, series P-60, no. 9, *Consumer Income*, (Washington, D.C.: Government Printing Office, 1952), Table 3, p. 23.
28. Simkins, *History of the South*, p. 594.

Chapter 10

1. John Hope Franklin, *From Slavery to Freedom* (New York: Alfred A. Knopf, 1965), p. 5.
2. U.S., Department of Labor, Bureau of Labor Statistics, *Black Americans—A Chartbook, 1971*, Bulletin 1699, (Washington, D.C.: Government Printing Office, 1971), p. 11.
3. Daniel O. Price, *Changing Characteristics of the Negro Population*, U.S. Bureau of the Census, 1960 Census Monograph (Washington, D.C.: Government Printing Office, 1969), p. 11.
4. U.S., Bureau of the Census, *Current Population Report*, P-20, No. 118, *Mobility of the Population of the United States: March 1960 to March 1961* (Washington, D.C.: Government Printing Office, 1962), Table 1, pp. 12–13.
5. Throughout this chapter we have used the term *black* for consistency. However, the data are for nonwhites and include some other minority groups. The black population is about 90 percent of the nonwhites.
6. It should be noted that "place of birth" data is indicative of cumulative migration not restricted to a particular time period.
7. Divisional data on the extent of migration provide somewhat more specificity to the general migration picture of the 1950s, e.g., the regions in which the various divisions are to be found.
8. Gladys K. Bowles and James D. Tarver, *Net Migration of the Population 1950–1960 by Age, Sex, and Color*, U.S. Department of Agriculture (Washington, D.C.: Government Printing Office, 1965), p. ix.
9. Daniel O. Price, "Urbanization of the Blacks, *Milbank Memorial Fund Quarterly* 48 (April 1970), p. 47.
10. Price, "Urbanization of the Blacks," p. 57.
11. U.S., Bureau of the Census, *Census of Population: 1960*, Subject Reports, Final Report PC(2)-2B, *Mobility of States and State Economic Areas* (Washington, D.C.: Government Printing Office, 1963), Table 2, p. 2.
12. Donald J. Bogue, *Principles of Demography* (New York: John Wiley & Sons, 1969), p. 764.
13. Ibid., p. 765.
14. Ibid., pp. 769–70.
15. Ibid., p. 769.
16. Ibid.
17. Price, *Negro Population*, p. 212.
18. Bogue, *Principles of Demography*, p. 768.
19. Ibid.
20. Daniel M. Johnson, "Black Return Migration to a Southern Metropolis: Birmingham, Alabama" (Ph.D. Diss., Univ. of Missouri, 1973) pp. 82–97.
21. J. A. Jackson, *Migration* (Cambridge: Cambridge University Press, 1969), p. 7.

22. Ibid.
23. C. E. Bishop, "Southern Agriculture in a Commercial Era," in John McKinney and Edgar Thompson, eds., *The South in Continuity and Change* (Durham, N.C.: Duke University Press, 1965), pp. 248–49.
24. Bishop, "Southern Agriculture," p. 255.
25. Harry C. Dillingham and David Sly, "The Mechanical Cotton Picker, Negro Migration and the Integration Movement," *Human Organization* 25 (Winter 1966): 346.
26. Ibid.
27. Ibid., pp. 346–47.
28. Daniel F. Capstick, *Economics of Mechanical Cotton Harvesting*, Bulletin 622, March 1960, Arkansas, Agricultural Experiment Station (Fayetteville: Univ. of Arkansas), p. 4, cited in Dillingham and Sly, "The Mechanical Cotton Picker," p. 347.
29. Dillingham and Sly, "Mechanical Cotton Picker," p. 347.
30. Ibid., p. 348.
31. Ibid., p. 349.
32. Paul F. Coe, "The Non-white Population Surge to our Cities," *Land Economics* 35 (Aug. 1959): 195–210.
33. One example of the many studies on this topic is Joseph J. Spengler's "Southern Economic Trends and Prospects" in McKinney and Thompson, *The South*, pp. 101–31.
34. Ibid.
35. Price, *Negro Population*, p. 113.
36. Ibid.
37. Benjamin Quarles, *The Negro in the Making of America* (New York: Collier Books, 1964), p. 239.
38. Ibid., pp. 239–40.
39. Ibid., p. 240.
40. Ibid.
41. Richard Raymond, "Determinants of Non-White Migration During the 1950s," *The American Journal of Economics and Sociology* 31 (1972): 9–20.
42. Gunnar Myrdal, *An American Dilemma* (New York: Harper and Brothers, 1944), pp. 186–87.
43. Raymond, "Determinants of Migration," p. 11.
44. Elaine M. Burgess, "Race Relations and Social Change," in McKinney and Thompson, *The South*, p. 344.
45. Nathan Glazer and Daniel P. Moynihan, *Beyond the Melting Pot* (Cambridge: The M.I.T. Press, 1963), p. 27.
46. Irving Kristol, "The Negro Today is Like the Immigrant Yesterday," *New York Times Magazine*, Sept. 11, 1966, p. 50.
47. Oscar Handlin, *The Newcomers* (Cambridge: Harvard Univ. Press, 1959). See also Marc Fried, "The Transitional Functions of Working-Class Communities," in Mildred Kantor, *Mobility and Mental Health* (Springfield, Ill.: Charles C. Thomas Publisher, 1965).
48. Glazer and Moynihan, *Beyond the Melting Pot*, p. 33.
49. Burgess, "Race Relations," p. 355.
50. J. A. Jackson, *Migration*, p. 7.
51. E. Franklin Frazier, *The Negro Church in America* (New York: Schocken Books, 1964), pp. 70–71.
52. Frazier, *Negro Church*, p. 71.
53. Lee Rainwater, "The Negro Lower Class Family, Crucible of Identity," *Daedalus* 95 (Winter 1966): 179.
54. Lee Rainwater and William L. Yancey, *The Moynihan Report and the Politics of Controversy* (Cambridge: M.I.T. Press, 1967), p. 107.
55. Glazer and Moynihan, *Beyond the Melting Pot*, p. 29.
56. Ibid., pp. 38–39.
57. Ibid., p. 38.
58. Karl E. Taeuber and Alma F. Taeuber, *Negroes in Cities* (Chicago: Aldine Publishing Co., 1965), p. 140.
59. Reynolds Farley, "Recent Changes in Negro Fertility," *Demography* 1 (1966): 190.
60. Ibid., p. 200.
61. Ibid., pp. 201–2.

62. W. E. B. DuBois, *The Philadelphia Negro* (Philadelphia: Univ. of Pennsylvania, 1899), p. 81, cited in Taeuber and Taeuber, *Negroes in Cities*, p. 144.
63. Philip M. Hauser, "Demographic Factors in the Integration of the Negro," *Daedalus* 94 (Fall 1965): 852.
64. Ibid., p. 852.
65. Taeuber and Taeuber, *Negroes in Cities*, pp. 31–43.
66. Ibid.
67. Oscar Handlin, *The Uprooted* (Boston: Little, Brown, 1973); Handlin, *The Newcomers*; Otis Dudley Duncan and Beverly Duncan, *The Negro Population of Chicago* (Chicago: Univ. of Chicago Press, 1957).
68. Taeuber and Taeuber, *Negroes in Cities*, p. 150.
69. Ibid.
70. James Q. Wilson, *Negro Politics* (New York: The Free Press, 1960), pp. 98–99.
71. Ibid., "The Negro in Politics," in Talcott Parsons and Kenneth B. Clark, *The Negro American* (Boston: Houghton Mifflin Co., 1966), p. 441.

Chapter 11

1. Walter T. K. Nugent, *Modern America* (Boston: Houghton Mifflin Co., 1973), pp. 298–300.
2. David Snowman, *America Since 1920* (New York: Harper and Row, 1968), p. 137.
3. See Bradford Chambers, *Chronicles of Negro Protest* (New York: Parents Magazine Press, 1968); Benjamin Muse, *The American Negro Revolution: From Nonviolence to Black Power* (Bloomington: Indiana Univ. Press, 1968); Lewis Killian, *The Impossible Revolution: Black Power and the American Dream* (New York: Random House, 1968).
4. Killian, *Impossible Revolution*, p. 148.
5. William McCord et al., *Life Styles in the Black Ghetto* (New York: W. W. Norton and Co., 1969), p. 31.
6. U.S. Bureau of the Census, *Historical Statistics of the United States, Colonial Times to 1970, Bicentennial Edition, Part I*, (Washington, D.C.: Government Printing Office, 1975), Table A 172–194, p. 22.
7. See Rex R. Campbell, Daniel M. Johnson, and Gary J. Stangler, "Return Migration of Black People to the South," *Rural Sociology* 39 (Winter 1974): 514–28; Daniel M. Johnson, Gary J. Stangler, and Rex R. Campbell, "Black Migration to the South: Primary and Return Migrants," Paper presented at the annual meeting of the Rural Sociological Society in Montreal, Canada, August 1974; Rex R. Campbell and Daniel M. Johnson, "Propositions on Internal Counterstream Migration," Paper presented at the Population Tribune 1974, Non-Governmental Forum-World Population Conference, Bucharest, Romania, August 1974; Rex R. Campbell, Daniel M. Johnson, and Gary J. Stangler, "Counterstream Migration of Black People to the South: Data from the 1970 Public Use Sample," *Review of Public Use Data* 3 (Jan. 1975): 13–21; Gary J. Stangler, Rex R. Campbell, and Daniel M. Johnson, "Black Return Migration to Two Non-Metropolitan Areas of the South," Paper presented at the Rural Sociological Society meeting of the Southern Association of Agricultural Scientists, New Orleans, Louisiana, February 1975; Rex R. Campbell and Daniel M. Johnson, "Propositions on Counterstream Migration" *Rural Sociology*, 41 (Spring 1976): 127–45.
8. E. G. Ravenstein, "The Laws of Migration," *Journal of the Royal Statistical Society* 52 (June 1889): 241–301, cited in Everett Lee, "A Theory of Migration," *Demography* 3 (1966): 1.
9. Henry Shryock, *Population Mobility Within the United States* (Chicago: Community and Family Study Center, 1964), p. 285.
10. Ibid.
11. Lester C. Thurow, *Poverty and Discrimination* (Washington, D.C.: The Brookings Institution, 1969), pp. 14–18.
12. U.S., Department of Labor, *Black Americans: A Chartbook*, (Washington, D.C.: Government Printing Office, 1971), pp. 38–45.
13. James Q. Wilson, "The War on Cities," *The Public Interest*, No. 3 (Spring 1966): 32.
14. Shane Davies and Gary L. Fowler, "The Disadvantaged Urban Migrant in Indianapolis," *Economic Geography* 48 (April 1972): 164.

15. For a full discussion of the 1967 Survey of Economic Opportunity, see Gladys K. Bowles, A. Lloyd Bacon, and P. Neal Ritchey, *Poverty Dimensions of Rural-to-Urban Migration: A Statistical Report*, Population-Migration Reports, Rural-Urban Migrants, Vol. 1, pt. 1 (Washington, D.C.: U.S. Government Printing Office, 1973).

16. Anne S. Lee and Gladys K. Bowles, "Contributions of Rural Migrants to the Urban Occupational Structure," *Agricultural Economics Research* 26 (April 1974): pp. 25–32.

17. Ibid., p. 32.

18. Zahava D. Blum, Charles C. Berry, and Aage B. Sorensen, "Migration and Household Composition: A Comparison Between Blacks and Nonblacks." Center for the Study of Social Organization of Schools, The Johns Hopkins University, Report No. 77, August 1970, p. 19.

19. P. Neal Ritchey and C. Shannon Stokes, "Residence Background, Migration and Fertility," *Demography* 9 (May 1972): 219–20.

Epilogue

1. U.S., Bureau of the Census, *Current Population Reports*, series P-20, no. 285, *Mobility of the Population of the United States: March 1970 to March 1975*, (Washington, D.C.: Government Printing Office, 1975), Table 30, p. 67.

2. Larry H. Long and Kristin A. Hansen, "Trends in Return Migration to the South," *Demography* 12 (Nov. 1975): 601–14.

Index